PORTRAITS IN LEADERSHIP

JEWISH LEARNING INSTITUTE

Printed in Canada
© Published and Copyrighted 2010 by
The Rohr Jewish Learning Institute
822 Eastern Parkway, Brooklyn, NY 11213

All rights reserved.
No part of the contents of this book
may be reproduced or transmitted in any form
or by any means
without the written permission of the publisher.

(888) YOUR-JLI/718-221-6900
www.myJLI.com

ב"ה

The **Rohr Jewish Learning Institute**
gratefully acknowledges
the pioneering support of

George and Pamela Rohr

SINCE ITS INCEPTION
the **Rohr JLI** has been
a beneficiary of the vision, generosity,
care and concern
of the **Rohr family**

In the merit of
the tens of thousands of hours of Torah study
by **JLI** students worldwide,
may they be blessed with health,
Yiddishe Nachas from all their loved ones,
and extraordinary success
in all their endeavors ❧

WE DEDICATE THE PRESENT COURSE, *Portraits in Leadership,* to a modern-day Jewish leader who had the courage and vision to dream big dreams and make them come true.

Jack Nash fled Nazi Germany with his family to the United States at the age of eleven. He was renowned for his brilliance and self-made success. As a philanthropist, he was bold, exacting, generous, and humble.

His philanthropy reflected his deep and steadfast core values, his creative and strategic genius, and his embrace and support for visionary ideas and leaders. He had an uncanny ability to intuit outstanding potential. Applying a venture capital approach to the causes he funded, he was distinguished by his willingness to back fledgling projects and provide the level of challenge and support necessary for success.

Jack was a man of few words with no interest in fanfare who accomplished so much for so many. Never one to pursue honor, honor followed him.

צִדְקָתוֹ עוֹמֶדֶת לָעַד
תהלים קי״ב,ט

His righteousness endures forever
(*Psalms* 112:9)

This course is lovingly dedicated
to the memory of

Jack Nash
יעקב בן יוסף ע״ה
Tamuz 27, 5768/July 30, 2008

who invested himself in the Jewish future

and who lives on in the hearts of all who were touched by his kindness.

May our study of Torah be a tribute to his legacy

and an everlasting monument to his name.

תנצב״ה

જ

Dedicated by his daughter and son-in-law
Pamela and George Rohr

Table of Contents

Lesson 1
Hillel

Introduction

Wisdom requires that we carefully choose the battles we wish to fight and the wrongs we feel we must right. Sometimes, it turns out that all we are defending is our pride.

Hillel managed to revive the fabric of Jewish life without antagonizing the ruling Roman powers of the time. What was the secret to his leadership?

We'll find out in Lesson 1.

הלל אומר
הוי מתלמידיו של אהרן אוהב שלום ורודף שלום אוהב
ומקרבן לתורה

הוא היה אומר עשה רצוני כרצונך כדי שישה
רצונך כרצוני וכו' מדי שיבטל
כתורה לך לא אמרו על דיום מורו ואל
חמורך עד שתגיע למקום
להשמע ואל תאמר לכשאפנה אשה שהיה

Historical Timeline

3412/349 BCE	Jews permitted to return to Jerusalem—Second Temple is built
3622/139 BCE	Chanukah
3649/111 BCE	Birth of Hillel
3725/36 BCE	End of the Hasmonean Dynasty and ascent of Herod to the throne
3729/32 BCE	Hillel returns to Israel
3769/9 CE	Passing of Hillel

ROMAN EMPERORS & NOTABLES IN THE TIME OF **HILLEL**

63 BCE–48 BCE	**POMPEY**
49 BCE–44 BCE	**JULIUS CAESAR**
42 BCE–30 BCE	**MARK ANTHONY**
27 BCE–14 CE	**AUGUSTUS**

- Hillel ascended to Israel the first time during the rule of Pompey.
- Shemaya and Avtalyon passed away during the rule of Julius Caesar.
- Hillel was appointed *nasi* during the rule of Mark Anthony.
- Hillel passed away toward the end of the reign of Augustus.

Brief Biographical Overview

Hillel was born in Babylonia in 111 BCE. He relocated to Israel to learn from Shemaya and Avtalyon around 71 BCE. This was shortly after the death of the Jewish king Alexander Jannaeus, whose two sons Hyrcanus II and Aristobulus II laid claim to the throne. A bloody civil war broke out in Israel in which many Jews died. The brothers presented their dispute to General Pompey of Rome, who ruled with Hyrcanus. The war continued for a while longer, but Hyrcanus eventually prevailed and was appointed king. During these difficult times, the rabbinate suffered great deprivation, and the sages were forced to teach Torah in small, unlit rooms. Despite the privation, Hillel flourished and returned to Babylonia an accomplished scholar.

The country was plagued by further civil war and by aggressive Roman intervention. Under Roman pressure, the *sanhedrin* was temporarily disbanded. After the passing of Shemaya and Avtalyon in 46 BCE, no one was appointed to succeed them. The family of Beteira was given leadership responsibilities, but there was no formal *sanhedrin* over which to preside.

Hillel returned to Israel eight years later (32 BCE) to find this sorry state of affairs. He was immediately recognized as the foremost pupil of Shemaya and Avtalyon, and the respected family of Beteira abdicated their position in favor of Hillel. Hillel, appalled by the terrible decline of Torah study in Israel, set about to reestablish the academies of old. Thousands flocked to his academy, and Hillel revitalized the study of Torah in Israel.

Hillel eventually established the *sanhedrin* and served as *nasi* [leader] for forty years. Shortly before Hillel's appointment, Herod ascended to the throne of Israel. Although Herod was a sworn enemy of the Torah scholars, there is no evidence of any negative interaction between Hillel and Herod. Perhaps this was due to the fact that Hillel never involved himself in politics but saw his role solely as a spiritual one. Likely, this was also due to Hillel's sincerity, kindness, and peaceful disposition. It is difficult to carry a grudge against a man who gives no offense, or to persecute a man who refuses to speak ill of you or anyone else. Hillel's humility allowed him to tend to the spiritual needs of his flock without being targeted by the harsh designs of Herod.

Hillel passed away in 9 CE, at the age of 120, and was succeeded by his son Shimon. For the next fifteen generations, the descendants of Hillel were leaders of Torah scholarship.

From Babylonia to Israel

Text 1a

אמרו עליו על הלל הזקן שבכל יום ויום היה עושה ומשתכר בטרפעיק
חציו היה נותן לשומר בית המדרש, וחציו לפרנסתו ולפרנסת אנשי ביתו
פעם אחת לא מצא להשתכר ולא הניחו שומר בית המדרש להכנס
תלמוד בבלי יומא לה,ב

Every day Hillel the Elder used to work and earn one tropaik [coin], half of which he would give to the guard at the house of study and the other half with which he purchased food for his family. Once he had [found no work and] earned nothing [all day long], and the guard at the house of study would not permit him to enter.

TALMUD YOMA 35B

Text 1b

עלה ונתלה וישב על פי ארובה
כדי שישמע דברי אלהים חיים מפי שמעיה ואבטליון
אמרו: אותו היום ערב שבת היה, ותקופת טבת היתה
וירד עליו שלג מן השמים
כשעלה עמוד השחר אמר לו שמעיה לאבטליון
אבטליון אחי, בכל יום הבית מאיר, והיום אפל, שמא יום המעונן הוא

הציצו עיניהן וראו דמות אדם בארובה, עלו ומצאו עליו רום שלש אמות שלג
פרקוהו, והרחיצוהו, וסיכוהו, והושיבוהו כנגד המדורה
אמרו: ראוי זה לחלל עליו את השבת
תלמוד בבלי יומא לה,ב

He climbed [to the roof] and stretched out on the skylight, to hear words of [Torah] from the mouths of Shemaya and Avtalyon. It was a wintery Friday night, and snow began to fall [covering him completely]. When dawn broke, Shemaya said to Avtalyon, "Brother Avtalyon, every day this house is light and today it is dark. Is it perhaps a cloudy day?"

They looked up and saw the figure of a man in the skylight. They went up and found him covered in three cubits of snow. They removed him, bathed, and anointed him. They placed him opposite the fire and said, "This man deserves that the Sabbath be desecrated on his behalf."

TALMUD YOMA 35B

Ascending to Leadership

Text 2a

פעם אחת חל ארבעה עשר להיות בשבת

שכחו ולא ידעו אם פסח דוחה את השבת אם לאו

אמרו: כלום יש אדם שיודע אם פסח דוחה את השבת אם לאו

אמרו להם: אדם אחד יש שעלה מבבל, והלל הבבלי שמו

ששימש שני גדולי הדור שמעיה ואבטליון

ויודע אם פסח דוחה את השבת אם לאו. שלחו וקראו לו

אמרו לו: כלום אתה יודע אם הפסח דוחה את השבת אם לאו . . .

מיד הושיבוהו בראש ומינוהו נשיא עליהם

והיה דורש כל היום כולו בהלכות הפסח

התחיל מקנטרן בדברים

אמר להן: מי גרם לכם שאעלה מבבל ואהיה נשיא עליכם

עצלות שהיתה בכם, שלא שמשתם שני גדולי הדור שמעיה ואבטליון

תלמוד בבלי פסחים סו,א

On one occasion, the fourteenth of Nisan fell on the Sabbath, and the Beteira family forgot whether the sacrifice of Passover overrides the Sabbath or not.

They inquired of the sages, "Does anyone know whether the Passover sacrifice overrides the Sabbath?"

They were told, "There is a certain man who has come up from Babylonia. Hillel the Babylonian is his name. He served Shemaya and Avtalyon, the two greatest men of the previous generation, and he knows whether the Passover sacrifice overrides the Sabbath."

They summoned him and asked whether the Passover sacrifice overrides the Sabbath. [Hillel replied in the affirmative and provided many compelling arguments in support of this position.]

[When the Beteira family recognized the extent of his scholarship,] they set him at their head and appointed him *nasi*; he sat and lectured the whole day on the laws of Passover. He began to rebuke them, "Why did you have to abdicate the leadership in my favor? It was because of your indolence in not studying diligently from the two greatest men of the time, Shemaya and Avtalyon."

TALMUD PESACHIM 66A

Questions **for Discussion**

What are your impressions of Hillel based on his response to the Beteira family? Is his criticism of them fair? What does it imply about his personality?

Text 2b

אמרו לו: רבי, שכח ולא הביא סכין מערב שבת מהו

אמר להן: הלכה זו שמעתי ושכחתי

תלמוד בבלי פסחים סו,א

[A question arose regarding carrying on the Sabbath and they asked of Hillel,]

66 **M**aster, what if a man forgot and did not bring a knife [to slaughter the lamb] on the eve of the Sabbath [may it be carried on the Sabbath]?"

"I have heard this law," he replied, "but I have forgotten it."

TALMUD PESACHIM 66A

Text 2c

אמר להן: הלכה זו שמעתי ושכחתי

אלא, הנח להן לישראל אם אין נביאים הן בני נביאים הן

למחר, מי שפסחו טלה תוחבו בצמרו, מי שפסחו גדי תוחבו בין קרניו

ראה מעשה ונזכר הלכה, ואמר: כך מקובלני מפי שמעיה ואבטליון

תלמוד בבלי פסחים סו,א

66 **I** have heard this law, but have forgotten it," replied Hillel. "However, leave it to [the children of] Israel; if they are not prophets, they are the children of prophets!"

On the morrow, he whose Passover offering was a lamb stuck [the knife] in its wool; he whose Passover offering was a goat stuck it between its horns. He saw this practice and was reminded of the *halachah* and he said, "This [practice does indeed reflect] the tradition I received from Shemaya and Avtalyon."

TALMUD PESACHIM 66A

A Humble Greatness

Text 3 📜

תנו רבנן: לעולם יהא אדם ענוותן כהלל ואל יהא קפדן כשמאי

מעשה בשני בני אדם שהמרו זה את זה

אמרו: כל מי שילך ויקניט את הלל יטול ארבע מאות זוז

אמר אחד מהם: אני אקניטנו

אותו היום ערב שבת היה, והלל חפף את ראשו

הלך ועבר על פתח ביתו

אמר: מי כאן הלל, מי כאן הלל. נתעטף ויצא לקראתו

אמר לו: בני, מה אתה מבקש. אמר לו: שאלה יש לי לשאול

אמר לו: שאל בני, שאל

מפני מה ראשיהן של בבליים סגלגלות

אמר לו: בני, שאלה גדולה שאלת, מפני שאין להם חיות פקחות

הלך והמתין שעה אחת, חזר ואמר: מי כאן הלל, מי כאן הלל

נתעטף ויצא לקראתו

אמר לו: בני, מה אתה מבקש, אמר לו: שאלה יש לי לשאול

אמר לו: שאל בני, שאל

מפני מה עיניהן של תרמודיין תרוטות

אמר לו: בני, שאלה גדולה שאלת, מפני שדרין בין החולות

הלך והמתין שעה אחת, חזר ואמר: מי כאן הלל, מי כאן הלל

נתעטף ויצא לקראתו

אמר לו: בני, מה אתה מבקש

אמר לו: שאלה יש לי לשאול. אמר לו: שאל בני, שאל

מפני מה רגליהם של אפרקיים רחבות

אמר לו: בני, שאלה גדולה שאלת—מפני שדרין בין בצעי המים

אמר לו: שאלות הרבה יש לי לשאול, ומתירא אני שמא תכעוס

נתעטף וישב לפניו, אמר לו: כל שאלות שיש לך לשאול—שאל

אמר לו: אתה הוא הלל שקורין אותך נשיא ישראל, אמר לו: הן

אמר לו: אם אתה הוא, לא ירבו כמותך בישראל. אמר לו: בני, מפני מה

אמר לו: מפני שאבדתי על ידך ארבע מאות זוז

אמר לו: הוי זהיר ברוחך

כדי הוא הלל שתאבד על ידו ארבע מאות זוז וארבע מאות זוז והלל לא יקפיד

תלמוד בבלי שבת ל,ב

ur Rabbis taught: "A man should always be gentle like Hillel, and not impatient like Shammai."

It once happened that two men made a wager with each other, saying, "He who goes and makes Hillel angry shall receive four hundred zuz."

One of them said, "I will go and provoke him."

It was Friday afternoon before Shabbat, and Hillel was bathing.

The man passed by Hillel's house and called out, "Who here is Hillel, who here is Hillel?" [*This is a rude and provocative way of summoning Hillel. Rashi.*]

Hillel dressed and went out to him, saying, "My son, what do you require?"

"I have a question," said the man.

"Ask, my son, ask," he prompted.

Thereupon he asked, "Why are the heads of the Babylonians round?"

"My son, you have asked a great question," replied Hillel. "It is because their midwives are not skillful."

He departed, tarried a while, returned, and called out, "Who here is Hillel, who here is Hillel?"

Hillel dressed and went out to him, saying, "My son, what do you require?"

"I have a question," said the man.

"Ask, my son, ask," he prompted.

Thereupon he asked, "Why do the Palmyreans have narrow eye slits?"

"My son, you have asked a great question," Hillel replied. "It is because they live in sandy places." [*The narrow slits protect their eyes from the sand driven by the wind. Rashi.*]

The man departed, tarried a while, returned, and called out, "Who here is Hillel, who here is Hillel?"

Hillel dressed and went out to him, saying, "My son, what do you require?"

"I have a question," said he.

"Ask, my son, ask" he prompted.

He asked, "Why are the feet of the Africans wide?"

"My son, you have asked a great question," said he. "It is because they live in watery marshes." [*The wide foot enables them to avoid the narrow marshes. Rashi.*]

"I have many questions to ask," said he, "but fear that you may become angry."

Thereupon he wrapped himself in a cloak, sat before him and said, "Ask whatever you want to ask."

"Are you the Hillel who is called the *nasi* of Israel?"

"Yes," he replied.

"If that is you," he retorted, "may there not be many like you in Israel."

"Why, my son?" queried Hillel.

"Because I have lost four hundred zuz through you," complained the man.

"Be wary of your moods," Hillel replied. "It is worth it that you should lose four hundred zuz and yet another four hundred zuz, yet Hillel shall not lose his temper."

TALMUD SHABBAT 30B

Discussion Questions

Does this portrait of Hillel seem consistent with the portrait we have painted up to now?

Based on these readings, how would you characterize Hillel?

Learning Activity 1

In the following reading, Hillel asserts that his greatness lies in his great humility:

Text 4

השפלתי היא הגבהתי הגבהתי היא השפלתי

ויקרא רבה א,ה

y humility is my greatness and my greatness is my humility.

Vayikra Rabah 1:5

1. Do you agree with this characterization? Review the first three texts with a partner, jotting down what you consider to be evidence for Hillel being humble vs. evidence against Hillel being humble.

Evidence for Humility	Evidence Against Humility

2. Do you see an inherent contradiction in Hillel asserting that his greatness lies in his humility? Why or why not?

There is/isn't a contradiction in Hillel declaring that his greatness is his humility because:

_____

_____

_____

_____

_____

_____

_____

_____

_____

_____

_____

_____

Text 5

One who is comfortable with his essence is moved neither by those greater than him nor by those lesser than him.

RABBI SHALOM DOV BER SCHNEERSON

Text 6

די מחסורו (דברים טו,ח) אתה מצווה עליו לפרנסו

ואי אתה מצווה עליו לעשרו

אשר יחסר לו (שם) אפילו סוס לרכוב עליו ועבד לרוץ לפניו

אמרו עליו על הלל הזקן שלקח לעני בן טובים אחד

סוס לרכוב עליו ועבד לרוץ לפניו

פעם אחת לא מצא עבד לרוץ לפניו, ורץ לפניו שלשה מילין

תלמוד בבלי כתובות סז,ב

The Torah requires that we provide for the poor in a manner that is "sufficient for his needs" (Deuteronomy 15:8), [which implies that] we are commanded [only] to maintain him [according to the standards he has grown accustomed to], but not to make him rich; [yet it is further written that we must provide] "that which he wants (ibid.)," [which implies an obligation to provide] even a horse to ride upon and a slave to run before him [if this is his want].

It was related that Hillel the Elder purchased for a poor man from an aristocratic family, a horse to ride upon and a slave to run before him. On one occasion, he could not find a slave to run before him, so Hillel himself ran before him for three *mil* (six thousand cubits).

TALMUD KETUBOT 67B

Text 7

The sages said regarding a [royal] slave, "the slave of a king is a king" (Sifri, Deuteronomy 1:7). [Being respected like a king] does not create a feeling of self-importance or pride in the slave, who realizes that his status is not due to his own importance or greatness, but rather due to the stature of the king. Similarly, feeling truly nullified to God does not preclude having power or a sense of personal exaltedness, since such power flows not from the self, but from God.

RABBI MENACHEM MENDEL SCHNEERSON, LIKUTEI SICHOT, VOL. 17

Text 8

אם אין אני לי מי לי וכשאני לעצמי מה אני ואם לא עכשיו אימתי
משנה אבות א,יד

If I am not for myself, who will be for me? And if I am only for myself, what am I? And if not now, when?

MISHNAH AVOT 1:14

Text 9

ובמקום שאין אנשים השתדל להיות איש
משנה אבות ב,ה

Where there is no other person, endeavor to become that person.

MISHNAH AVOT 2:5

Seeing the Best in Others

Text 10a 📖

אמר רבי אבא אמר שמואל

שלש שנים נחלקו בית שמאי ובית הלל

הללו אומרים הלכה כמותנו והללו אומרים הלכה כמותנו

יצאה בת קול ואמרה: אלו ואלו דברי אלהים חיים הן, והלכה כבית הלל

וכי מאחר שאלו ואלו דברי אלהים חיים

מפני מה זכו בית הלל לקבוע הלכה כמותן

מפני שנוחין ועלובין היו, ושונין דבריהן ודברי בית שמאי

ולא עוד אלא שמקדימין דברי בית שמאי לדבריהן

תלמוד בבלי עירובין יג,ב

Rabbi Abba stated in the name of Shmuel: For three years, there was a dispute between the school of Shammai and the school of Hillel, the former asserting the *halachah* is in agreement with their views, and the latter contending the *halachah* is in agreement with their views. Then a heavenly voice announced, "Both opinions are words of the living God, but the *halachah* agrees with the school of Hillel." [The Talmud asks:] If both were the words of the living God why was the school of Hillel entitled to have the *halachah* [decided in accordance with their view]? Because they were kindly and modest; they studied their own rulings and those of the school of Shammai, and were even so humble as to cite Shammai's views before their own.

TALMUD ERUVIN 13B

Text 10b

ללמדך, שכל המשפיל עצמו הקדוש ברוך הוא מגביהו

וכל המגביה עצמו הקדוש ברוך הוא משפילו

כל המחזר על הגדולה, גדולה בורחת ממנו

וכל הבורח מן הגדולה, גדולה מחזרת אחריו

תלמוד בבלי עירובין יג,ב

This teaches you that he who humbles himself is exalted by the Holy One, blessed be He, and he, who exalts himself, is humbled by the Holy One, blessed be He. From he who seeks greatness, greatness flees, but he who flees from greatness, greatness pursues.

TALMUD ERUVIN 13B

Text 11a

תנו רבנן: מעשה בנכרי אחד שבא לפני שמאי

אמר לו: כמה תורות יש לכם. אמר לו: שתים, תורה שבכתב ותורה שבעל פה

אמר לו: שבכתב אני מאמינך, ושבעל פה איני מאמינך

גיירני על מנת שתלמדני תורה שבכתב

גער בו והוציאו בנזיפה

בא לפני הלל—גייריה

יומא קמא אמר ליה: א״ב ג״ד, למחר אפיך ליה

אמר ליה: והא אתמול לא אמרת לי הכי

אמר לו: לאו עלי דידי קא סמכת, דעל פה נמי סמוך עלי

תלמוד בבלי שבת לא,א

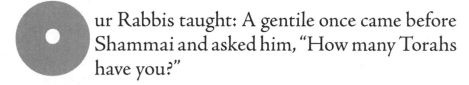ur Rabbis taught: A gentile once came before Shammai and asked him, "How many Torahs have you?"

"Two," he replied. "The written Torah and the oral Torah."

"I believe you with respect to the written, but not with respect to the oral Torah. Convert me on condition that you teach me only the written Torah."

Shammai scolded and repulsed him.

He then went before Hillel, who accepted him as a proselyte. On the first day, he taught him, "Alef, Bet, Gimmel, Daled." The following day he reversed [the letters].

"But yesterday you taught them to me differently," protested the proselyte.

"Must you then not rely on my tradition [in order to read the written text]? Then rely on me with respect to the oral [Torah] too," replied Hillel.

Talmud Shabbat 31a

Text 11b ▌

שוב מעשה בנכרי אחד שבא לפני שמאי

אמר לו: גיירני על מנת שתלמדני כל התורה כולה כשאני עומד על רגל אחת

דחפו באמת הבנין שבידו

בא לפני הלל—גייריה

אמר לו: דעלך סני לחברך לא תעביד

זו היא כל התורה כולה, ואידך פירושה הוא, זיל גמור

תלמוד בבלי שבת לא,א

n another occasion, a gentile came before Shammai and said to him, "Convert me on condition that you teach me the whole Torah while I stand on one foot."

[Shammai] repulsed him with the builder's cubit in his hand.

When [the gentile] went before Hillel, Hillel said to him, "What is hateful to you, do not to your neighbor, that is the whole Torah, the rest is the commentary thereof; go and learn it."

TALMUD SHABBAT 31A

Text 11c ▌

שוב מעשה בנכרי אחד שהיה עובר אחורי בית המדרש

ושמע קול סופר שהיה אומר

ואלה הבגדים אשר יעשו חשן ואפוד (שמות כח,ד)

אמר: הללו למי, אמרו לו: לכהן גדול

אמר אותו נכרי בעצמו, אלך ואתגייר, בשביל שישימוני כהן גדול

בא לפני שמאי, אמר ליה: גיירני על מנת שתשימני כהן גדול

דחפו באמת הבנין שבידו

בא לפני הלל—גייריה

אמר לו: כלום מעמידין מלך אלא מי שיודע טכסיסי מלכות

לך למוד טכסיסי מלכות

הלך וקרא, כיון שהגיע והזר הקרב יומת (במדבר א,נא)

אמר ליה: מקרא זה על מי נאמר

אמר לו: אפילו על דוד מלך ישראל

נשא אותו גר קל וחומר בעצמו: ומה ישראל שנקראו בנים למקום

ומתוך אהבה שאהבם קרא להם בני בכרי ישראל (שמות ד,כב)

כתיב עליהם והזר הקרב יומת

גר הקל שבא במקלו ובתרמילו—על אחת כמה וכמה . . .

לימים נזדווגו שלשתן למקום אחד, אמרו . . .

ענוותנותו של הלל קרבנו תחת כנפי השכינה

תלמוד בבלי שבת לא,א

O n another occasion, a certain gentile was passing behind a study hall, when he heard a voice
reciting, "And these are the garments which they
shall make: a breastplate, and an apron" (Exodus 28:4).

"For whom are these?" [he asked].

"For the High Priest," he was told.

The gentile said to himself, "I will go and convert so that
I may be appointed High Priest."

He went before Shammai and said to him, "Convert me
on condition that you appoint me High Priest."

But [Shammai] repulsed him with the builder's cubit in
his hand.

He then went before Hillel, who made him a proselyte. [Hillel] then said to him, "Can any man be made a king before he learns the art of government? Go and study the art of [Jewish] government!"

He went and read [the Torah]. When he came to [the verse], "And the stranger that approaches [the sanctuary] shall be put to death" (Numbers 1:51), he asked Hillel, "To whom does this verse apply?"

"Even to David, King of Israel," was the answer.

Thereupon that proselyte reasoned to himself, "If regarding [the people of] Israel, who are the sons of God, and He lovingly designated them as 'Israel, my son, my firstborn' (Exodus 4:22), it is written 'and the stranger that approaches [the sanctuary] shall be put to death,' how much more so a mere proselyte, who comes with his staff and wallet!"...

Some time later the three [proselytes] met in one place and reflected, "... Hillel's gentleness brought us under the wings of the divine presence".

TALMUD SHABBAT 31A

Text 11d 📕

שבית שמאי אומרים אל ישנה אדם אלא למי שהוא חכם ועניו ובן אבות ועשיר

ובית הלל אומרים לכל אדם ישנה

שהרבה פושעים היו בהם בישראל

ונתקרבו לתלמוד תורה ויצאו מהם צדיקים חסידים וכשרים

אבות דרבי נתן ב,ט

The School of Shammai said one should teach [only those who are] wise, humble, from good parentage and wealthy. The School of Hillel said one may teach any person, for there are many Jews who were [once] sinners but came to learn Torah, and their children were righteous, pious, and reliable Jews.

AVOT DEREBBI NATAN 2:9

Key Points

1. Hillel traveled from Babylonia to Israel, enduring great poverty, in order to learn Torah directly from the masters, Shemaya and Avtalyon.

2. So devoted was he to his studies that when he did not have the funds to enter the house of study, he climbed on the roof.

3. When Hillel remembered a law regarding the paschal lamb that the Beteira family had forgotten, they abdicated their position of leadership in favor of Hillel.

4. Although Hillel was humble, he also was aware of his capabilities and knew how to be assertive and forceful when necessary.

5. Where Shammai was critical and exacting, Hillel saw potential for growth.

6. Hillel's tolerant attitude allowed him to attract many students to the academy without arousing the antagonism of the ruling authorities.

Additional Readings

The Case of the Floating Skull
Ethics 1:6

By **Yosef Marcus**

A man had gone for a stroll along the river when he noticed an unusual and ghoulish sight: a skull floating on the surface of the water. His reaction was unusual. He reached neither for his cellphone nor for his digital camera.

Instead, he turned to the skull and uttered the following six Aramaic words: *Ahl d'ateift aftfuch, v'sof mitofayich yitufun*. Had he spoken to it in English, he might have said this: "You were drowned because you drowned others. And ultimately, those who drowned you will also drown." Less poetic in English, yet essentially the same point.

The reason he used Aramaic was because at the time the incident occurred—some time toward the end of the Second Temple era—Aramaic was not yet a deceased language. In fact, it was very much alive, especially among Jews who lived in Babylonia.

The man walking along the river had lived in Babylonia until the age of forty. He then migrated to the holy city of Jerusalem to study at the feet of Shma'ayah and Avtalyon, two brothers of Greek extraction, who had converted to Judaism and rose to become the leading Judaic scholars of their day.

The man was Hillel, the author of better known statements, such as "If I am not for myself who is for me", "What is hateful to you do not do unto your friend" and others. He was known for his profound knowledge and extraordinary patience. Like Moses, he was known for his humility; and, like Moses, he lived for one hundred and twenty years. According to kabbalistic tradition he and Moses shared the same soul.

Maimonides and the Skull

Another man by the name of Moses, Moses Maimonides, who lived some 1,000 years after the skull story, wrote the following in his commentary on Tractate Avot ("Ethics of the Fathers") where the skull story is recorded (paraphrased):

There are consequences to our actions—consequences that reflect those actions. If you commit murder and drown others in a river to hide your crime, you will receive your punishment in the form of your crime. If you invent an unjust thing to benefit yourself at the expense of others, that unjust thing will ultimately be used against you. On the positive side, if you introduce something that benefits others, that thing will ultimately come to benefit you as well. In Hebrew it is called: *midah k'neged midah*—measure for measure.

This is how Maimonides and other commentators explain Hillel's message.

Pharaoh vs. Moses round II

Maimonides' grandson, Rabbi David Hanagid, cites a tradition handed down by "the early ones" that the floating skull belonged to none other than Pharaoh himself. Hillel therefore told him: "Because you commanded that Jewish children be drowned in the Nile, you were drowned." It was specifically Hillel who confronted Pharaoh's skull, since as a reincarnation of Moses he was fit to confront Pharaoh.

According to this interpretation, says Rabbi Isaac Luria, the renowned 16th century Safed mystic known as "the Holy Ari", the second half of Hillel's statement is addressed not to Pharaoh but to the Jewish people: "Just as Pharaoh was drowned, so all persecutors of Israel will ultimately be drowned."

The Lubavitcher Rebbe, Rabbi Menachem Mendel Schneerson of blessed memory, saw in the Ari's comment words of comfort to the tired soul of the exiled

Jew, to the soul of one who feels that he or she is up against an insurmountable challenge, an impenetrable cloud of darkness. Hillel, the great leader of Israel, turns to this person and says: "If Pharaoh, the embodiment of evil, the man who cast fear even into the heart of Moses, so much so that God had to reassure him and say, 'Come to Pharaoh—I will accompany you,' ended up drowned in a river, certainly all the Pharaohs of history, all the great serpents that tried and will try to drown you through physical and spiritual persecution—they will be drowned as well. For evil has no leg to stand on. Like smoke it obscures our vision for a time but must ultimately disappear."

Mocking the Poor

If that were all we could learn from Hillel's statement, it would be enough. But there's more. Here's another beautiful thought:

It seems strange that Hillel, the man of kindness, humility and impossible patience, would rebuke a dead man! According to Jewish tradition, one ought not perform any mitzvah in a graveyard. Doing so is considered "mocking the poor" (*loeg la'rash*), since those that dwell in the earth are no longer capable of performing *mitzvot*. Just as you would not partake of a gourmet dinner in the face of one unable to afford a slice of bread, so one should not show one's *tzizit*, for example, in the presence of those who can no longer fulfill that commandment.

Why, then, did Hillel, the man of kindness and humility, rebuke this poor dead person, who could do nothing with this rebuke?

The answer, says the Rebbe, is that when Hillel came across the skull of Pharaoh, he though to himself: "Why has God arranged for me to see this sight?" He then came to the conclusion that the time had finally come for the soul of Pharaoh to find peace. And by using Pharaoh as an example with which to teach a meaningful message, Hillel uplifted Pharaoh's soul and granted it the ability to find peace.

In summation

So what starts out as an innocent stroll along the river turns out to be a passage filled with meaningful lessons:

• What goes around comes around.

• Even the most formidable evil is transient.

• Everything that comes your way has a purpose and you should fulfill that purpose. Not always is that purpose apparent but we should at least take advantage of those situations when the purpose is apparent.

• Even a Pharaoh can ultimately be redeemed and should be redeemed when that time arrives.

And that's the story of the floating skull.

Reprinted with permission from chabad.org.

Tetzaveh: The High Priest's Clothes and the Convert

The Talmud [Shabbat 31a] tells the story of three Gentiles who wished to convert. In each case, they were initially rejected by the scholar Shamai, known for his strictness, but they were later accepted and converted by the famously modest Hillel.

The Convert Who Wanted to be High Priest

In one case, a Gentile was walking near a synagogue when he heard the Torah being read and translated:

"These are the clothes that you should make: the jeweled breast-plate, the *ephod*-apron . . . " [Ex. 28:4]

His interest was piqued. "For whom are these fancy clothes?' he asked. "They are special garments for the 'Kohen Gadol,' the High Priest. The Gentile was excited. "For this, it's worth becoming a Jew. I'll go convert and become the next High Priest!'

The Gentile made the mistake of approaching Shamai. "I want you to convert me,' he told Shamai, "but only on condition that you appoint me High Priest.' Shamai rebuffed the man, pushing him away with a builder's measuring rod.

Then he went to Hillel with the same proposition. Amazingly, Hillel agreed to convert the man. Hillel, however, gave him some advice. "If you wanted to be king, you would need to learn the ways and customs of the royal court. Since you aspire to be the High Priest, go study the appropriate laws.'

The new convert began studying Torah. One day, he came across the verse, "Any non-priest who participates (in the holy service) shall die" [Num. 3:10]. "To whom does this refer?' he asked. Even King David, he was told. Even David, king of Israel, was not allowed to serve in the holy Temple, as he was not a descendent of Aaron the *kohen*.

The convert was amazed. Even those born Jewish, and who are referred to as God's children—even they are not allowed to serve in the Temple! Certainly, a convert who has just arrived with his staff and pack may not perform this holy service. Recognizing his mistake, he returned to Hillel. "May blessings fall on your head, humble Hillel, for drawing me under the wings of the Divine Presence."

A fascinating story, but one that requires some explanation. Why did Shamai use a builder's measuring rod to send away the potential convert? What did Hillel see in the Gentile that convinced him to perform the conversion?

Shamai's Rejection

Shamai felt that the man lacked a sincere motivation to convert. By chance, he had overheard the recitation of the High Priest's special garments. The garments, beautiful though they may be, represent only an external honor. His aspirations were shallow and superficial, like clothing that is worn on the surface.

Furthermore, the chance incident did not even awaken within the Gentile a realistic goal. How could conversion to Judaism, with all of the Torah's obligations, be based on such a crazy, impossible fancy—being appointed High Priest? The foundations of such a conversion were just too shaky. Shamai pushed him away with a builder's measuring rod, hinting that he needed to base his goals on solid, measured objectives.

Hillel's Perspective

Hillel, however, looked at the situation differently. In his eyes, the very fact that this man passed by the synagogue just when this verse was being read, and that this incident should inspire him to such a lofty goal—converting to Judaism—such a person must have a sincere yearning for truth planted deeply in his heart. He was not seeking the honor accorded to the rich and powerful, but rather the respect granted to those who serve God at the highest level. The seed of genuine love of God was there, just obscured by false ambitions, the result of profound ignorance. Hillel was confident that as he advanced in Torah study, the convert would discover the beauty and honor of divine service that he so desired through the sincere observance of the Torah's laws.

Both Traits Needed

Once, the three converts who were initially rejected by Shamai and later accepted by Hillel, met together. They all agreed: "The strictness of Shamai almost made us lose our (spiritual) world; but the humility of Hillel brought us under the wings of God's Presence."

Rav Kook noted that the converts did not talk about Shamai and Hillel. Rather, they spoke of the "strictness of Shamai" and the "humility of Hillel". These are two distinct character traits, each one necessary in certain situations. In order to maintain spiritual attainments, we need the traits of firmness and strictness. On the other hand, in order to grow spiritually, or to draw close those who are far away, we need the traits of humility and tolerance. The three converts recognized that it was Hillel's quality of humility that helped bring them 'under the wings of God's Presence'.

[adapted from Ein Eyah vol. III, pp. 144-147]

Reprinted with permission from ravkooktorah.org and Chanan Morrison.

There's So Much Hypocrisy!

By **Tzvi Freeman**

Question:

I've been getting into Torah lately. But the more I learn, the more I see how everyone around me is doing it all wrong. I don't mean the people that are not observant. I mean the people that have committed to an observant life. There's so much hypocrisy!

Answer:

Don't get so excited. It's just a personality thing. You're probably one of those School of Shamai souls. Remember the story with the Talmudic sage Shamai? A man came and asked, "Convert me to Judaism on condition that you tell me the entire Torah while I stand on one foot!" Shamai chased the mocker out with a yardstick.

So he went to Hillel. Hillel converted him on the spot and then told him: "That which is hateful to you, don't do to others. This is the entire Torah. The rest is commentary. Now go and learn it!"

Some people tie their shoelaces a little looser. Some tie them real tight. Some let the world come in as one big blur. Others focus on every detail and weigh and measure with a precise rule.

Problem is, the world is a messy place.

It all began when we ate from the Tree of Knowing Good With Evil—our world became a place of compounds and mixtures. Wherever you find beauty, there's going to be ugliness. You won't find joy without sorrow, pleasure without pain. You cannot invent a thing that will provide benefit without threat of harm, or find a man on this earth who does only good without fault.

Wherever you will find one form of good, you're going to find another sort of evil. And where that evil does not lie, another takes its place. You want to find pure and simple goodness in a single being? It will be rare, very, very rare.

This is what wise King Solomon had to say: Don't reject any thing for the harm it could cause. Don't despise any man for the ugliness inside him. Rather, use each thing towards the purpose God conceived it for, and learn from each man all he has to offer.

But you are doing the Shamai thing—both to all the people around you and to yourself as well: You're creating a model in your mind of how things should be, and measuring everything according to that yardstick. And guess what? Things don't line up.

I'm not telling you to throw the yardstick out. Just be a little more practical with its use. This is an imperfect world. We're not there yet. Measure accordingly. Both yourself and others.

Have you ever done any carpentry or one of those Ikea do-it-yourself jobs? They always tell you not to tighten the bolts until the whole thing's been put together.

Hillel summed it all up:

Don't chase people out with measuring sticks.

You don't like being measured to perfection, so don't do that to others.

Now go and learn. Dig deeper and deeper.

Reprinted with permission from chabad.org.

On Humility

By Jonathan Sacks

How virtues change! Moses, the greatest hero of Jewish tradition, is described by the Bible as "a very humble man, more humble than anyone else on the face of the earth." By today's standards he was clearly wrongly advised. He should have hired an agent, sharpened up his image, let slip some calculated indiscretions about his conversations with the Almighty and sold his story to the press for a six-figure sum. With any luck, he might have landed up with his own television chat show, dispensing wisdom to those willing to bare their soul to the watching millions. He would have had his fifteen minutes of fame. Instead he had to settle for the lesser consolation of three thousand years of moral influence.

Humility is the orphaned virtue of our age. Charles Dickens dealt it a mortal blow in his portrayal of the unctuous Uriah Heep, the man who kept saying, "I am the 'umblest person going." Its demise, though, came a century later with the threatening anonymity of mass culture alongside the loss of neighbourhoods and congregations. A community is a place of friends. Urban society is a landscape of strangers. Yet there is an irrepressible human urge for recognition. So a culture emerged out of the various ways of "making a statement" to people we do not know, but who, we hope, will somehow notice. Beliefs ceased to be things confessed in prayer and became slogans emblazoned on t-shirts. A comprehensive repertoire developed of signalling individuality, from personalized number-plates, to in-your-face dressing, to designer labels worn on the outside, not within. You can trace an entire cultural transformation in the shift from renown to fame to celebrity to being famous for being famous. The creed of our age is, "If you've got it, flaunt it." Humility, being humble, did not stand a chance.

This is a shame. Humility—true humility—is one of the most expansive and life-enhancing of all virtues. It does not mean undervaluing yourself. It means valuing other people. It signals a certain openness to life's grandeur and the willingness to be surprised, uplifted, by goodness wherever one finds it. I learned the meaning of humility from my late father. He had come over to this country at the age of five, fleeing persecution in Poland. His family was poor and he had to leave school at the age of fourteen to support them. What education he had was largely self-taught. Yet he loved excellence, in whatever field or form it came. He had a passion for classical music and painting, and his taste in literature was impeccable, far better than mine. He was an enthusiast. He had—and this was what I so cherished in him—the capacity to admire. That, I think, is what the greater part of humility is, the capacity to be open to something greater than oneself. False humility is the pretence that one is small. True humility is the consciousness of standing in the presence of greatness, which is why it is the virtue of prophets, those who feel most vividly the nearness of God.

As a young man, full of questions about faith, I travelled to the United States where, I had heard, there were outstanding rabbis. I met many, but I also had the privilege of meeting the greatest Jewish leader of my generation, the late Lubavitcher Rebbe, Rabbi Menachem Mendel Schneerson. Heir to the dynastic leadership of a relatively small group of Jewish mystics, he had escaped from Europe to New York during the Second World War and had turned the tattered remnants of his flock into a worldwide movement. Wherever I travelled, I heard tales of his extraordinary leadership, many verging on the miraculous. He was, I was told, one of the outstanding charismatic leaders of our time. I resolved to meet him if I could.

I did, and was utterly surprised. He was certainly not charismatic in any conventional sense. Quiet, self-effacing, understated, one might hardly have noticed him had it not been for the reverence in which he was held by his disciples. That meeting, though, changed my life. He was a world-famous figure. I was an anonymous student from three thousand miles away. Yet in his presence I seemed to be the most important person in the world. He asked me about myself; he listened carefully; he challenged me to become a leader, something I had never contemplated before. Quickly it became clear to me that he believed in me more than I believed in myself. As I left the room, it occurred to me that it had been full of my presence and his absence. Perhaps that is what listening is, considered as a religious act. I then knew that greatness is measured by what we efface ourselves towards. There was no grandeur in his manner; neither was there any false modesty. He was serene, dignified, majestic; a man of transcending humility who gathered you into his embrace and taught you to look up.

True virtue never needs to advertise itself. That is why I find the aggressive packaging of personality so sad. It speaks of loneliness, the profound, endemic loneliness of a world without relationships of fidelity and trust. It testifies ultimately to a loss of faith—a loss of that knowledge, so precious to previous generations, that beyond the visible surfaces of this world is a Presence who knows us, loves us, and takes notice of our deeds. What else, secure in that knowledge, could we need? Time and again, when conducting a funeral or visiting mourners, I discover that the deceased had led a life of generosity and kindness unknown to even close relatives. I came to the conclusion—one I never dreamed of before I was given this window into private worlds— that the vast majority of saintly or generous acts are done quietly with no desire for public recognition. That is humility, and what a glorious revelation it is of the human spirit.

Humility, then, is more than just a virtue: it is a form of perception, a language in which the "I" is silent so that I can hear the "Thou", the unspoken call beneath human speech, the Divine whisper within all that moves, the voice of otherness that calls me to redeem its loneliness with the touch of love. Humility is what opens us to the world.

And does it matter that it no longer fits the confines of our age? The truth is that moral beauty, like music, always moves those who can hear beneath the noise. Virtues may be out of fashion, but they are never out of date. The things that call attention to themselves are never interesting for long, which is why our attention span grows shorter by the year. Humility—the polar opposite of "advertisements for myself"—never fails to leave its afterglow. We know when we have been in the presence of someone in whom the Divine presence breathes. We feel affirmed, enlarged, and with good reason. For we have met someone who, not taking himself or herself seriously at all, has shown us what it is to take with utmost seriousness that which is not I.

Reprinted with permission from chabad.org.

Towards A Definition Of Humility

By **Sol Roth**

Judaism requires humility on both religious and human grounds. It is a necessary ingredient in the religious perspective and is indispensable in social relations. The importance assigned to this character trait is considerable. In the Torah—the written and the oral—humility is associated prominently with Judaism's most outstanding representatives. No one was ever as humble as Moses.[1] One shall strive to be as humble as Hillel.[2] Rabbi Judah the Prince, redactor of the Mishnah, was so proficient in this virtue that, by comparison, none of his survivors were to be regarded as humble. As the Talmud put it, "When Rebbe died, humility disappeared."[3]

The idea of humility is rich in content and inextricably bound to other principles and precepts included in the complex system of Jewish ethics. In this essay, its wealth of meaning will be explored and its centrality in that system will be exhibited. This essay is offered as a proposal for the characterization of the Jewish conception of humility.

I

A careful analysis reveals two independent conceptions of humility expounded in Talmudic literature: (1) The religious conception—the humble person is one who believes that his achievements and acquisitions are the result of Divine benevolence rather than personal power or merit. (2) The moral conception—the humble person is one who believes that his personal achievements and acquisitions, whatever they may be, provide no grounds for the judgment that he is superior to his fellow men.

The first conception is formulated in the *Semag*. He explains the verse "Take heed lest you forget the Lord your God"[4] as a warning that "the children of Israel shall not feel pride when the Holy One, blessed be He, brings them blessing and they shall not say that they accumulated these blessings through their own effort and thus fail to acknowledge the good which they received from the Holy One, blessed be He, because of their pride."[5]

Rabbeinu Yonah, on the other hand, on the verse which commands the king that "his heart be not lifted up above his brethren"[6] declares "We are warned in this command to remove from our souls the quality of pride and that the big man shall not behave with arrogance towards the small man but that he shall always be of humble spirit."[7] This statement is an expression of the moral conception. Both conceptions are formulated as prohibitions against pride but humility admits of degrees and, at its lowest, it is simply the negation of pride.

The claim that these formulations represent two conceptions rather than one is based, first, on the fact that they are factually and logically independent. One may, in behavior, exhibit the religious attitude without the moral and vice versa. One may recognize his attainments and possessions as the products of Divine grace and display humility in relation to God and yet treat men with contempt if, in his judgment, their successes fall short of his. On the other hand, it is possible that a person does not believe his attainments to be in any way superior and yet, meager though they are, to identify himself as their sole and exclusive cause—in which case he is religiously arrogant and morally humble. Both types are numerous and abundantly available to human experience.

But, secondly, it should be noted that humility is a relational conception, that is to say, it does not denote a *quality* that may be affirmed or denied of an individual but a *relation* into which an individual enters merely as a term. For, it is evident that, from the philosophic point of view, the declaration of the humble, namely "I am unimportant," does not assert that he possesses a certain quality as is the case, for example, with the statement "I am white." Rather does it assert a relation in the same way as the declaration: "I am tall!" Tallness is not an intrinsic property of an individual. It designates a relation that obtains between the individual and some standard or some other individual. Analogously, unimportance denotes a relation to some standard or to some entity. The humble person may therefore assert unimportance either in relation to God or in comparison with man. But in the two cases the meaning of unimportance differs. In one it means dependence on God; in the other it signifies that success is no basis for the judgment of superiority. These two conceptions are independent. It should also be noted, in passing, that this relational aspect of humility makes it logically possible for a person to experience simultaneously the polar sentiments of importance and unimportance. But more of this later.

By way of further clarification, it should be added that the claim that there are two conceptions of humility should not be construed as the suggestion that there are differences of opinion among the interpreters of Torah as to which of these two is an imperative of Halakhah. The dispute among the sages focuses exclusively on the question as to which of the two should be assigned primacy. Some include the prohibition on one form of arrogance among the 613 commandments and some include the other in that list;[8] none removes from his conception of the *humble personality* the element stressed by the other. Thus, Ramban, whose emphasis coincides with that of *Rabbeinu Yonah* and who maintains that the Biblical root of the prohibition on arrogance deals with human relations, writes, "I will therefore explain how you shall conduct yourself as a humble man…. Every man shall be greater than you in your eyes . . . In all your speaking, acting and thinking regard yourself as though you were in the presence of God."[9] A full characterization of the humble personality must therefore, according to Ramban, take into account man's relation to God as well.

Further, arrogance and humility, at their lowest level, are correlative notions. A person is arrogant if he regards himself as the cause of his achievements or if he believes them to be the ground of his superiority. One who avoids these attitudes is humble.

The arrogant person is intellectually in error. One who exemplifies the religious conception of arrogance may declare either "My power and the might of my hand hath gotten me this wealth"[10] or "For my righteousness the Lord hath brought me to possess this land,"[11] that is, he asserts that his achievements are due to his own power or personal merit. In the first case he errs in that he fails to recognize the Almighty as at least a part cause of his success—one may plant the seeds but he cannot produce the rain—and even as the ultimate source of all the powers he is able to activate. In the second case, he errs in that he overemphasizes the good of which he is the source and underestimates the evil of which he is also the origin.

The morally arrogant person contends that he is better than others. This claim presupposes a standard by which he may be compared with others. It may be a standard of physical strength, material accumulation, intellectual achievement, social status, etc. But whatever may be the standard that impresses him as most important, the arrogant individual believes that he ranks higher on the scale than those by whom he is surrounded and that consequently he is the better man. His error, in this case, may be rooted in any of three misconceptions. He may be mistaken in his value system. If, for example, he regards material accumulation to be of highest value, he errs in the standard he selects. He may also stray from the truth in his judgment. If piety and morality should be his choice of the ultimate standard, his estimate of his own attainments in relation to those of others may not be accurate. Finally, if human life is of unlimited value, one may, if his standard is good and his judgment right, maintain "My deeds are better than his" but he is not generally justified in declaring "I am better than he." He simply has no way of estimating the value of his life in comparison with the life of another in order to make the invidious comparison.

Two important conclusions which contribute to the understanding of the idea of humility follow from this discussion. First, humility is a function of two things: attainments and attitudes. If one who has lived a life filled with failures refrains from attributing whatever meager success he has accumulated to his own competence or avoids the sentiment that he is to his own competence or avoids the sentiment that he is superior to others, his attitude, while praiseworthy, cannot be identified as one of great humility—no matter how small the value he assigns to himself. To be outstanding in humility, one must first be outstanding in achievements. "Now the man Moses was very meek, above all men that were upon the face of the earth."[12] To match the humility of Moses, one must first reach his greatness.

Second, the sense of humility is not the same as the psychological sense of inferiority. If a person suffers from the latter sentiment, he feels incapable and incompetent. His very feeling may interfere with his performance. The humble person believes himself to be—not incompetent—but unimportant. He recognizes the successes he has achieved; he is even aware of their value; he simply avoids attaching great importance to himself because of these successes. When Moses declared, "Who am I that I should go unto Pharaoh and that I should bring forth the children of Israel out of Egypt,"[13] he was expressing humility; when he insisted, "For I am slow of speech and of a slow tongue"[14] he was declaring incompetence. The humble person, notwithstanding his humility, is capable of great achievement.

II

The *beliefs* described above however, do not exhaust the meaning of humility. Humility is exhibited in *feeling* as well. It is clear that the sentiment that should be experienced by the personality who exemplifies the religious conception of humility is gratitude. If I must credit God with my success, if I am obligated to acknowledge Him as the ultimate source of all powers I am able to activate, then I should be grateful for all the blessings that He has seen fit to bestow upon me. On the other hand, the individual who exemplifies the moral conception of humility should experience what we may call the sentiment of equality. If no matter what his attainments may be, he is not to judge himself superior—and, according to the definition offered in the preceding section, there is no requirement to assign to himself a value that will reduce him to a level that is inferior—he should experience himself to be the equal of others.

These two attitudes, namely, gratitude to God and equality in relation to man are in fact mandatory. Rambam declares that, as part of prayer, we are obligated "to give praise and thanksgiving to the Almighty for the good that he bestowed upon us."[15] The demand that we cultivate a sense of equality was put in the Talmud in the form of a suggestion. "A favorite saying of the Rabbis of Yavneh was: I am God's creature and my fellow is God's creature. My work is in town and his work is in the country. I rise early for my work and he rises early for his work. Just as he does not presume to do my work so I do not presume to do his work. Will you say that I do much and he does little? We have learned: One may do much or one may do little, it is all one provided he directs his heart to heaven."[16]

But, an examination of Biblical and rabbinic declarations reveals that more is required than the sentiments that are the concomitants of the beliefs here described.

Thus the *Semag,* in elaborating upon the religious conception of humility applauds the attitude exhibited by King David who declared, "But I am a worm and no man"[17] and adds "I am obligated to view myself as a worm who hides beneath the dust in shame."[18] We may also recall the patriarch's expression when he was appealing to God in behalf of the people of Sodom, "But I am dust and ashes."[19] It is characteristic of the religious personality when contemplating or addressing Deity to regard himself as of an infinitesimal quantity, as a speck of dust in a vast ocean of unlimited space, as a thoroughly insignificant entity. A philosopher expressed this well. "Returning to himself, let man consider what he is in comparison with all existence; let him regard himself as lost in a remote corner of nature; and from the little cell in which he finds himself lodged, I mean the universe, let him estimate at their true value the earth, kingdoms, cities, and himself. What is man in the Infinite?"[20] Now this attitude seems to be the counterpart of another belief altogether, not that God is the source of all my blessings but that in relation to God I am an infinitesimal and wholly meaningless entity.

Under the heading of the moral conception of humility, it appears that more is required than the feeling of equality. Ramban, for example, demands of the humble personality that he direct attention to his own failings and that he stress the achievements of others. "Every man should be great in your eyes. If he is wise or wealthy, it is your duty to honor him. If he is poor and you are richer or wiser than he, consider that you are more guilty than he and he more innocent than you."[21] This posture seems to involve, not so much an objective belief as the deliberate adoption of an attitude. The humble personality does not prepare a balance sheet of assets and liabilities which are evaluated and weighted in order to arrive at a total which may be compared with that of somebody else. He deliberately under scores his own weaknesses while emphasizing the strengths of others. He adopts an attitude which is both subjective and selfless.

We must conclude that each of the two conceptions— the religious and the moral—may be exemplified in the humble personality in various degrees. Humility is a quantitative conception. In the preceding section attention was directed to the lowest levels at which the

concept of humility may be exemplified. We are now concerned with the ultimate in humble behavior. Under the heading of the religious conception, the individual who has attained to the first level believes that God is, at least, a partial cause of his achievements, while the one who has reached the highest level declares that he is totally insignificant in comparison with God. In the category of the moral, the humble personality, on the lower level, believes that his successes do not justify the judgment of superiority, while on the higher level, he is determined to demonstrate that he is inferior. Each of these beliefs is accompanied by the appropriate feelings—the feelings of gratitude and insignificance in relation to God, and the sentiments of equality and inferiority in relation to man.

It seems appropriate, in each of the two conceptions, to distinguish between the *anav* and the *shefal ruach.* The *anav* is grateful and accepts the idea of equality. The *shefal ruach* goes beyond the *anav by* insisting on his own insignificance and on his weaknesses in relation to others. Rambam directed attention to these extremes in humble behavior in the following passage: "It is not good that a man shall be humble *(anav)* alone, but that he shall be meek *(shefal ruach)* and that his spirit shall be very low."[22]

III

The concept of humility requires further clarification. It has been said that the humble person entertains certain beliefs and experiences certain feelings. But these, in the genuinely humble personality, must be translated into actions. How then shall we define humility behaviorally? To what kind of actions do these beliefs and feelings give rise?

It is not possible within the limited scope of this essay to give an exhaustive account of all the behavioral patterns that should be associated with the posture of humility. A few illustrations, however, will suffice for the purpose of elucidation.

One who is humble *(anav)* in the religious sense would, among other things, be satisfied with his portion in the world *(sameach bechalko).* If to God belongs the credit of human achievement, man may not claim or demand anything he does not possess as a matter of right. Humility then sets the boundary to human ambition in the material domain. Thus *Baachya* declares that one who is humble "should be contented with whatever means of livelihood present themselves and with whatever he finds."[23] The *shefal ruach,* however, in addition to behavior of the type just described must also be prepared to act in a manner that would express his sense of personal insignificance when relating to the Almighty. Thus *Baachya* cites, in order to illustrate, the act of Aaron the High Priest who performed the menial task of collecting the ashes of the burnt offering which the fire had consumed, and the leaping and dancing of King David, behavior unbecoming to a man of his stature, when he was expressing gratitude to God.[24]

One who is an *anav* in a moral sense, i.e., he does not believe that his achievements justify the judgment that he is superior, does not wish to exercise authority over others. Thus, Shemaya urged us to "hate lordship."[25] But the *shfal ruach* who emphasizes his own weakness and the strengths of others, is one who is patient with human failings. He accepts their foibles and their insults. The Talmud recommends that we shall be as humble as Hillel. The essence of the entire tale which follows the precept and which is intended to illustrate the humility of Hillel is that he refused to respond with anger to deliberate provocation."[26] He was patient. The Talmud also praises those "who are put to shame and do no put others to shame, hear themselves reviled and do not retort; do everything out of love and rejoice in their own suffering."[27] The patience of the humble leads to forgiveness.

In sum, the humble person entertains certain beliefs, experiences certain feelings and performs certain actions. In the characterization of humility in this essay, all three—beliefs, feelings, and actions—have been taken into account.

IV

The feeling of self importance which is, under certain conditions, a manifestation of pride is not entirely proscribed. According to one view in a Talmudic debate, a minimal quantity of pride is required for a specified group of people. In a passage of the Mishnah, a variety of the sense of self-importance is declared to be mandatory for all.

In a well known passage of the Talmud we are told. "R. Hiyya b. Ashi said in the name of Rab: A disciple of

the sages should possess an eighth (of pride) R. Huna the son of R. Joshua said: (This small amount of pride) crowns him like the awn of the grain. Raba said: (a disciple of the sages) who possesses (haughtiness of spirit) deserves excommunication, and if he does not possess it he deserves excommunication. R. Nahman b. Isaac said: He should not possess it or part of it."[28]

Setting aside the question as to how this debate fares in the Halakhah, the following observations are relevant. First, it is the *Talmid Chacham* who is permitted to display the minimum amount of pride even according to those sages cited in the a passage who condone it. Second, Rashi views the grounds of justification for such pride as entirely practical. He declares in his commentary that the *talmid chacham* must have a little arrogance in order that the simple minded will accept his authority. It would be appropriate to suggest that, under the circumstances, it is only the *act* of pride that should be deemed necessary, not the corresponding feeling or belief.

This last point is stressed by the *Meiri* who discussed at great length the suggestion that certain individuals must exhibit pride on practical grounds. In addition to the class of *talmidei chachamim* he recognizes the importance of pride for that smaller group of people who carry on their shoulders the burden of political authority. They too must arouse, even to a greater degree than the *talmid chacham,* reverence and respect. In support of this contention he cites the advice given by Rabbi Judah the Prince (himself outstanding in humility) to his son who was to be his successor, "conduct your patriarchate with pride"[29] and the *Meiri* explains that this quality was not to be become part of his nature; he was merely urged to act in a mannerAnother form of proud behavior was urged by the *Meiri*, and also for practical reasons, for the average person. It is the type of pride that prompts an individual to dissociate himself from those in society whose behavior is deficient by moral and religious standards. To verify the legitimacy of this category of practical pride, he cites the Talmudic passage, "The fair minded of the people in Jerusalem used to act thus: They would not sign a deed without knowing who would sign with them; they would not sit in judgment unless they knew who was to sit with them; and they would not sit at a table without knowing their fellow diners."[31]

By way of further clarification of the permissible forms of pride, the following observations are in order. First, these forms describe exceptions to the requirements of the moral variety of humility, not the religious variety. They describe circumstances in which one may act with pride in relation to his fellow man, not in relation to God.

Second, the sanction for these exceptions to humble behavior derives from the necessity to enforce moral and religious values upon society and to preserve such values in one's personal behavior. The *Talmid Chacham* and the *Nasi* are obligated to inspire and enforce obedience to laws that express the values of Torah. The individual must refrain from exposing himself to environmental conditions, e.g., the company of scoundrels, that would weaken his inclination to moral and religious behavior. Proud actions that are approved are therefore motivated by *commitment* rather than by the *sense of self-importance.*

It follows that if proud behavior is irrelevant to the enforcement or preservation of value it cannot be countenanced. This will perhaps explain Maimonides' endorsement of an extreme instance of humility in which a man of deep piety traveling on a ship responded with joy in a situation in which he experienced great humiliation.[32]

The Mishnah, however, in another well-known passage, declares that the feeling of self importance is a necessity for all. "Therefore, every single person is obliged to say: The world was created for my sake."[33] And Rashi explains this declaration to mean "I am as important as the entire world. I will not therefore banish myself from the world even with a single transgression."

It should be noted, in the first place, that this feeling of self-importance is required universally, for all. Further, it is not a minimal quantity of self-importance that is urged but a maximum amount. According to Rashi, each man shall regard himself as equal in value to the entire natural world. Finally it is not merely the *act* which expresses self-importance that is demanded but the correlative feeling and belief as well.

It is also noteworthy that the words which mean pride or arrogance do not occur at all in the Mishnah's formulation of precept. The Mishnah then does not appear to regard this judgment as at all relevant to the question of pride. On the contrary, the very same circumstance which is cited by the Mishnah in justification of the demand that everyone experience a sense of self-importance is also described as the basis for a sentiment which belongs among the experiences of humility. The circumstance is that man was created alone. This is taken by the Mishnah to imply many things—among them that "one might not say to his fellow, 'my father was greater than thine' (i.e., he shall be humble about his ancestry) and that each person shall believe himself to be of highest value (an experience which apparently belongs to the category of pride).

This merely apparent inconsistency may be easily resolved. Its resolution turns on the fact that humility is a relational conception. The humble individual experiences himself as unimportant in relation to God (the religious conception) and to man (the moral conception). But there is no objection to a feeling of self-importance, even to a maximum degree, by any standard and in relation to any object, which is consistent with the experience of unimportance in relation to God and man. In one relation it is even required.

Consider a standard according to which the animate is assigned greater value than the inanimate, the rational is considered superior to the merely animate, etc. This criterion would clearly assign to man, a being created in the image of God, a very high rank on the scale of value. An individual cannot, in virtue of the possession of this quality, regard himself as important in relation to God who is its ultimate source, or to his fellow man who is endowed with the identical quality. On the contrary, it is possible—it is even required that—he deem himself unworthy in these relations because man is nothing in the infinite and because he should always seek excellence in others while diverting attention to his own weaknesses. Nevertheless, by the standard here described, he is obligated to experience a profound sense of self-importance in virtue of his location in the scheme of creation. Thus King David who, in addressing God, compared himself to a worm groveling in the dust, in comparison to the rest of creation, judged himself (and others) to be but a little less than angels.[34]

This sense of self-importance is required. Rashi, in his comment in the Mishnah cited above, stated that a man's sense of self-esteem will help him to avoid sin. We may generalize this view. Man's behavior will depend, to a large extent, on the image he projects of himself. It makes a great deal of difference in terms of human action—if we may use some ancient distinctions—whether man regards himself as a rational animal or as a two-legged animal without feathers. There is a vast difference in the individual and social behavior patterns of those who believe themselves to be the bearers of the *Tzelem E-lo-kim* (the image of God) and those who regard themselves as structured bits of matter, complex though they may be, or as brothers to the apes.

The human being logically and psychologically can and morally must view himself as of unlimited value in one relation though he believes himself unworthy and insignificant in relation to the Divine source of all being.

V

In Rabbinic literature, humility is not counted as merely one of a number of virtues—each with equal status. Rather is it judged to be a central virtue[35]—and for several reasons. First, its centrality is due to its moral status. Again, we turn to a discussion on arrogance to shed light on its correlative, humility. The Talmud declares[36] that, on one view, arrogance is the moral equivalent of adultery and incest. According to another opinion, it is equivalent to idolatry or atheism. As the Talmud puts it, the arrogant person is to be viewed "as though" *(K'ilu)* he enjoyed illicit relations with those who are forbidden to him; "as though" he served the gods of the heathens, "as though" he denied the existence of God. On these conceptions, a true estimate of the character of arrogance compels the conclusion that it belongs in the same category as adultery, incest, idolatry and atheism. If we take into account the moral standard formulated in the literature of the Talmud, we arrive at the result that arrogance is among the most serious violations of the precepts of Torah. It belongs in the category of those precepts which we are not permitted to violate even when threatened with death.

If humility is as much a virtue as arrogance is vice, we may infer that, by the same moral standard, humility ranks among those virtues that are highest on the scale. This is what Ramban intended when he wrote that "humility is the best of all the virtues."[37] *Baachya* echoed the same sentiments when he wrote, "It follows that all virtues are secondary to humility which is the head and front of them all."[38]

But, secondly, humility is judged to be central in the Jewish system of ethics because of its practical consequences. Ramban regards the virtue of humility as sufficient for the exemplification of the attitude of reverence which in turn leads to fear of God and avoidance of sin. "Through humility there will emerge in your heart the virtue of reverence for you will consider always from whence you came and where you are going... and when you will think of all this, you will fear your Maker and you will avoid sin." [39]

The Talmud, furthermore, cites the view that arrogance *leads* to adultery. "Anyone who is arrogant will ultimately stumble with another man's wife."[40] The attitude of arrogance is thus declared to be psychologically adequate to the commission of a serious crime. Another major consequence of arrogance is cited in the Torah. "Your heart will be lifted up and you will forget the Lord your God,"[41] a circumstance which, in turn, may lead to a denial of His existence. All qualities of character involve behavioral consequences but arrogance leads to results which, by the Jewish standard of morality, are the most serious of all, namely, atheism and adultery.

These two grounds of the centrality of humility are, however, not independent of each other. A distinction that is relevant to this discussion will serve to clarify their relationship. We must separate virtues (or traits of character) from the actions that illustrate the virtues. A person may be said to possess a certain moral quality if the habit to act in accordance with the related moral rule has become part of his psychological anatomy. Such a person is expected to exhibit the quality in question, in *most* instances, when the occasion arises. A just man acts justly out of habit, out of an acquired inclination. An action, on the other hand, need not be motivated by a corresponding moral habit, i.e., by a quality of character. It may reflect a passing impulse. An unjust individual does, on occasion, act justly.

Now a moral theory may include the formulation of a standard by which both actions and habits may be evaluated. Or, the moral theory may concern itself exclusively with action. While the primary interest of Halakhah is the specification of rules for action, habits which give rise to behavior in conformity with these rules are endorsed and those that result in violations of the precepts are rejected. In the case of arrogance, that rejection may take the form of assigning to the habit the identical moral status that belongs to the actions to which it gives rise. This is the view of those who declare that the person with whom arrogance is a habit is to be viewed "as though" he had committed the cardinal crimes of adultery, idolatry, etc.[42] Or, the rejection may take the form of pointing out the consequences of this trait and encouraging its avoidance. Thus, according to another interpretation, arrogance *leads* to adultery. Analogously, humility may be assigned the moral status identical to that possessed by the actions to which it gives rise; or it may be encouraged on the grounds that it leads to these actions.

In one sense, therefore, humility is central because it results in actions to which Judaism has assigned the highest moral status, and, on one view, because it also belongs to the same oral category. Baachya, however, suggested another ground for its centrality.

Baachya identifies humility as a necessary condition for the possession of any of the other virtues, that is to say, a person cannot exemplify in his behavior any other virtue if he does not possess humility. "It also follows that no virtue can exist in anyone whose heart is devoid of humility before God."[43] According to Baachya, therefore, though, for example, not every humble person is penitent, no one can be penitent if, he is not humble.

Baachya's claim, however, is not clear. Two questions are relevant. First, did Baachya insist on "humility before God" as a necessary condition, for the exercise of all virtues including those that are characteristic of human relations or did he have in mind only those that belong under the heading of piety. The virtue that he used to illustrate his point is penitence which surely belongs to the category of piety. But of even greater significance is the second question which incidentally is not unrelated to the first. When Baachya demands humility as a necessary ingredient of all virtues, is he making a factual claim or proposing a definition? Is he

declaring that, on the Jewish view, humility enters into the definition of each virtue?—in which case, no quality of character that is not accompanied by humility could be a virtue by definition. Or, are the various virtues sufficiently defined without the inclusion of' the element of humility?—in which case the statement that humility is a necessary condition of all virtues, i.e., that wherever one *finds* virtue, there one *finds humility,* is a factual generalization in regard to human nature.

It would appear, from factual considerations, that Baachya's claim can be defended only if it formulates a generalization about the definition of the virtues in the context of Jewish ethical theory. Consider the illustration that Baachya employed viz. repentance. Suppose repentance meant no more than regret for past transgressions accompanied by a resolution to avoid similar violations in the future. Experience provides illustrations of those who are not endowed with the virtue of humility before God (atheists, for example), but who recognize and acknowledge the sanction of certain moral rules, are guilt stricken when they violate them, experience a sense of regret on those occasions, and affirm the appropriate resolutions. If Baachya's claim is correct, however, this sequence would not be a genuine example of repentance. This conclusion could be maintained, only, if Judaism were held to define the virtues in such a way that nothing can be a virtue if it does not include the sense of "humility before God."[44]

On this interpretation, it is probable that Baachya regards "humility before God" as an ingredient, not merely of the virtues in the category of piety, but of all virtues. For Baachya is not engaged in the task of psychological analysis of moral conceptions but in their religious definitions. Accordingly, by way of illustration, one may on the basis of purely social considerations extend the hand of generosity to the poor. But it would not be *tzedakah* unless the act was also motivated or, at least, accompanied by "humility before God."

VI

This essay is not offered as a detailed account of the entire domain of human behavior to which the qualities of pride and humility are relevant, but as a brief survey of its landmarks and major approaches. It is a preface to humility.

NOTES

[1]Numbers 12:3.

[2]*Shabbat,* 306.

[3]*Sotah,* 49a.

3a.In *Sefer Hamaspik* (Jerusalem, Alpha, 1965), p. 53 Avraham ben Ha Rambam distinguishes between what I have designated the religious and moral conceptions of humility.

[4]Deuteronomy 8:11.

[5]*Sefer Mitzvot Gadol*—negative commandment 64.

[6]Deuteronomy 17:20.

[7]*Sharei Teshuva*—Gate 3, letter 34.

[8]Some, Rambam, for example, exclude both conceptions from list of 613 commandments.

[9]*Kitvei Rambam*—(Jerusalem, Mosed Harav Kook, 1963) Book I, p. 374.

While the concept of humility formulated here belongs under a heading that will be characterized in the next section of this essay, it is clear that Ramban regards the humble personality as exemplifying both the religious and themoral conceptions.

[10]Deuteronomy 8:17.

[11]*Ibid.,* 19:4.

[12]Numbers 12:3.

[13]Exodus 3:11.

[14]*Ibid.,* 4:10.

[15]*Yad,* Hilkhot Tefillah I, 2.

[16]*Berakhot,* 17a.

[17]Psalms, 22:7.

[18]*Op. Cit.,* Negative commandment 64.

[19]Genesis 18:27.

[20]Pascal, *Pensees,* par. 72.

[21]Ramban, *op. cit.*

[22]*Yad.,* Hilkhot Deot. II, 3.

[23]*Chovot Halevovot,* Sixth Treatise, ch. VI.

[24]*Ibid.*

[25]*Avot* I, 11.

[26]*Shabbat,* 31a.

[27]*Pesachim,* 88b.

[28]*Sotah,* 5a.

[29]*Ketuvot,* 103b.

[30]*Chibur Hateshuvah* (Talpiot, Yeshiva U. 1963), p. 121 ff

[31]*Sanhedrin,* 23a.

[32]Maimonides' Comments on *Ethics of the Fathers,* Ch. IV, par. 4.

[33]*Sanhedrin,* 37a.

[34]Psalms 8:6.

[35]There is a Talmudic debate *(Avodah Zorah* 20b) as to whether *chasidut* or *anavah* is the greatest of all virtues.

Even if one chooses in favor of *chasidut,* humility may still be regarded as central.

Note too that the distinction drawn in the body of this essay between two conceptions of humility will not be applied in this section. In the sources that will be quoted that distinction is not explicitly made (with the exception of the passage taken from the *Chovot Holevovot).* Further, the Talmudic passages to which reference will be made speak—not of the concepts of arrogance and humility—but of the arrogant and humble *personalities.* It may be assumed that the typical arrogant or humble personality exemplifies both conceptions.

[36]*Sotah* 4b ff.

[37]Ramban, *op. cit.*

[38]Baachya, *op. cit.,* Ch. VIII.

[39]Ramban, *op. cit.*

[40]*Sotah* 4b.

[41]Deuteronomy 8:14.

[42]The Talmudic passage in question speaks of *mi she-yesh lo gassie haruach.* Two interpretations of this phrase, as it is employed here, are, in fact, possible.

(1) It refers to a person who is *actually* experiencing the feeling of arrogance.

(2) It refers to a person who has cultivated the *habit* of arrogance, though he may not at the moment be experiencing the relevant sentiments. The severity of the pronouncements, however, lend support to interpretation that it is the habit rather than an individual act is the subject of the judgment.

[43]Baachya, *op. cit.*

[44]This conclusion seems to be suggested by the passage in Baachya as well. After making the point that "no moral quality can possibly exist in any one whose heart is devoid of humility before God," he writes, "Thus also the beginning of repentance is loneliness, submissiveness and humility, as Scripture saith 'If my people which are called by my name, shall humble themselves and pray and seek my face' (II Chronicles 7:14). Further it is said, 'They have humbled themselves; I will not destroy them' *(ibid.,* 12:7)."

In this passage, as Baachya apparently interpreted it, Divine forgiveness which is a response to repentance is described as following on humility. Humility is then at the core of the act of repentance; it is not something that stands at the periphery of penitence and with which it is merely invariably connected.

Reprinted with permission from lookstein.org.
This article originally appeared in TRADITION, Volume 13, 1973.

Lesson 2
Rabban Yochanan ben Zakai

Introduction

Many of us have had a special teacher in our lives—someone who we trusted utterly to put our interests first and who may have gone out on a limb to ensure that we got the support we needed.

Rabban Yochanan ben Zakai was a scholar, a visionary leader, but most of all, a devoted teacher to the generations.

At times, he hovered in the background, trusting his students to rise to the challenge and act on their own. At times, he rose up like a fiercely protective lioness defending her cubs. But always, the needs of his students came first. And he considered everyone a beloved student.

מ שחרב בית המקדש התקין רבן יוחנן בן זכאי שיהו תוקע
בכל מקום שיש בן בית דין אמר רבי אלעזר לא התקין ר...
בן זכאי אלא ביבנה בלבד אמרו לו אחד יבנה ואחד כל מקום
בית דין

משחרב בית המקדש התקין רבן יוחנן בן זכאי שיהא לולב נ...
במדינה שבעה זכר למקדש ושיהא יום הנף כולו אסור

משחרב בית המקדש התקין רבן יוחנן בן זכאי שיהו מקבלין
החדש כל היום אמר רבי יהושע בן קרחה ועוד זאת התקין רב...
זכאי שאפילו ראש בית דין בכל מקום שלא יהא העדים הולכ...
למקום הוועד

Historical Timeline

3769/9 CE	Passing of Hillel
3776/16 CE	Birth of Rabbi Akiva
3810/50 CE	Rabban Yochanan ben Zakai is installed as *av bet din* in Yerushalayim
3716/56 CE	Rabbi Akiva departs for yeshiva
3826/66 CE	Beginning of the Great Revolt
3828/68 CE	Rabban Yochanan Ben Zakai escapes the siege of Yerushalayim to establish the academy at Yavneh
3829/69 CE	Second Temple is destroyed
3834/74 CE	Passing of Rabban Yochanan ben Zakai

Roman Emperors

27 BCE–14 CE	**AUGUSTUS**
14–37 CE	**TIBERIUS**
37–41 CE	**CALIGULA**
41–54 CE	**CLAUDIUS**
54–68 CE	**NERO**
68 CE	**YEAR OF THE FOUR EMPERORS: GALBA, OTHO, VITELLIUS, AND VESPASIAN**
69–79 CE	**VESPASIAN**

- Hillel passed away toward the end of the reign of Augustus.
- Rabban Yochanan was in the Galilee during the reign of Tiberius.
- Rabban Yochanan joined the *sanhedrin* during the reigns of Gaius (Caligula) and Claudius.
- Vespasian led his armies against Yerushalayim during the reign of Nero.
- Rabban Yochanan passed away during the reign of Vespasian.

Brief Biographical Overview

Shortly after Hillel's passing in 9 CE, Rabban Yochanan moved to the Galilee, where he lived for eighteen years, during which time Judea was ruled by a series of procurators appointed by Rome. On the whole, the procurators were greedy, ruthless, and oppressive. With the exception of a brief respite from 37-44 CE, during which time Agrippa I was appointed king over Judea, the cruel oppression of the Jews continued unabated.

Rabban Yochanan returned to Yerushalayim at some point between 27 and 34 CE. Yerushalayim was wilting under dual pressure: the tyrannical rule of Rome from outside and fierce factionalism from within. The Sadducees, Essenes, early Christians, and the Zealots each posed a separate challenge for the *sanhedrin*. Lawlessness and murder were daily fare; it was a terrible time for the Jews.

Rabban Yochanan addressed these issues with wise counsel and courageous leadership. In the year 34 CE, Rabban Yochanan joined the *sanhedrin* and in time was appointed chief justice. He thus found himself in Yerushalayim during the Great War and the siege of Yerushalayim. Rabban Yochanan, who believed that the city would fall, escaped Yerushalayim and persuaded Vespasian to grant the establishment of a Torah academy in Yavneh.

The Temple fell in the year 69 and Yavneh became the new center of Torah study. Six years later, his mission accomplished, Rabban Yochanan returned his soul to G-d.

Prologue:
Father to the Generations

Text 1

תנו רבנן: שמונים תלמידים היו לו להלל הזקן

שלשים מהם ראוים שתשרה עליהם שכינה כמשה רבינו

ושלשים מהן ראוים שתעמוד להם חמה כיהושע בן נון, עשרים בינונים

גדול שבכולן—יונתן בן עוזיאל, קטן שבכולן—רבן יוחנן בן זכאי

אמרו עליו על רבן יוחנן בן זכאי שלא הניח מקרא ומשנה, תלמוד, הלכות ואגדות

דקדוקי תורה ודקדוקי סופרים, קלים וחמורים וגזרות שוות

תקופות וגימטריאות, שיחת מלאכי השרת ושיחת שדים ושיחת דקלים

משלות כובסין, משלות שועלים, דבר גדול ודבר קטן

דבר גדול—מעשה מרכבה, דבר קטן—הויות דאביי ורבא

תלמוד בבלי סוכה כח,א

ur Rabbis have taught: Hillel the Elder had eighty disciples, thirty of whom were worthy of the Divine Spirit resting upon them, as [it did upon] Moses our Master, thirty of whom were worthy that the sun should stand still for them [as it did for] Joshua the son of Nun, and the remaining twenty were ordinary. The greatest of them was Yonatan ben Uziel, the least of them was Yochanan ben Zakai. They said of Rabban Yochanan ben Zakai that he did not leave [unstudied] Scripture, Mishnah, Gemara, Halachah, Aggadah, details of the Torah, details of the Scribes, inferences of *kal vachomer*, analogies, calendrical computations, *gematria*, the speech of ministering angels, the speech of spirits, and the speech of palm-trees, fullers' parables and fox fables, great matters or small matters; "great matters" are the *Ma'aseh Merkavah*, "small matters" are the discussions of Abaye and Raba.

TALMUD SUKAH 28A

Text 2

אמרו עליו על רבן יוחנן בן זכאי: מימיו לא שח שיחת חולין

ולא הלך ארבע אמות בלא תורה ובלא תפילין

ולא קדמו אדם בבית המדרש

ולא ישן בבית המדרש לא שינת קבע ולא שינת עראי

ולא הרהר במבואות המטונפות, ולא הניח אדם בבית המדרש ויצא

ולא מצאו אדם יושב ודומם אלא יושב ושונה

ולא פתח אדם דלת לתלמידיו אלא הוא בעצמו

ולא אמר דבר שלא שמע מפי רבו מעולם

ולא אמר הגיע עת לעמוד מבית המדרש

חוץ מערבי פסחים וערבי יום הכפורים

תלמוד בבלי סוכה כח,א

They said concerning Rabban Yochanan ben Zakai that [from the time he devoted himself fully to Torah study] he never engaged in mundane talk; nor did he walk four cubits without [studying] Torah or without *tefilin*; nor was any man earlier than him in the house of study; nor did he sleep or doze in the house of study; nor did he meditate [Torah thoughts] in unclean alleyways; nor was anyone ever still left in the house of study when he went out; nor did anyone ever find him sitting in silence, as he was always engaged in study; nor did anyone but he ever open the door for his disciples; he never in his life said anything which he had not heard from his teacher; and except on the eve of Passover and on the eve of the Day of Atonement, he never said, "It is time to arise and leave the house of study."

TALMUD SUKAH 28A

Text 3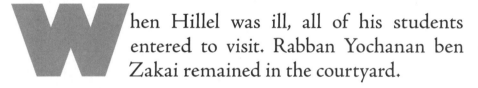

פעם אחת חלה ונכנסו כולן לבקרו

עמד לו רבן יוחנן בן זכאי בחצר

אמר להן: היכן הוא הקטן שבכם אב לחכמה ואב לדורות . . .

אמרו לו: הרי הוא בחצר, אמר להן: יכנס

כיון שנכנס אמר להן: להנחיל אוהבי יש ואוצרותיהם אמלא (משלי ח,כא)

תלמוד ירושלמי נדרים ה,ו

When Hillel was ill, all of his students entered to visit. Rabban Yochanan ben Zakai remained in the courtyard.

Hillel inquired, "Where is the minor one, the father of wisdom, the father of generations . . . ?"

They replied, "He is in the courtyard."

Said Hillel, "Allow him to enter." Once he entered, Hillel said to them, "[Of him it is written (Proverbs 8:21)] 'To bequeath plenty to my beloved ones and their storehouses I shall fill.'"

JERUSALEM TALMUD NEDARIM 5:6

Arav

Text 4 📖

אמר רבי יוסי בן קיסמא

פעם אחת הייתי מהלך בדרך ופגע בי אדם אחד ונתן לי שלום והחזרתי לו שלום

אמר לי: רבי מאיזה מקום אתה

אמרתי לו: מעיר גדולה של חכמים ושל סופרים אני

אמר לי: רבי רצונך שתדור עמנו במקומנו

ואני אתן לך אלף אלפים דינרי זהב ואבנים טובות ומרגליות

אמרתי לו: בני אם אתה נותן לי כל כסף וזהב ואבנים טובות ומרגליות שבעולם

איני דר אלא במקום תורה

פרקי אבות ו,ט

Rabbi Yosei the son of Kisma said, "Once, I was traveling and I encountered a certain man. He greeted me and I returned his greetings."

He said to me, "Rabbi, where are you from?"

I said to him, "I am from a great city of sages and scholars."

He said to me, "Rabbi, would you like to dwell with us in our place? I will give you thousands of dinars of gold, precious stones, and pearls."

I said to him, "If you were to give me all the silver, gold, precious stones, and pearls in the world, I would not dwell anywhere but in a place of Torah."

PIRKEI AVOT 6:9

Text 5

שמונה עשר שנין עביד הוי יהיב בהדא ערב

ולא אתא קומוי אלא אילין תרין עובדיא

אמר: גליל גליל שנאת התורה סופך לעשות במסיקין

תלמוד ירושלמי שבת טז,ח

abban Yochanan ben Zakai lived in Arav (in the Galilee) for eighteen years. In all that time, only two questions of Halachah were brought before him. [When he departed Arav,] he exclaimed, "Galilee, Galilee, your hatred for Torah will deliver you to thieves."

JERUSALEM TALMUD SHABBAT 16:8

Yerushalayim

Text 6

ואת כל בית הגדול שרף באש (מלכים ב כה,ט) זה מדרשו של רבן יוחנן בן זכיי
ששם היו מתנין גדולותיו של הקדוש ברוך הוא

תלמוד ירושלמי מגילה ג,א

"And every great house was burned by fire" (II Kings 25:9). This refers to the academy of Rabban Yochanan ben Zakai, for there they studied the greatness of G-d.

JERUSALEM TALMUD MEGILAH 3:1

Text 7

תני ארבעים שנה עד שלא חרב בית המקדש...
והיו נועלין דלתות ההיכל מבערב ומשכימין ומוצאין אותן פתוחין
אמר לו רבן יוחנן בן זכיי: היכל למה אתה מבהלינו
יודעין אנו שסופך ליחרב
שנאמר (זכרי' יא,א) פתח לבנון דלתיך ותאכל אש בארזיך

תלמוד ירושלמי יומא ו,ג

Our Rabbis taught: During the last forty years before the destruction of the Temple, they would lock the doors of the sanctuary at night and would rise to find the doors [of the sanctuary] open. Rabban Yochanan ben Zakai rebuked them, saying: "Sanctuary, why do you alarm us? We know that that in the end you will be destroyed, as it says, 'Open your doors, O Lebanon, the fire will devour your cedars'" (Zechariah 11:1).

JERUSALEM TALMUD YOMA 6:3

Text 8 📖

בראשונה היו קושרין לשון של זהורית על פתח אולם מבחוץ

הלבין היו שמחין, לא הלבין היו עצבין

התקינו שיהו קושרין אותו על פתח אולם מבפנים

ועדיין היו מציצין ורואין, הלבין היו שמחין, לא הלבין היו עצבין

התקינו שיהו קושרין אותו חציו בסלע וחציו בין קרניו של שעיר המשתלח

תלמוד בבלי ראש השנה לא,ב

riginally they would fasten the thread of scarlet on the outside of the door to the [Temple] court. If it turned white they would rejoice; if not, they were sad. [Later] they [began] to fasten it to the inside of the door to the [Temple] court. Some still peeped in and saw, and if it turned white they rejoiced; and if not, they were saddened. They then determined that half of the thread should be fastened to the rock and half between the horns of the goat that was sent [to the wilderness].

TALMUD ROSH HASHANAH 31B

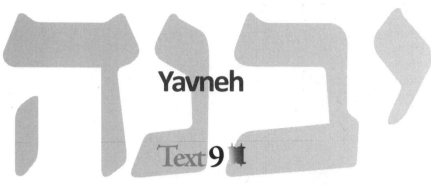

Yavneh

Text 9

אמר להם: שוטים מפני מה אתם מבקשים להחריב את העיר הזאת

ואתם מבקשים לשרוף את בית המקדש

וכי מה אני מבקש מכם

אלא שתשגרו לי קשת אחת או חץ אחת ואלך לי מכם

אמרו לו: כשם שיצאנו על שנים ראשונים שהם לפניך והרגנום כך נצא לפניך ונהרגך

כיון ששמע רבן יוחנן בן זכאי שלח וקרא לאנשי ירושלים

ואמר להם: בני מפני מה אתם מחריבין את העיר הזאת

ואתם מבקשים לשרוף את בית המקדש

וכי מהו מבקש מכם

הא אינו מבקש מכם אלא קשת אחת או חץ אחת וילך לו מכם

אמרו לו: כשם שיצאנו על שנים שלפניו והרגנום כך נצא עליו ונהרגהו

אבות דרבי נתן ד,ה

Vespasian sent word [to the defenders of the city], "Fools! Why do you seek to destroy the city and burn down the Temple? All I ask is that you send me one bow or arrow [as a sign of submission]."

They sent word [in reply], "Just as we attacked and destroyed the two armies that preceded you, so shall we attack and kill you."

Rabban Yochanan summoned the men of Yerushalayim and said, "My children, why do you destroy this city and seek to burn the Temple? All he demands is a single bow or arrow and he will depart." They replied, "As we attacked and killed the two armies that preceded him, so shall we attack and kill him."

Avot DeRebbi Natan 4:5

Text 10

כי מטא להתם, אמר: שלמא עלך מלכא, שלמא עלך מלכא

אמר ליה: מיחייבת תרי קטלא, חדא דלאו מלכא אנא וקא קרית לי מלכא . . .

אמר ליה: דקאמרת לאו מלכא אנא, איברא מלכא את

דאי לאו מלכא את לא מימסרא ירושלים בידך

דכתיב: (ישעיהו י,לד) והלבנון באדיר יפול

ואין אדיר אלא מלך, דכתיב: (ירמיהו ל,כא) והיה אדירו ממנו וגו׳

ואין לבנון אלא בית המקדש

שנאמר: (דברים ג,כה) ההר הטוב הזה והלבנון . . .

אדהכי אתי פריסתקא עליה מרומי

אמר ליה: קום, דמית ליה קיסר, ואמרי הנהו חשיבי דרומי לאותיבך ברישא . . .

אמר ליה: מיזל אזילנא ואינש אחרינא משדרנא, אלא בעי מינאי מידי דאתן לך

אמר ליה: תן לי יבנה וחכמיה, ושושילתא דרבן גמליאל

ואסוותא דמסיין ליה לרבי צדוק

קרי עליה רב יוסף, ואיתימא רבי עקיבא

משיב חכמים אחור ודעתם יסכל (ישעיהו מז,כה)

איבעי למימר ליה לשבקינהו הדא זימנא

והוא סבר דלמא כולי האי לא עביד, והצלה פורתא נמי לא הוי

תלמוד בבלי גיטין נו,א

When Rabban Yochanan reached [Vespasian] he said, "Peace unto you, O King, peace unto you, O King."

Vespasian said, "You are deserving of death, because I am not a king and you call me king . . ."

He replied, "In truth you are a king, since if you were not a king, Yerushalayim would not be delivered into your hands, as it is written, 'And Lebanon shall fall by a mighty one' (Isaiah 10:34). Mighty one [is an epithet] applied only to a king, as it is written, 'And their mighty one shall be of themselves etc.' (Jeremiah 30:21). And Lebanon refers to the Sanctuary, as it says, 'This goodly mountain and Lebanon' (Deuteronomy 3:25). . ."

Vespasian Coin

[As they were speaking a messenger arrived from Rome to inform Vespasian that he had been appointed Emperor.]

Vespasian said, "I will now be going, and will send someone to take my place. You can, however, make a request of me and I will grant it."

Rabban Yochanan ben Zakai said to him, "Give me Yavneh and its wise men, the family chain of Rabban Gamliel, and physicians to heal Rabbi Tsadok."

Rabbi Yoseph, or some say Rabbi Akiva, applied to him the verse, "[God] turns wise men backward and renders their knowledge foolish" (Isaiah 44:25). He ought to have petitioned Vespasian for deliverance of the Temple.

Obverse of coin:
Judea Capta, "Judea is captured" with palm tree signifying Judea

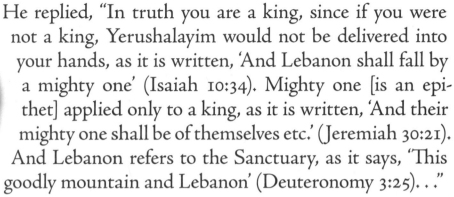

Rabbi Yochanan, however, thought that [Vespasian] would not grant such a large request, and then even a little would not be salvaged.

Talmud Gitin 56a

Epilogue

Text 11 📜

וכשחלה רבי יוחנן בן זכאי, נכנסו תלמידיו לבקרו

כיון שראה אותם התחיל לבכות

אמרו לו תלמידיו: נר ישראל, עמוד הימיני, פטיש החזק, מפני מה אתה בוכה

אמר להם: אילו לפני מלך בשר ודם היו מוליכין אותי, שהיום כאן ומחר בקבר

שאם כועס עלי אין כעסו כעס עולם, ואם אוסרני אין איסורו איסור עולם

ואם ממיתני אין מיתתו מיתת עולם, ואני יכול לפייסו בדברים ולשחדו בממון

אף על פי כן הייתי בוכה

ועכשיו שמוליכים אותי לפני מלך מלכי המלכים הקדוש ברוך הוא

שהוא חי וקיים לעולם ולעולמי עולמים, שאם כועס עלי כעסו כעס עולם

ואם אוסרני איסורו איסור עולם, ואם ממיתני מיתתו מיתת עולם

ואיני יכול לפייסו בדברים ולא לשחדו בממון

ולא עוד, אלא שיש לפני שני דרכים, אחת של גן עדן ואחת של גיהנם

ואיני יודע באיזו מוליכים אותי, ולא אבכה

תלמוד בבלי ברכות כח,ב

When Rabban Yochanan Ben Zakai fell ill, his disciples went to visit him. When he saw them, he began to weep.

His disciples said to him, "Lamp of Israel, pillar of the right hand, mighty hammer! Why do you weep?"

He replied, "If I were being taken today before a human king who is here today and tomorrow in the grave, whose anger, if he is angry with me, does not last forever; who, if he imprisons me does not imprison me forever; and who, if he puts me to death does not put me to everlasting death; and whom I can persuade with words and bribe with money; even so I would weep. Now that I am being taken before the supreme King of Kings, the Holy One, blessed be He, who lives and endures forever and ever; whose anger, if He is angry with me, is an everlasting anger; who if He imprisons me, imprisons me forever; who if He puts me to death puts me to death forever, and whom I cannot persuade with words or bribe with money; moreover, when there are two paths before me, one leading to Paradise and the other to Gehinnom, and I do not know by which I shall be taken; shall I not weep?"

TALMUD BERACHOT 28B

We are each given a mission to fulfill during the course of our lives. We are also allocated the requisite number of days in which to fulfill this mission; we are given neither one moment too many nor one moment too few. Every day or moment that is not utilized in fulfillment of its particular mission is not only a waste of that particular moment, but an abuse of the mission entrusted to us by the King of all Kings, Almighty G-d blessed be He. This is true even if we are engaged in a good endeavor, but not related to our particular mission.

Rabban Yochanan invested every moment of his life into his particular mission, which was to teach Torah and encourage observance of *mitzvot*. So engrossed was he in the engagement and fulfillment of his mission that he had not a moment to spare in which to pause and reflect on his personal spiritual progress. Because how could he pause to think of personal progress when the moment during which he would pause was designated for the fulfillment of a particular aspect of his mission.

Only on his death bed, when he had just about completed his mission . . . did he pause to take stock of his personal spiritual life (for, as he was taught by his teacher Hillel, if not now, when). This sudden realization (that he had no knowledge of his spiritual station in life) moved him to tears.

RABBI MENACHEM MENDEL SCHNEERSON, LIKUTEI SICHOT VOL. 16 P. 272

Key Points

1. Although Rabban Yochanan was the most junior of Hillel's students, Hillel assigned him the role of preserving Torah for the generations because of his prodigious memory, his faithfulness to the tradition, and his exceptional leadership qualities.

2. Rabban Yochanan was a teacher par excellence, drawing the best out of his students by asking them questions and analyzing their answers.

3. Rabban Yochanan spent eighteen years in Arav, despite the fact that it was not a learned community.

4. With the passing of Hillel's older students and the worsening of the political situation with Rome, Rabban Yochanan returned to Yerushalayim.

5. Rabban Yochanan tried to keep the people calm as long as possible in the face of the impending destruction so that the study of Torah could be maintained.

6. When the Zealots tried to force the Jews to war against the Romans, Rabban Yochanan stole out of the city and negotiated with the Roman general for the preservation of Yavneh and its sages.

7. Within two years of the destruction of the Beit HaMikdash, the center of study moved to Yavneh under the leadership of Rabban Gamliel.

8. Rabban Yochanan was instrumental in instituting new practices to take account of the changes brought about by the destruction of the temple.

9. He spent the end of his life in Beror Chayil.

Additional Readings

Shhh, the Neighbors are Listening

By **Elana Mizrahi**

I had spent the past ten days at home with my sick son who was very cranky (and rightfully so). My baby was crying and I myself didn't feel well. My son started to cry and whine and have a tantrum—about what, I don't even know. I burst out screaming, "Will you stop crying? What is it that you want from me?" I lifted my head from his startled gaze and my eyes rested upon the open windows. Probably everyone in my apartment building had heard me scream. I instantly lowered my voice and told him in a near whisper, "Let's make a deal. Avraham Nissim will stop whining and Mommy will stop screaming." He nodded his head in agreement.

Shhh, the neighbors are listening, what will they think?

I would awake to the sounds of people screaming below us. I grew up in a large house, oblivious to what was going on around me. Every scream, shout or negative comment stayed within the four walls of our home or trapped within my heart. We never worried about what the neighbors would think. When I was first married, we rented an apartment in a large apartment building in the heart of Mexico City. At two o'clock in the morning, I would awake to the sounds of people screaming below us. After two months, I told my husband I couldn't take it anymore and we moved to a different apartment, leaving behind a big deposit. It was worth it. I wonder to myself how many homes would be saved if only the occupants had thought to themselves, "Shhh, the neighbors are listening, what will they think?"

On occasion, by the time Thursday or Friday rolls around I'm so exhausted from the week, I can't even think about preparing for Shabbat. I have thoughts of serving peanut butter and jelly sandwiches or store-bought cold cuts instead of my usual home-cooked meals that are infused with love and holiness. Just then, the phone will ring, as it does almost every week, and it's someone asking to come over for a meal on Shabbat. I tell the caller "yes" and breathe a sigh of relief. Thanks to the Shabbat guest, my home will radiate, sparkle, and shine and the smell of good food will fill it... after all, what would the Shabbat guest think?

Even when the windows are closed shut in the middle of the winter or during the week when we don't have a single caller, I say to myself, "The windows are open, what will the neighbors think. You might have an unexpected guest, what will he/she think?"

Have you ever noticed how easy it is to get upset with your family and how difficult it is to display the same anger for a stranger? How your home looks impeccable when you know that visitors are coming, and if not, it would look like a disaster? You might ask, why do you need the neighbors or a Shabbat guest to do what you should be doing anyways? Isn't it like living a lie or putting on a show? One might call it pretend or make-believe to always be thinking that someone is listening or that someone is visiting, but, in fact, it is reality. The first law in the famous compilation of codified Jewish law, the Shulchan Aruch, states, "*shiviti Hashem linegdi tamid*"—I am always dwelling in front of G-d.

We always have Someone listening and observing our actions. The Talmud (Tractate Brachot 28:b) relates that when Rabbi Yochanan ben Zakai was on his deathbed, his students asked him to give them a blessing. He told them, "Have the same fear of Heaven as you have of man."

"That's it, Rabbi? [Only the same, not more?]"

"If only it would be the same as it is for man!" he answered.

We seem to forget that we are never alone; we always have Someone listening and observing each and every one of our actions. I always tell the brides I counsel to speak in a tone with their husbands as they would if the neighbors were listening, to treat their spouses and future children with the same patience as they would a guest.

Once again my son taught me a valuable lesson and reminded me that everything I do does make a difference, because, after all, "Shhh, the neighbors are listening, what will they think?"

"Shiviti Hashem linegdi tamid"—I am always dwelling before G-d.

Reprinted with permission from chabad.org.

Great Leaders of Our People: Rabbi Yochanan ben Zakkai

Rabbi Yochanan ben Zakkai was one of the great heroes of the Jewish People. He lived at the time of the destruction of Jerusalem and the Temple by the Romans in approximately the year 70 CE.

He realized the futility of resisting the Romans at that time, but that it was possible for the Jewish People to survive even exiled from its spiritual center, Jerusalem, and its heart, the Holy Temple and its homeland, the Land of Israel. That ability was based on the fact that it had in its possession the Torah, the Law of G-d, that could not be taken from them.

When Vespasian, the Roman General, soon-to-be-Emperor, offered to grant him three wishes, he did not request the salvation of the City nor the Temple, for he realized that the Romans were too deeply committed to their destruction, and would never grant him those. He did, however, request that the Romans spare Yavneh,

the new home of the "Sanhedrin," the Jewish Supreme Court, and its Torah Sages.

He realized that the study of the Torah and observance of its "Mitzvot," Commandments, would allow the Jewish People to continue to exist wherever they were exiled to in the world, and it would enable them to keep the memory of the Temple burning in their hearts, so that it would never be forgotten. When HaShem would have mercy on His People, and allow them to return to their land, they would be ready.

As "Nasi," or "Prince," he made enactments and instituted customs for the specific purpose of serving as memory-aids for the People, so that they would never forget what life was like when they had their Temple.

But the ultimate uncertainty of human life is reflected in the Talmudic account that upon his deathbed, he wept and said, "I don't know on what road I will be taken." For even though history seems to have strongly corroborated the truth of his analysis, he was never absolutely certain that he had not erred by not requesting it all—the salvation of the Temple and Yerushalayim!

He was a descendant of the House of David and his family has kept alive through the ages the hope of the People of Israel for the arrival of their Anointed King, the Mashiach, may he arrive soon, and in our days.

Reprinted with permission of ou.org.

R' Yochanan ben Zakkai

Rebbi Yochanan ben Zakkai was born approximately 110 years before the destruction of the second Bais Ha'mikdosh. He saw it in its great beauty and, unfortunately, witnessed its destruction. He lived to the ripe old age of 120 years, spending his first forty years in business, the next forty years in study and the last forty years as the leader of Klal Yisroel. (Sanhedrin 41)

He studied under the great giants of the time, Hillel and Shammai. (Pirkei Avos) He is mentioned as the least of Hillel's eighty students. The greatest amongst them being Yonasan ben Uziel (Targum Yonason) who was so holy, that a bird flying overhead would instantly be burned. Yet, even he, being the smallest of all Hillel's students had the power to be *mechayeh meysim*—bring the dead back to life. One wonders what the Rebbi's power was?

He was knowledgeable in every area of Torah, be it Mikrah, Mishnah, Gemorah, Halacha, Aggadah, Tekufos, gematrios, the language of angels, *sheidim*, palm trees, and knew the secrets of creation (*Maaseh Beraishis*) and *Maaseh Merkavah* (secrets of the Chariot). (Sukkoh 28)

Yet, despite his great Torah knowledge, he would always tell his students that if you have studied much Torah do not take credit for yourselves, for this was the purpose for which you were created. (Avos 2)

As he was once riding on a donkey, his great student Rebbi Eliezer ben Aroch asked him to teach him the secrets of *Maaseh Merkavah*. "I'm sorry" said Rebbi Yochanan "but one is not permitted to teach these secrets to anyone but may only give hints to those great enough to figure things out on their own." Thereupon Rebbi Eliezer asked his Rebbi to permit him to say some of the things he had learned, whereupon Rebbi Yochanan granted him permission. Rebbi Yochanan now got off his donkey, covered himself with his cloak, and sat down on a rock under an olive tree as his student began to expound on the deep secrets of Merkavah. The sky blackened, powerful winds began to blow and the heavenly angels lit up the sky as they came to listen to the holy words of Rebbi Eliezer as he revealed the secrets of the heavenly Chariot.

Upon hearing his student's great grasp of these hidden secrets, Rebbi Yochanan was so overcome with emotion that he kissed him and said "Blessed be G-d who has given such a great son to Avrohom Ovinu that is able to expound and understand these great secrets."

It was said of Rebbi Yochanan ben Zakkai that in his entire life he never engaged in idle talk; for the words of Torah were constantly on his lips. Never did he even take four steps (amos) without speaking in Torah or without wearing tefillin. He was always the first to enter the Bais Medrash and the last to leave. He learned uninterruptedly and never even for a moment would he be found dozing or sleeping in the Bais Medrash. He would personally open the door for his students to enter. Never would he say something that he did not hear from his Rebbi. The only time he closed the doors of his yeshivah was on Erev Pesach and Erev Yom Kippur. He was always the very first one to greet people, including a goy, in the street.

Once, when his son was very sick he asked his student Rebbi Chaninah ben Dosa to pray that he get well. Rebbi Chaninah put his head between his feet, prayed for him and he recuperated. When his wife asked him why he had asked this of his student and did not pray for him himself, he answered, "he is likened to a servant in front of His Master (and so has constant access), while I am like a governor in front of His Master."

Already forty years before the destruction of the Bais Hamikdosh there were many heavenly signs that it would soon be destroyed. The usual ten miracles didn't take place. That's when Rebbi Tzodok began his forty year fast, praying fervently to overturn the terrible decree. When the gates of the Heichal automatically opened wide as if inviting the enemy to enter, he shouted at them and they quickly shut closed.

For three years, the Roman General Vespasian set siege to the city of Yerushalayim but was unable to get her to surrender. Rebbi Yochanan was of the opinion that armed resistance against the Romans was useless and the only chance for survival was to make peace with them. However, there was a large group of people, called the Baryonim who thought they could fight against the mighty Roman army rather than surrender. Yerushalayim still had a large supply of oil, wine, and wood and could easily hold out against an enemy siege. The Baryonim deliberately set fire to these storehouses in hope of forcing the people to fight the enemy.

Rebbi Yochanan ben Zakkai called his nephew, Abba Sikrah, who was the leader of this rebellious group and tried to reason with him. "We'll all die if you continue this madness," he told him. Abba Sikrah told him that there was really nothing he can do for he had lost all control of his followers. Were he to dare suggest that they make peace, they would have his head. Rebbi

Yochanan pleaded with him to find him a way to get out of the city so that he could go and negotiate with the Roman general.

Abba Sikrah gave him the following advice. He was to pretend that he was very sick and allow only his most trusted students into his room. "After a few days let it be known that you have died." Only the dead were permitted to be taken out of the city and buried outside. The plan worked perfectly and his coffin was taken out of the city without any mishap. Rebbi Yochanan ben Zakkai immediately made his way to the Roman general and was granted entry. Upon entering into the general's presence, he bowed graciously and proclaimed, "Blessed be you my King, blessed be you my King."

The general looked at him in great anger and said "You now deserve to be killed twice. Once, for addressing me as the king when I am only the general, and secondly, if it be true that I am the king then why did you not come earlier?"

Rebbi Yochanan ben Zakkai replied, "Undoubtedly you must be the King because our prophets have prophesied that Yerushalayim will fall into the hands of a King, and the reason I haven't come earlier is because the Baryonim would not permit me to leave the city."

At that very moment a Roman nobleman arrived on horseback with an urgent message for the general. It stated that the king had died and that Vespasian had been proclaimed the new ruler. Vespasian was amazed at this turn of events and told Rebbi Yochanan to make any request of him and it would be granted.

Rebbi Yochanan, of course, realized that if he asked for too much he may get nothing at all, so he make just three requests. He asked to be given the city of Yavneh and its great scholars. He asked that the leadership of the princely family of Rebbi Gamliel should be allowed to continue, and he requested that a doctor be given to heal Rebbi Tzodok.

The king graciously agreed to all three requests.

And so, while Rebbi Yochanan could not save the city of Yerushalayim itself, he at least rescued the great Torah Sages and thereby insured that the study of Torah would continue uninterruptedly. (Gittin 56)

As he was once walking in Yerushalayim and saw the Bais Hamikdosh laying in ruins, his student Rebbi Yehoshua remarked, "Woe to us that the place where we were able to obtain our forgiveness lies in ruins." "My son," answered Rebbi Yochanan. "We must always remember that we are still left with one method of forgiveness that is her equal, and that is *gemilas chasodim*—doing good deeds."

He would tell his students that there are three things that merit a person with a share in the world to come and they are: a) Living in Eretz Yisroel b) Bringing up one's children to Torah Study c) Reciting Havdala on wine on Motzoei Shabbos. (Pesochim 113)

Once, when he was told that a certain family of *kohanim* were all dying before they reached the age of eighteen, he immediately suspected that they came from the family of Eli Ha'kohen that had been cursed with short life. He advised them to devote themselves to Torah study and they would merit longer life. His advice paid off and the family called their children Yochanan in honor of the great *tzadik*.

He had five students that stood out from amongst all the rest. He praised Rebbi Eliezer ben Horkenus as being like a lime pit that doesn't lose a drop of its water. About Rebbi Yehosuah ben Chananyah he said, "Praise worthy is the mother that gave birth to such a special son." Rebbi Yossi HaKohen was praised as the pious one, and Rebbi Shimon ben Nesanel as one who truly feared sin. Rebbi Elozor ben Aroch was likened to a spring whose waters came gushing forth with great strength. If all the scholars would be put on one side of a scale and Rebbi Eliezer ben Horkinus would be put on the other side, he would outweigh them all.

He instituted many important enactments. After the Bais Hamikdosh was destroyed he instituted that the *lulov* and *esrog* be taken all seven days of Sukkos in all cities around the world. During the time of the Bais Hamikdosh it was taken only for one day. The only place it was taken for all seven days was in the Bais Hamikdosh itself. He instituted many other important enactments in order to strengthen Torah law and remember the Beit Hamiikdosh.

When Rebbi Yochanan ben Zakkai became sick, his students came to visit him. When he saw them enter, he began to cry. "Rebbi, the light of Yisroel, the right pillar, the strong hammer," said his students, "why do you cry?" Answered Rebbi Yochanan, "If I would have to appear in front of an ordinary King who rules only temporarily and whose anger is not lasting and whose death penalty is only of short duration, wouldn't I be terrified? Now that I must come before the King of Kings, Whose rule is eternal and Whose anger is eternal and Whose punishment of death remains everlasting, should I not be frightened?" "Furthermore," he said, "there are two paths in front of me, one leads to Gan Eden while the other leads to Gehenom, and one can never be sure on which path he will be led, shouldn't I therefore cry?"

Thereupon they said to him "Rebbi, please bless us." He thereupon told them, "If only your fear of heaven be equal to your fear of man." "And not more?" they asked. "When a person sins he is always afraid lest a person see him," was his reply. "If only you realize that HaShem is always watching."

As he was about to return his *neshomah* to the One Above he told his students. "Empty the house of any objects that can become *tomei* and prepare a chair for Chizkiyahu King of Yehudah who is coming to greet me." (Berochos 28)

When he died it was said "that the shine of wisdom has gone."

He lies buried in the city of T'verya, right alongside where the Rambam would be buried 1,100 years later.

Reprinted with permission from campsci.com.

Lesson 3
Rabbi Eliezer

Introduction

Although revolutionaries may take on unpopular causes, they are generally nurtured by a group of friends or mentors that provide strength and support as they wage the war of ideas. But how many people can stand up to the censure of others when they are totally alone?

Rabbi Eliezer was a man of rare integrity, willing to leave behind home and financial security to join those who shared his passion for Torah. But the greatest test of his life was yet to come. Would he be willing to part from the colleagues who meant everything to him to defend absolute truth?

רבי אליעזר בן הורקנוס

Historical Timeline

3810/50 CE	Rabban Yochanan ben Zakai is installed as *av bet din* in Yerushalayim
3716/56 CE	Rabbi Akiva departs for Yeshiva
3826/66 CE	Beginning of the Great War
3828/68 CE	Rabban Yochanan ben Zakai founds Yavneh
3829/69 CE	Second Temple is destroyed
3834/74 CE	Passing of Rabban Yochanan ben Zakai
3840/80 CE	Rabbi Akiva returns home with 24,000 students
3842/82 CE	Rabbi Eliezer is banned from the academy

ROMAN EMPERORS

241–54 CE	**CLAUDIUS**
54–68 CE	**NERO**
68 CE	**YEAR OF THE FOUR EMPERORS: GALBA, OTHO, VITELLIUS, AND VESPASIAN**
69–79 CE	**VESPASIAN**
79–81 CE	**TITUS**
81–96 CE	**DOMITIAN**

- Rabbi Eliezer likely came to Jerusalem during the reign of Claudius.
- He escaped Jerusalem with Rabban Yochanan during the year of the four emperors.
- The great debate occurred just after the reign of Titus at the beginning of the reign of Domitian.

Brief Biographical Overview

The year of Rabbi Eliezer's birth and the age of his passing are unknown. He was twenty-eight when he first arrived in Jerusalem and quickly became one of Rabban Yochanan's main disciples. Rabbi Eliezer's time in Jerusalem was marked by Roman oppression and bloody uprisings. One such uprising resulted in the defeat of the local Roman garrison and the Jews established an independent government. This rebellion sparked the Great War that culminated with the destruction of the Temple.

During the siege, Rabbi Eliezer's teacher, Rabban Yochanan ben Zakai, sought to establish a safe place for Torah learning outside of Jerusalem. Along with his colleague Rabbi Yehoshua, Rabbi Eliezer secretly spirited Rabban Yochanan out of Jerusalem and accompanied him to Yavneh.

Rabbi Eliezer was renowned for his brilliant memory and was appointed by Rabban Yochanan as the primary conduit of Torah for the next generation. Later generations paid homage to his brilliance by adding to his name the epithet *hagadol*—the great one.

Loyal to his mandate, Rabbi Eliezer insisted on teaching only that which he had heard from his teachers and never taught anything he had not learned from the previous generation. His commitment to his tradition placed him at odds with many of the new rulings promulgated by the *sanhedrin* and matters came to a head in the year 82 CE during the great debate.

As a result of that debate, Rabbi Eliezer was banned from the Yeshiva for the rest of his life. He lived to a ripe old age, but his age and date of passing are unknown.

Introductory Text

Aaron M. Feuerstein, the inventor of Polartec fleece, became a certifiable corporate folk hero by paying workers out of his own pocket after his family-owned Malden Mills factory burned to the ground in 1995. Six years later, however, he lost control of the company when it declared bankruptcy, a victim of excessive debt it took on to recover from the fire.

Now Mr. Feuerstein, 78, wants to buy back his company from its current owners. A storybook ending, right? Not quite. His offer, which would keep 1,000 jobs in the Merrimac Valley of northeastern Massachusetts and provide low-cost housing to area residents, has been rejected by the board of Malden Mills and its largest shareholder, GE Capital, the giant financing arm of General Electric.

NY TIMES, OCT. 24, 2004

Questions for Discussion

Would you use your personal resources to pay workers who were laid off due unforeseeable circumstances beyond your control?

If you would end up bankrupted as a result of your kind actions, would you regret your actions, or grow bitter that your good deed has not been rewarded?

Rabbi Eliezer's Youth

Text 1 📜

מעשה ברבי אליעזר בן הורקנוס שהיו לאביו חורשין

והיו חורשין על גבי המענה והוא היה חורש בטרשין

ישב לו והיה בוכה, אמר לו אביו: מפני מה אתה בוכה

שמא מצטער אתה שאתה חורש בטרשין

עכשיו הרי אתה חורש עמנו על גבי המענה

ישב לו על גבי המענה והיה בוכה

אמר לו אביו: מפני מה אתה בוכה

שמא מצטער אתה שאתה חורש על גבי המענה

אמר לו: לאו, אמר לו

ולמה אתה בוכה, אמר לו: איני בוכה אלא שאני מבקש ללמוד תורה

אמר לו: והרי בן שמנה ועשרים שנה אתה ואתה מבקש ללמוד תורה

אלא קח לך אשה והוליד בנים ואתה מוליכן לבית הספר . . .

עמד ועלה לו אל ירושלם אצל רבן יוחנן בן זכאי, ישב לפניו והיה בוכה

אמר לו: מפני מה אתה בוכה, אמר לו: מפני שאני מבקש ללמוד תורה

אמר לו: בן מי אתה, ולא הגיד לו

אמר לו: מימיך לא למדת לא קריית שמע ולא תפלה ולא ברכת המזון

אמר לו: לאו, אמר לו: עמוד ואלמדך שלשתן . . .

והיה אומר לו שתי הלכות כל ימי השבוע, והיה חוזר לו עליהן ומדבקן . . .

אמר לו: בני בן מי אתה, אמר לו: בן הורקנוס אני

אמר לו: והלא בן גדולי עולם אתה, ולא היית מגיד לי

אמר לו: חייך היום אתה סועד אצלי

אמר לו: כבר סעדתי אצל אכסניא שלי

אמר לו: ומי הוא אכסניא שלך

אמר לו: רבי יהושע בן חנניא ורבי יוסי הכהן

שלח ושאל אכסניא שלו, אמר להם: אצלכם סעד אליעזר היום

אמרו לו: לאו, והלא יש לו שמנה ימים שלא טעם כלום

אחר כן הלכו רבי יהושע בן חנניא ורבי יוסי הכהן

ויאמרו לרבן יוחנן בן זכאי: הרי יש לו שמנה ימים שלא טעם כלום

פרקי רבי אליעזר א

I t is told of Rabbi Eliezer ben Hyrcanus that his father had ploughmen who ploughed the furrows while he was made to plough the stony land. He sat down and cried.

"Why are you crying?" asked his father. "Are you pained because you are ploughing the stony land? From now on, you will plough the furrows."

[But] he sat down amid the furrows and cried [some more].

"Why are you crying?" asked his father.

"Is it possible that you are pained because you are ploughing the furrows?"

Rabbi Eliezer replied, "No."

"Then why are you crying?"

"My soul desires [to study] Torah," he replied.

His father said to him, "You are twenty-eight years old and you want to study Torah!? It would be better if you got yourself a wife, had children, and took *them* to school."...

Rabbi Eliezer got up and went to Rabban Yochanan ben Zakai in Jerusalem. He sat down and cried.

Rabban Yochanan asked, "Why are you crying?"

Rabbi Eliezer replied, "Because I want to learn Torah."

Rabban Yochanan asked, "Whose son are you?" but he did not tell him.

Rabban Yochanan asked, "Have you in all your days never learned *Shema*, the prayers, or the Grace after Meals?"

Rabbi Eliezer replied, "No."

"Stand up and I will teach you all three," said Rabban Yochanan. . . .

He would teach him two *halachot* every day of the week, and Rabbi Eliezer would repeat them and affix them in his memory. . . .

(Once again) Rabban Yochanan asked, "My son, whose son are you?"

Rabbi Eliezer replied, "I am the son of Hyrcanus."

Rabban Yochanan said, "You are the son of one of the great [wealthy] ones of the world and you didn't tell me? I insist that you eat with me today."

Rabbi Eliezer replied, "I have already eaten at my lodgings."

Rabban Yochanan asked, "With whom do you lodge?"

Rabbi Eliezer replied, "With Rabbi Yehoshua ben Chananya and Rabbi Yossi HaKohen."

Rabban Yochanan sent a messenger who said to them, "Did Eliezer eat with you today?"

They replied, "No. He must not have tasted anything for eight days!"

Later, Rabbi Yehoshua ben Chananya and Rabbi Yossi HaKohen came and testified to Rabban Yochanan that he had indeed gone eight days without tasting anything.

Pirkei Rabbi Eliezer ch. 1

Text 2

אמרו בניו של הורקנוס לאביהם: עלה לך לירושלים ונדה את בנך אלעזר מנכסיך

ועלה לירושלים לנדותו ומצא שם יום טוב לרבן יוחנן בן זכאי

והיו כל גדולי המדינה סועדים אצלו . . .

ועשו לו מקום והושיבו אותו אצלו, ונתן עיניו ברבי אליעזר

אמר לו: אמור לנו דבר אחד מן התורה

אמר לו: רבי אמשול לך משל למה הדבר דומה

לבור הזה שאינו יכול להוציא מים יותר ממה שהוא מכניס

כך איני יכול לומר דברי תורה יותר ממה שקבלתי ממך

אמר לו: אמשול לך משל, למה הדבר דומה

למעיין שהוא נובע ומוציא מים ויש בכחו להוציא יתר ממה שהוא מכניס

כך אתה יכול לומר דברי תורה יתר ממה שקבלו מסיני

אמר לו: שמא ממני אתה מתבייש, הריני עומד מאצלך

עמד רבן יוחנן בן זכאי והלך לו לחוץ

והיה רבי אלעזר יושב ודורש ופניו מאירות כאור החמה

וקרנותיו יוצאות כקרנותיו של משה

ואין אדם יודע אם יום ואם לילה

בא רבי יוחנן בן זכאי מאחוריו ונשקו על ראשו

אמר לו: אשריכם אברהם יצחק ויעקב שיצא זה מחלציכם

אמר הורקנוס אביו: למי אמר כך, אמרו לו: לאלעזר בנך

אמר להם: לא כך היה לו לומר אלא אשרי אני שיצא זה מחלצי

היה רבי אליעזר יושב ודורש ואביו עומד על רגליו

כיון שראה אביו עומד על רגליו נבהל

אמר לו: אבא שב שאיני יכול לומר דברי תורה ואתה עומד על רגליך

אמר לו: בני לא על כן באתי אלא לנדותך מנכסי

ועכשיו שבאתי לראותך וראיתי כל השבח הזה

הרי אחיך מנודים מהם והם נתונים לך במתנה

אמר לו: והרי אני איני שוה כאחד מהם

אילו קרקעות בקשתי מלפני הקב"ה היה לפניו ליתן לי

שנאמר (תהלים כד,א) לה' הארץ ומלואה תבל ויושבי בה

ואלו כסף וזהב בקשתי היה נותן לי

שנאמר (חגי ב,ח) לי הכסף ולי הזהב נאום ה' צבאות

אלא לא בקשתי מלפני הקב"ה אלא תורה בלבד

שנאמר (תהלים קיט,קכח) על כן כל פקודי כל ישרתי כל אורח שקר שנאתי

פרקי רבי אליעזר ב

Hyrcanus' sons said to their father, "Go up to Jerusalem and disinherit your son Eliezer." He went up to Jerusalem to disinherit him but found that Rabban Yochanan ben Zakai was having a celebration, and all the prestigious men of the city were feasting with him . . . They made a place [for Hyrcanus], and placed him [up front] near Rabban Yochanan.

Rabban Yochanan set his eyes on Rabbi Eliezer and said to him, "Expound for us some teaching from the Torah."

Rabbi Eliezer said to him, "Rabbi! I will give you an example of what this is like. A cistern cannot yield more water than that which was put into it. In the same way, I cannot say any more words of Torah than those I received from you."

Rabban Yochanan said to him, "I will give you an example: A spring that gushes forth water has in its power to bring forth more water than what was put into it. In the same way, you will be able to say more words of Torah than what was given at Sinai."

Rabban Yochanan then asked, "Are you embarrassed before me? I will leave you."

Rabban Yochanan got up and went outside, and Rabbi Eliezer sat and expounded, his face radiant like the light of the sun, emanating rays of light like Moses, so that no one knew whether it was day or night. Rabban Yochanan ben Zakai came from behind and kissed him on his head. He proclaimed, "How happy you should be, Abraham, Isaac, and Jacob, that one such as this has descended from you!"

Hyrcanus said, "Of whom did he say that?"

They said to him, "Of Eliezer, your son."

He said to them, "That's not what he should have said. He should have said how happy I should be that one such as this has descended from me."

Rabbi Eliezer sat and expounded, and his father stood on his feet. When he saw his father standing on his feet, he was upset and said, "Father, sit, for I cannot say words of Torah while you stand on your feet."

Hyrcanus said to him, "My son, this is not why I came.

I came to disinherit you. But now that I have come and I see this great honor, it is your brothers who are disinherited, and their portion is given to you."

Rabbi Eliezer replied, "I am not equal to even one of them. Had I asked God for land, it would have been for Him to give it, as it says (Psalms 24:1), 'The land and its fullness is God's, the earth and those who dwell on it.' Had I asked for gold and silver, He would have given it to me, as it says (Haggai 2:8), 'The silver is Mine and the gold is Mine says the God of Hosts.' But all I asked of the blessed Holy One was Torah alone, as it says (Psalms 119:128), 'Therefore all of the laws I have kept uprightly, and I have hated every path of lying.'"

PIRKEI RABBI ELIEZER CH. 2

His Mission

Text 3a

הוא היה אומר: אם יהיו כל חכמי ישראל בכף מאזנים
ואליעזר בן הורקנוס בכף שניה
מכריע את כולם

משנה אבות ב,ח

Rabban Yochanan used to say, "If all the sages of Israel were on one pan of a balance scale and Rabbi Eliezer ben Hyrcanus was on the other, he would outweigh them all."

MISHNAH AVOT 2:8

Text 3b

הוא היה מונה שבחן: רבי אליעזר בן הורקנוס בור סיד שאינו מאבד טפה

משנה אבות ב,ח

He (Rabban Yochanan) enumerated their praises. Of Rabbi Eliezer ben Hyrcanus he would say, "A cemented cistern that loses not a drop."

MISHNAH AVOT 2:8

Text 4a

משמת רבי אליעזר נגנז ספר תורה

תלמוד בבלי סוטה מט,ב

With Rabbi Eliezer's passing, the Torah scroll was laid to rest.

TALMUD SOTAH 49B

Text 4b

שהיה בעל הלכות מפי שמועה הרבה וסדורות בפיו כאילו כתֻוב בספר

רש"י שם

He was fluent in all *Halachah* and was a master of tradition. The laws were as well ordered in his mind as if they were clearly documented on a scroll.

RASHI AD LOC.

Text 4c

פעם אחת נכנס רבי יהושע . . .

ואמר: האבן הזאת דומה להר סיני, וזה שישב עליה דומה לארון הברית

שיר השירים רבה א

Once, [after Rabbi Eliezer's passing,] his colleague Rabbi Yehoshua, entered [Rabbi Eliezer's study hall] . . . and said, "This stone

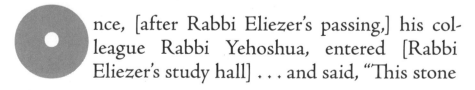

[on which Rabbi Eliezer sat] is like Sinai and he who sat on it is like the Holy Ark."

SHIR HASHIRIM RABAH I

Text 5 📖

תנו רבנן: מעשה ברבי אליעזר ששבת בגליל העליון

ושאלוהו שלשים הלכות בהלכות סוכה

שתים עשרה אמר להם שמעתי, שמונה עשר אמר להם, לא שמעתי . . .

אמרו לו: כל דבריך אינן אלא מפי השמועה

אמר להם: הזקקתוני לומר דבר שלא שמעתי מפי רבותי

מימי לא קדמני אדם בבית המדרש

ולא ישנתי בבית המדרש לא שינת קבע ולא שינת עראי

ולא הנחתי אדם בבית המדרש ויצאתי, ולא שחתי שיחת חולין

ולא אמרתי דבר שלא שמעתי מפי רבי מעולם

תלמוד בבלי סוכה כח,א

It happened that Rabbi Eliezer spent Shabbat in the Upper Galilee. He was asked thirty questions regarding the laws of Sukah.

Of twelve of these, he said, "I heard [them from my teachers]."

Of eighteen, he said, "I have not heard [these from my teachers]."

They said to him, "Are all your words only reproductions of what you have heard?"

He answered them, "You wish to force me to say something which I have not heard from my teachers. During all my life, no man came earlier than me to the house of study. I never slept or dozed in the house of study, nor did I ever leave a person [behind] in the house of study when I left, nor have I ever engaged in idle chatter, nor have I ever in my life said a thing which I did not hear from my teachers."

TALMUD SUKAH 28A

תנור של עכנאי

The Great Debate

Text 6

תנא: באותו היום השיב רבי אליעזר כל תשובות שבעולם ולא קיבלו הימנו

אמר להם: אם הלכה כמותי חרוב זה יוכיח

נעקר חרוב ממקומו מאה אמה, ואמרי לה: ארבע מאות אמה

אמרו לו: אין מביאין ראיה מן החרוב

חזר ואמר להם: אם הלכה כמותי אמת המים יוכיחו

חזרו אמת המים לאחוריהם. אמרו לו: אין מביאין ראיה מאמת המים

חזר ואמר להם: אם הלכה כמותי כותלי בית המדרש יוכיחו

הטו כותלי בית המדרש ליפול

גער בהם רבי יהושע, אמר להם

אם תלמידי חכמים מנצחים זה את זה בהלכה, אתם מה טיבכם

לא נפלו מפני כבודו של רבי יהושע

ולא זקפו מפני כבודו של רבי אליעזר, ועדין מטין ועומדין

חזר ואמר להם: אם הלכה כמותי מן השמים יוכיחו

יצאתה בת קול ואמרה: מה לכם אצל רבי אליעזר שהלכה כמותו בכל מקום

עמד רבי יהושע על רגליו ואמר: לא בשמים היא (דברים ל,יב)
מאי לא בשמים היא

אמר רבי ירמיה: שכבר נתנה תורה מהר סיני, אין אנו משגיחין בבת קול
שכבר כתבת בהר סיני בתורה (שמות כג,ב) אחרי רבים להטת
תלמוד בבלי בבא מציעא נט,ב

I t has been taught: On that day Rabbi Eliezer
brought forward every imaginable argument, [to
prove that the oven of Achnai is not subject to ritual
defilement] but the sages did not accept his arguments.

Said Rabbi Eliezer, "If the *Halachah* agrees
with me, let this carob tree prove it."

Thereupon the carob tree was uprooted
and moved a distance of a hundred
cubits; others say, four hundred
cubits.

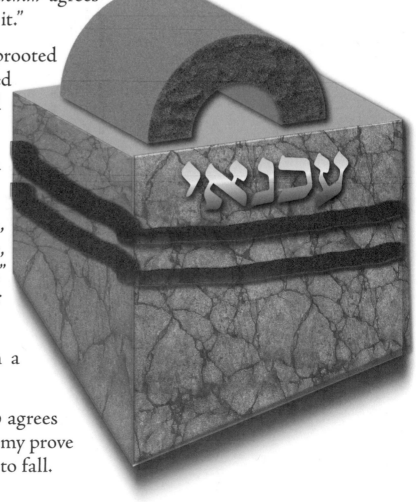

"No proof can be brought from a
carob tree," they retorted.

Again Rabbi Eliezer said to them,
"If the *Halachah* agrees with me,
let the stream of water prove it,"
whereupon the stream of water
began to flow backwards.

"No proof can be brought from a
stream of water," they rejoined.

Again he urged, "If the *Halachah* agrees
with me, let the walls of the academy prove
it," whereupon the walls inclined to fall.

But Rabbi Yehoshua rebuked the [walls], saying, "Scholars are engaged in *halachic* dispute; what right have you to interfere?"

[The Talmud recounts that] The walls did not cave in completely to honor the words of Rabbi Yehoshua, nor did they resume their upright position to honor the words of Rabbi Eliezer; and they are still standing thus inclined.

Again he said to them, "If the *Halachah* agrees with me, let the heaven prove it," whereupon a heavenly voice proclaimed, "Why do you dispute with Rabbi Eliezer, when the *Halachah* agrees with him in all matters?"

But Rabbi Yehoshua arose and exclaimed, "The Torah is not in heaven!" (Deuteronomy 30:12).

What did he mean by this?—Said Rabbi Yirmiyahu, "Ever since the Torah was given at Mount Sinai, we pay no attention to a heavenly voice, but adjudicate matters in accordance with the law of majority opinion as is written in the Torah, 'After the majority must one incline'" (Exodus 23:2).

TALMUD BAVA METSIA 59B

Text 7 📜

ונמנו עליו וברכוהו, ואמרו: מי ילך ויודיעו

אמר להם רבי עקיבא: אני אלך . . .

מה עשה רבי עקיבא

לבש שחורים, ונתעטף שחורים, וישב לפניו בריחוק ארבע אמות

אמר לו רבי אליעזר: עקיבא, מה יום מיומים

אמר לו: רבי, כמדומה לי שחבירים בדילים ממך

אף הוא קרע בגדיו וחלץ מנעליו, ונשמט וישב על גבי קרקע זלגו עיניו דמעות

לקה העולם שליש בזיתים, ושליש בחטים, ושליש בשעורים . . .

תנא: אך גדול היה באותו היום, שבכל מקום שנתן בו עיניו רבי אליעזר, נשרף

תלמוד בבלי בבא מציעא נט,ב

They took a vote and [when Rabbi Eliezer refused to accept the ruling they] excommunicated him.

They said, "Who shall go and inform him?"

"I will go," answered Rabbi Akiva. . . .

He donned black garments and wrapped himself in black, and sat at a distance of four cubits from him.

"Akiva," said Rabbi Eliezer to him, "What particular event has happened today?"

"Master," replied Rabbi Akiva, "It appears that your colleagues have separated themselves from you."

Thereupon Rabbi Eliezer rent his garments, removed his shoes, and sat on the earth, while tears streamed from his eyes.

The world was then smitten: A third of the olive crop, a third of the wheat, and a third of the barley crop [was destroyed on that day]. . . A *tanna* (a sage from the Mishnah period) taught: A great calamity befell the world on that day, for everything on which Rabbi Eliezer cast his eyes was consumed by fire.

TALMUD BAVA METSIA 59B

The End of the Story

Text 8a

כשחלה רבי אליעזר נכנסו רבי עקיבא וחביריו לבקרו . . .

נכנסו וישבו לפניו מרחוק ארבע אמות. אמר להם: למה באתם

אמרו לו: ללמוד תורה באנו. אמר להם: ועד עכשיו למה לא באתם

אמרו לו: לא היה לנו פנאי . . .

נטל שתי זרועותיו והניחן על לבו

אמר: אוי לכם שתי זרועותיי שהן כשתי ספרי תורה שנגללין

הרבה תורה למדתי, והרבה תורה לימדתי

הרבה תורה למדתי—ולא חסרתי מרבותי אפילו ככלב המלקק מן הים

הרבה תורה לימדתי—ולא חסרוני תלמידי אלא כמכחול בשפופרת

ולא עוד אלא שאני שונה שלש מאות הלכות בבהרת עזה

ולא היה אדם ששואלני בהן דבר מעולם

ולא עוד אלא שאני שונה שלש מאות הלכות

ואמרי לה שלשת אלפים הלכות, בנטיעת קשואין

ולא היה אדם שואלני בהן דבר מעולם, חוץ מעקיבא בן יוסף . . .

מנעל שעל גבי האמוס מהו. אמר להן: הוא טהור. ויצאה נשמתו בטהרה

עמד רבי יהושע על רגליו ואמר: הותר הנדר, הותר הנדר

תלמוד בבלי סנהדרין סח,א

When Rabbi Eliezer fell sick, Rabbi Akiva and his colleagues went to visit him . . . The sages entered [his chamber] and sat down at a distance of four cubits.

"Why have you come?" he asked them.

"To study the Torah," they replied.

"And why have you not come before now?" he asked.

They answered, "We had no time. . . ."

"He then put his two arms over his heart, saying, "Woe to you, two arms of mine, that are like two scrolls of the law that are being wrapped up."

"Much Torah have I studied, and much have I taught.

"Much Torah have I studied, yet I have but skimmed from the knowledge of my teachers as much as a dog lapping from the sea.

"Much Torah have I taught, yet my disciples have only drawn from me as much as a painting stick from its tube.

"Moreover, I have studied three hundred laws on the subject of *baheret*, yet no man has ever asked me about them.

"Moreover, I have studied three hundred laws, some say, three thousand laws, about the planting of cucumbers [by magic] and no man, excepting Akiva ben Yosef, ever questioned me thereon. . . ."

[His visitors then asked him] "What [is the law] of a shoe that is on the last?"

He replied, "It is *tahor*, [pure]" and in pronouncing this word, his soul departed.

Then Rabbi Yehoshua arose and exclaimed, "The vow is annulled, the vow is annulled!"

TALMUD SANHEDRIN 68A

Text 8b

למוצאי שבת פגע בו רבי עקיבא מן קיסרי ללוד

היה מכה בבשרו עד שדמו שותת לארץ

פתח עליו בשורה ואמר: אבי אבי רכב ישראל ופרשיו (מלכים ב ב,יב)

הרבה מעות יש לי ואין לי שולחני להרצותן

תלמוד בבלי סנהדרין סח,א

On the conclusion of the Sabbath, Rabbi Akiva met [Rabbi Eliezer's bier] being carried from Caesarea to Lydda. [In his grief] he beat his flesh until the blood flowed down upon the earth.

Then Rabbi Akiva commenced [his eulogy], the mourners being lined up about the coffin, and said: "My father, my father, the chariot of Israel and the horsemen thereof (II Kings 2:12). I have many coins, but no money changer to accept them."

TALMUD SANHEDRIN 68A

Text 8c

לאחר פטירתו של רבי אליעזר נכנסו ארבעה זקנים להשיב על דבריו . . .
אמר להן רבי יהושע: אין משיבין את הארי לאחר מיתה

תלמוד בבלי גיטין פג,א

After Rabbi Eliezer's passing, four elders entered the academy to dispute (overturn) Rabbi Eliezer's words (rulings) . . . Rabbi Yehoshua [intervened] and said to them, "One does not engage a lion posthumously."

TALMUD GITIN 83A

Key Points

1. Rabbi Eliezer was willing to leave his family and study Torah at great personal sacrifice.

2. Rabbi Eliezer saw his mandate as preserving the Torah in unadulterated fashion just as he learned it from his teachers, so that future generations would have access to this authentic wisdom.

3. In the aftermath of the destruction of the temple, it was critical for the nascent academy in Yavneh to establish its unequivocal authority if Torah was to be preserved.

4. The debate regarding the oven of Achnai pitted Rabbi Eliezer's dedication to faithful transmission of the tradition against the academy's responsibility to provide leadership and a united *halachic* voice.

5. Despite heavenly signs supporting Rabbi Eliezer's opinion, the rabbis of the academy maintained that they did not see the logic of his view, and the majority vote must be followed.

6. Rabbi Eliezer refused to retract his view because to do so might compromise the trust people could place in the authenticity of his teachings.

7. As a result, the academy banned Rabbi Eliezer from taking part in further *halachic* debate for they felt it would result in confusion and dissension.

8. Rabbi Eliezer humbly accepted consequences of maintaining his view, and though he continued to respond to questions, he no longer played an active role with the academy life.

9. After his passing, the ban was lifted so that he could be given the respectful burial that a man of his stature deserved.

Additional Readings

The Oven Of Achnai Re-Deconstructed

By **Nachman Levine**

The interpreters of the enigmatic narrative of the oven of Achnai incident (b *Baba Metzia* 59b) attempt to explicate its halachic (and legalistic), historical, philosophical, theological, and mystical import.[1] But it is also a very literary text which can be read for its form, imagery, and allusions to other texts.[2] The debate of both traditional commentaries and modern historians over whether it is a "fictitious" allegory or a literal historical legal discussion is irrelevant to reading the text and its elements, certainly a text so grounded in allusion and metaphor and with so much literary texture.[3]

---

[1] **Halachic**: R. Aharon HaLevi, *Sefer HaHinuch,* 408, R. Haim Yosef David Azulai, *Birchei Yosef*, Livorno 1774, no. 32, *Petah Einayim,* Livorno 1790 ,*Bava Metzia 59b*, *Rosh David,* Mantua 1776, *Nitzavim*, R. Reuven Margaliot, *Mehkarim BiDarchei HaTalmud VeHidotehav,* Jerusalem, 1967, pp 34. **Legalistic:** Julius Stone, *Human Law and Human Justice*, Stanford 1965; Edmund Cahn, "Authority and Responsibility" 51 *Columbia Law Review* p. 38, Ascarelli, *Problemi Giuridici* (Milan, 1959) 14, 157-58; Ronald R. Garet, "Natural Law and Creation Stories", *Nomos XXX: Religion, Morality, and the Law*, (New York University Press:New York 1988) pp. 218-262, Moshe Silberg, "Law and Morals in Jewish Jurisprudence", *Talmudic Law and the Jewish State,* New York 1973, Menahem Elon, *Mishpat Halvri, Toldotav, Mekorotav, Ikaronotav,* Magnes Press: Jerusalem 1973, pp. 875-876 (*Jewish Law: History, Sources, Principles*, Philadelphia 1990), Bernard Jackson, "Religious Law in Judasim", *ANRW* II 19/1 (Berlin, 1979), Robert A. Burt, "Precedent and Authority in Antonin Scalia's Jurisprudence, 12 *Cardozo Law Review* 1685-(1991), Suzanne Last Stone, "In Pursuit of the Counter-Text: The Turn to the Jewish Legal Model in Contemporary Legal Theory", *Harvard Law Review* 106:4, Feb. 1993 pp. 855-894, Daniel J. H. Greenwood, "Akhnai", *Utah Law Review* 1997:309, No. 2, pp. 309-358. **Historical:** Yitzhak Isaac HaLevi, *Dorot HaRishonim,* (Frankfort 1902), Vol: II pp. 286-296, R. David Lurya, *Kuntres Emek Brachah* in *Pirkei DiRabbi Eliezer,* Warsaw 1852, p. 1-5, Gedaliah Allon, *The Jews in their Land in the Talmudic Age*, 1980, 314-315, E. E. Urbach, *The Sages their Concepts and Beliefs,* Jerusalem 1969, p. 99, Yitzhak D. Gilat, *The Teachings of R. Eliezer b. Hyrcanus and their Position in the History of Halakhah,* Ramat Gan 1968), *R. Eliezer b. Hyrcanus: A Scholar Outcast*, (Ramat Gan 1984), M. Aberbach, "Did Rabban Gamliel II Impose the Ban on Rabbi Eliezer ben Hyrcanus" 54 (1964) *JQR* 201, David Kraemer, *The Mind of the Talmud,* (Oxford University Press; Oxford 1990) pp. 140-141, David W. Halivni, *Peshat and Derash: Plain and Applied Meaning in Rabbinic Exegesis* (Oxford 1991), pp. 101-125. **Theological:** Among others: Maharal, *Netivot Olam*, Prague 1596, *Netiv Ahahvat Reah*, 2, *Hidushei Agadot*, *Beeir HaGolah*, 4, Maharsha, *Hidushei Agadot*, R. Menahem Mali Tzintzenet HaMan,Offebach, 1723, R. Yitzhak Sasson, *Shemen Sason*, Vilna 1859, R. Yosef of Pinczov, *Rosh Yosef*, Kiten, 1717, R. Yitshak Luzzato, *Kaftor VeFerah*, Basil 1581, R. Yosef Hayim, *Ben Yehoyada* Jerusalem 1898, R. Menaham Azariah of Fano *Asarah Maamarot*, Venice 1597, *Hikur HaDin* 2:18, R. Isaiah Hurvitz, *Shnei Luhot HaBrit* ,Amsterdam 1649, p. 335, R. Moshe Cordevero, *Pardes Rimonim,* Venice 1586, R. Moshe of Bisenz, *Darash Mosheh,* Cracow, 1589, p.59, R. Yosef Shlomoh HaRofe Delmedigo, *Taalumot Hochmah,* Basilia 1629, p. 22, R. Elijah of Vilna, *Aderet Eliyahu,* 1859, and extensive sources cited in Izhak England's comprehensive classic survey, "The Oven Of Achnai: Interpretation of an Agadah", *Shenaton HaMishpat Halvri* I, p. 45-56, 1974, "Majority Decision vs. Individual Truth: The Interpretations of the "Oven of Achnai" Aggadah", 15 *Tradition,* (1975) pp. 137-152; see also Erich Fromm, *Psychoanalysis and Religion,* (New Haven 1950) p. 45.

[2] S.L. Stone, "In Pursuit of the Counter-Text", p.855, observes that it is rarely considered in its literary context, noting that the same point was made by England, "Majority Decision vs. Individual Truth", nearly twenty years before, but "requires reiteration in light of the renewed fascination with the story."

[3] See also Yonah Fraenkel, "Time and Its Shaping in Aggadic Narratives", *Studies in Aggadah in Memory of Joseph Heinemann* (Jerusalem 1976) pp. 147-53, Judah Goldin, "On the Account of the Banning of R. Eliezer ben Hyrcanus: An Analysis and Proposal", *Journal of the Ancient Near East Society*, 16-17, 1984-85; Eliezer Segal, "Law As Allegory: An Unnoticed Device In Talmudic Narratives", *Prooftexts* 8 (1988), pp. 245-246, David Stern, "Midrash and Indeterminacy", 15 *Critical Inquiry* 132, 1988, Daniel Boyarin, *Intertextuality and*

The *Achnai* story is no less enigmatic for the meaning it conveys than for the way in which it conveys it.[4] Generally, interpreters of the story have, for good reason, concentrated on the legal/theological implications of its startling core metaphor ("It is not in heaven", God laughing, "My sons have defeated Me") and core message, or classically, on the allegorical interpretation of the elements of R. Eliezer's miraculous proofs, etc. My interest here is simply to unpack and catalog the enigmatic constituent literary elements used to tell the story and create its meaning. Among these devices are its literary motifs and internal structure, symmetry, parallelism, wordplay, oppositions, self-referentiality, editorial framing, allusions to other Talmudic sources, and more.[5] Its import may be discerned in these if the story's form and devices are part of its own commentary.

Furthermore, the story has parallels as well as sequels about the aftermath and resolution in other Talmudic sources. Reading them as a composite whole reveals significant intertextual relationships and parallels.[6]

While earlier commentators use "allegorical" exegesis in interpreting the narrative (and guardedly, concluding "all this is far fetched"[7]), it is possible to read it structurally or "semiotically" for *what* it says in *how* it says it. For example, there is the question of the literary relationship of the narrative elements to the underlying legal controversy.[8] The question of the status of an oven assembled from different pieces could reflect a literary question about the narrative's import in being, "symbolic of a question of unity within a diversity of opinions."[9]

The story is dense with allusions to *other* debates of its protagonists and mediators, some within several months of it, also involving deposings and questioning leadership at this crucial historical time.[10] And while the ban's narrative and parallels have a resolution of sorts, the narrative is structured to suggest that its issues are *not* at all resolved or finalized: the walls of the House of Study, "neither *fall* nor *stand* but still *incline*."

Perhaps this is what its literary devices imply. And as the text raises questions about *authority of interpretation* and *interpretation of authority* in a self-referentiality evoking deconstructive infinite regression, self-referentiality may be one of its strongest metaphors: in several connected *halachic* debates their subjects become metaphors for the debates themselves. The story's form and devices may be its commentary if the details which demand interpretation are those that *describe* the catastrophic effects of interpretation winning out. The text, about the interpretation of texts, that itself demands interpretation becomes an allegory for itself. In it Heaven laughingly affirms the process of interpretation but also laughs at it.

---

the Reading of Midrash, (Bloomington, 1991), p. 34-37, Jeffrey Rubenstein, *Talmudic Stories: Narrative Art, Composition, and Culture* (Johns Hopkins Press: Baltimore, 1999) p. 34-64, Charlotte Elisheva Fonrobert, "When The Rabbi Weeps: On Reading Gender In Talmudic Aggadah", *Nashim: A Journal of Jewish Women's Studies and Gender Issues*, 2001, pp. 56-83 .

[4] "This is a very difficult text to understand in many ways; there is no need to elaborate on its difficulties" (Maharal, *Netivot Olam, Netiv Ahahvat Reah,* 2); "Whoever examines this narrative finds the sages' words very exact in precision and wisdom; the more we delve into their words the more wisdom we find" (Maharal, *Beeir HaGolah* 4).

[5] On literary details, structural symmetry, and chiasmus in Aggadah: Y. Frankel,*The Ways Of The Agadah And Midrash*, (Jerusalem 1991), *Studies in the Spiritual World of the Aggadic Story*, (Tel Aviv 1981), "The Structures of Aggadic Narratives", *Studies of The Center for the Study of Folklore* 7 1983, pp. 45-97; Midrashic (and Talmudic/halachic) alliteration and wordplay: Frankel, "Paronomasia in Aggadic Narratives", *Scripta Hierosolymitana* XXVII, Jerusalem 1978, pp. 27-51, *Darcheï HaAgadah* I, pp. 436-8, S. Lieberman, *Sifrei Zuta* (NY 1968) p. 120. Rubenstein, *Talmudic Stories*, and Fonrobert, "When The Rabbi Weeps", deal with *literary* implications of the *Achnai* editorial framing.

[6] Parallels: y*Moed Katan* 3:1; aftermath and resolution: y*Shabbat* 2:5, *Avot DiRabbi Natan* 19,25, b*Sanhedrin* 68a. A. Guttman, "The Significance of Miracles for Talmudic Judaism", (1974) *HUCA* 20, p. 363 discusses the differences

of the ban narratives. See also D. Kraemer, *The Mind of the Talmud,* pp.122-124. Y. Frankel, "Time and Its Shaping in Aggadic Narratives" mentions differences in the Bavli (*Sanhedrin* 67-68) and Yerushalmi (*Shabbat* 2:5) versions of R. Eliezer's death and the resolution.

[7] Maharam Schiff, Commentary to b *Bava Metzia* 59a.

[8] See Stone, "In Pursuit of the Counter-Text", p. 859, note 245.

[9] Segal, "Law As Allegory", pp. 245-246. Segal similarly interprets legal elements of the ban's resolution. See also Fonrobert, "When The Rabbi Weeps", p. 76, no. 3.

[10] HaLevi, *Dorot HaRishonim*, ibid..

The Narrative

They taught there [m Kelim 5:10][11]: "They cut rings [in an oven] and put sand between each ring: R. Eliezer [b. Hyrkanos] declared it [ritually] pure and the sages declared it impure. [R. Eliezer held the rebuilt oven unlike a whole is not susceptible to ritual impurity.] This is the "oven of Achnai." What is Achnai? . . . that they surrounded it with words [of debate] like an Achnai: snake",[12] and declared it impure. On that day R. Eliezer answered all the answers on earth and they did not accept it from him.

He said "If the law is as I say the carob tree will prove it"; the carob tree moved one hundred Amah from its place, some say four hundred Amah. They said: "We do not bring proof from a carob tree."

He returned and said "If the law is as I say the water channel will prove it"; the water channel flowed in reverse direction. They said: "We do not bring proof from a water channel."

He returned and said "If the law is as I say the walls of the House of Study will prove it"; they inclined to fall.

R. Yehoshua rebuked them, saying "If scholars argue what business is it of yours?" They did not fall because of the honor of R. Yehoshua and they did not straighten, because of the honor of R. Eliezer, and they still incline and stand.

R. Eliezer returned and said, "If the law is as I say, from Heaven they will prove it"; a heavenly voice came out and said, "What have you with R. Eliezer, who the law is like him in every place?" R. Yehoshua stood on his feet and said. "The torah is not in heaven," (Deut. 30:12).

R. Yirmiyah [fourth-century Amora] said: "That the torah was already given at Sinai, we do not pay attention to a heavenly voice, since You already wrote at Sinai in the torah, "After the majority to incline," (Ex. 23:2).

R. Natan [a later Tana] met the prophet Elijah and said to him, "What did the Holy One Blessed be He do in that hour?" He said to him: "He smiled and said, "My sons defeated Me, My sons defeated Me.""

On that day they burned all the pure things R. Eliezer had declared pure; they voted upon him and excommunicated him. They asked "Who will go and inform him?"; R. Akiva said, "I will go, lest an improper person inform him and all the earth will be destroyed." What did R. Akiva do? He dressed in black and sat before him at a distance of four Amot. R. Eliezer said: "Akiva, what is today from all days?" He said, "My master, it appears to me your friends distanced themselves from you." R. Eliezer too tore his clothes, removed his shoes and sat on the ground and his eyes flowed tears.

The earth was stricken, a third in olives, a third in wheat, a third in barley. Some say: even dough in a woman's hand spoiled. Great was that day that every place R. Eliezer put his eyes was burned.

And even R. Gamliel was on a ship; a wave stood upon him to drown him. He said: It appears to me this is only because of R. Eliezer b. Hyrkanos. He stood on his feet and said, "Master of the world, it is revealed and known before You that not for my honor I did nor for the honor of my father's house but for Your honor that controversies not multiply in Israel." The sea rested from its anger.

Ima Shalom, wife of R. Eliezer, was R. Gamliel's sister; from then she did not allow R. Eliezer to fall on his face in prayer. One day the New Moon became miscalculated for her between a twenty-nine or thirty day month. Some say: a poor man came and stood at the gate, she brought out bread to him. She found R. Eliezer fallen in prayer and said, "Get up, you have killed my brother." Meanwhile a ram's horn blast went out from R. Gamliel's house [to announce] that he died. R. Eliezer asked, "How did you know?" She said, "So I have received a tradition from the house of my father's father: "All gates are closed but the gates of oppression.""

Internal Protagonists And Commentators—As Metaphor
The narrative's elements can be read as *metaphor*[13] or

---

[11] And *mEduyot* 8:7. What the debate was is itself the subject of debate: see Rashi, b*Bava Metzia* 59b, Maimonides, *Perush HaMishnayot*, Kelim, Raavad, *Commentary on mEduyot* 8:7, and *Ritva, Shitah Mekubetzet, b*Bava Metzia* 59b.

[12] Snake: *echida*: εχιδνα. It is a literary name as well as of an actual person; similarly the other case in *Kelim m* 5:10: is called "the oven of *Dinai*", "because they surrounded it with *litigation*" ["*Dinim*" (Maimonides, *Perush HaMishnayot*, op. cit.) while also being the name of an actual person (R. Asher b. Yehiel, citing b *Sotah* 9:9); see also Tosafot, "*Zeh*", b*Bava Metzia* 59b.

[13] As metaphoric allusion (not allegory) the carob which takes

allusion to related events rather than as strict *allegory*,[14] (as it has been read: the carob is R. Hanina, the spring is R. Elazar b. Arach,[15] the walls are the students,[16] R. Eliezer's miracles as symbolic of his qualities. But R. Hanina b. Dosa does not appear here, nor does R. Elazar b. Arach who never came to Yavneh where the debate was.[17])

If anything, instead of the miracles or *motifs* being allegory *for people* in the narrative, *the individuals in it* can be *its metaphor.*

Fascinatingly, *everybody* in this narrative about banishment over issues of methodology was himself once banished or banned, usually from a Beit Midrash, *even those* appearing *as commentators* in the text:

R. Eliezer (here and at his career's beginning, *Pirkei DeRabi Eliezer* 1),[18] R. Yehoshua (b *Bechorot* 36a, *Berachot* 28a, *Rosh HaShanah* 25a), R. Gamliel (b*Berachot* 28a), R. Akiva

(banned and disowned at his career's beginning just as R. Eliezer was (b *Nedarim* 60a, b*Ketubot* 62b), even R. Natan who lived later, banished for methodological disputes with leadership (b *Horayot* 13b)[19] and the commenting fourth-century *Amora* R. Yirmiyah, banished and almost banned for methodological questions (b *Bava Batra* 23b, y *Moed Katan* 3:1)[20]. Strikingly, A. Heiman defends the banishment of R. Yirmiyah, because it was: "similar to the incident of R. Eliezer b. Hyrkanus"(!).[21]

Even Elijah's heavenly testimony, mediating between heaven and earth, is rejected in the earthly Beit Midrash and *other* legal contexts.[22] His testimony that Heaven said "My sons defeated Me" can serve as the narrative's inherent paradox: why should that testimony be given any weight if it itself reports Heaven's exclusion from the interpretive process?[23] Testimony from heaven that heaven laughed legally obligates us to ignore that laughter.

Editorial Framing As Opposed Metaphor

The editorial framing and construction of the *Sugya*/story creates a dynamically unresolved counter-metaphor. On one hand comments of the *banned* internal commentators are used ironically to *support the banning*. The *Amora* R. Yirmiyah (banished for methodological questions) comments that we do not follow a heavenly voice since the torah says, "After the majority to incline," (Ex. 23:2.), supporting the majority ruling against Heaven and the *methodology* of R. Eliezer's whose position is rejected and banned. R. Natan (banished for methodological disputes with leadership) testifies that heaven agreed with earth's authority against R. Eliezer, justifying the ban.

On the other hand, in the narrative's describing of the subsequent fates of the individual *protagonists*— the banners—Heaven defends R. Eliezer against their injustice. R. Gamliel is stricken. R. Yehoshua who initiated discussion against R. Eliezer is himself deposed

---

seventy years to grow (b*Taanit* 23a, b*Bechorot* 8a; *Midrash Tehilim* 126) invokes both R. Elazar b. Azariah and R. Yehoshua describing themselves as "like a man of *seventy* years" after *R. Gamliel's* deposing (b*Berachot* 28b; *Mechilta Bo* 15); R. Yehoshua is associated with *walls* after *his* distancing *by* R. Gamliel (b*Berachot* 26b). In *Pirkei DiRabbi Eliezer* 2 R. Eliezer is compared to a *spring*; R. Akiva is identified with "*springs of torah*" (*Avot DeRabbi Natan* 6), imagery framed by that of torah as water (water penetrating the rock at the beginning *Avot DeRabbi Natan* 6), the parable of the fox and the fishes leaving the water at the end (*Berachot* 61b)). Alon Goshen-Gottstein,"R. Elazar b. Arach: Symbol and Reality", *Jews and Judaism in the Second Temple, Mishnaic, and Talmudic Periods*, Jerusalem 1992, *The Sinner and the Amnesiac: The Rabbinic Invention of Elisha ben Abuya and Eleazar ben Arach* (Stanford University Press, 2000) argues some Agadot about R. Elazar b. Arach reflect those of R. Akiva.

[14] See R. Yehezkel Feivel, *Toledot Adam,* Dierenfurth 1801, p. 108, R. Menahem of Taksin, *Orah Yesharim, Bava Metzia* 59a, Maharam Schiff.

[15] Maharam Schiff: R. Hanina "is satisfied with carobs" (b*Berachot* 17b, b*Taanit* 24b, b*Hulin* 86a.); R. Elazar is an overflowing *spring* (m*Avot* 2:8).

[16] Maharal, *Netivot Olam, Netiv Ahavat Reiah,* 2; Maharam Schiff, *Bava Metzia* 59b.

[17] *Avot DiRabbi Natan* 14:6, *Ecc. Rabah* 7:2. Halevi, *Dorot HaRishonim,* Vol. III ch. 26.

[18] And *Avot DiRabbi Natan* 6, Ver. 2:13, *Gen. Rabah* 42:1, *Tanhuma LechLecha* 10.

[19] See R. Yisachar Ber Eilenberg, *Beer Sheva*, Frankfort 1709) to b*Horayot* 13b, the Lubavitcher Rebbe, *Likutei Sihot*, Kehoth: Brooklyn 1999, Vol. 13, pp. 122-124.

[20] Also b*Bava Batra* 165b, b*Sotah* 16b.

[21] *Toledot Tanaim VeAmoraim,* "R. Yirmiyah." Heiman feels the b*Bava Batra* 23b banishment caused the y*Moed Katan* 3:1 ban.

[22] b *Yevamot* 102a, b *Avodah Zarah* 36a, b *Shabbat* 108a.

[23] Greenwood, "Akhnai" p. 316. R.Z.H. Chajes, *Berachot* 3b asks why Elijah's halachic teachings in Aggadot have legal significance.

by R Gamliel in b *Berachot* 28a, where R. Gamliel's relationship with R. Yehoshua inversely parallels his relationship with R. Eliezer as he himself is deposed for insulting R. Yehoshua.[24] The debate's protagonists and commentators serve as *metaphor* for its irresolution. Literary *oppositions* structure the debate interpreted to be about any number of oppositions: majority rule/individual truth[25], School of Hillel/School of Shamai,[26] tradition/interpretation,[27] quality/quantity,[28] potential/actual,[29] etc. And in the core conflict the sages appear to outvote heaven (as if vaguely antinomian) yet in fact they paradoxically defend the Torah against *any force* that would question it, citing the Torah from heaven even against heaven in order to affirm heaven: they affirm God's Torah which says that it is not in heaven.

Form, Motif, And Symmetry: The Ban and Its Earthly Effects

The narrative appears *within* a legal discussion on oppression which begins with the tradition that *all gates of prayer are locked but the gates of tears,* and ends symmetrically with the *narrative's* tradition: *"all gates are closed but the gates of oppression."* [30] In the story R. Eliezer's position

is defeated and he is banned because the torah is not in heaven—and heaven supports that position. Yet the narrative ends symmetrically with the catastrophic retribution for the ban's oppression which is felt on *earth*.[31] R. Eliezer first invokes earthly elements, the carob tree (*vegetation*), the river (*water*), and then Heaven. At the end the resultant ban affects *vegetation* ("the earth was stricken a third in *olives*, a third in *wheat*, a third in *barley*") as a *wave* (*water*) endangers the ban's initiator, R. Gamliel. The invoked carob, stream, walls, have been interpreted as corresponding to the elements of which the earth is composed.[32]

(Similarly in the aftermath [b *Sanhedrin* 67b, *Avot DiRabbi Natan* 26] as the ban is rescinded R. Eliezer tells of his torah's effect on earth: when R. Akiva asked him to teach him three hundred laws of planting cucumbers an adjacent field became full of cucumbers;[33] when he asked about the laws of their *uprooting* they all *gathered to one place,* as if a metaphor for the unity which R. Gamliel argues motivated the *ban.* (At that time according to the version in *Avot DiRabbi Natan* 26, R. Eliezer fears they will die a death "from *heaven.*")

The Bread And The Oven

The narrative begins with a dispute about (the contents of) an *oven* and ends symmetrically with the effect on "*dough* in the hand of a woman", and then Ima Shalom, a *woman,* goes to give *bread* (dough from the oven) to a poor man, causing R. Gamliel to die for invoking the ban. And symmetrically, she *brought out* bread and the ram's horn blast *went out* announcing R. Gamliel's death, *kindness* counterpointing the results of hurtful *wrongdoing.* (Symmetrically, as she would distract R.

---

[24] Noted by Greenwood, "Akhnai", pp. 322 and 347.

[25] See sources in England, "Majority Decision vs. Individual Truth", *"Tanur Shel Achnai."*

[26] R. Margaliot, *Mehkarim BiDarchei HaTalmud,* p. 45, Gilat, *The Teachings of R. Eliezer,* pp. 328-329.

[27] Urbach, *The Sages,* pp. 600-601, Gilat, *The Teachings of R. Eliezer b. Hyrcanus,* pp. 320-329, G. Allon,*The Jews in their Land in the Talmudic Age,* 1980, 314-315, J. Goldin, "On the Account of the Banning of R. Eliezer ben Hyrcanus", p. 85.

[28] *Maharal, Beer HaGolah, Beer* 4, R. Reuven Margaliot, *Mehkarim BiDarchei HaTalmud,* pp. 34-45.

[29] Gilat, *The Teachings of R. Eliezer,* pp. 26-29, 313 (citing *Hidushei Ritva bEruvin* 12a, *Shaagat Aryeh* 70), see also R.S.Y. Zevin, "On the Methods of the House Of Shamai and the House of Hillel" *LeOr HaHalachah,* 1957, pp. 302-309 .

[30] It begins with King David's complaint of hurt; the tradition at the *end*, of the House of R. Gamliel going back to the House of David, mirrors its *beginning.* Rashi feels it is the *same* tradition derived from the *Psalms* prooftext at the beginning. Rubenstein, *Talmudc Stories,* p.43, and C.E. Fonrobert, "When the Rabbi Weeps" p. 63, note the parallel between the statement of Rav in the introductory legal *Sugya:* "A person must always be careful about wronging his wife because her tears are frequent . . . for R. Eleazar taught that . . . that *all gates of prayer are locked but*

---

the gates of tears," as foreshadowing R. Eliezer's tears. Fonrobert contributes many valuable insights to the story's reading but I'm not convinced that gender is at the heart of it. Thus I see the story of the effects of R. Eliezer's crying as simply the amplification of the teaching that all gates of prayer are locked except the gates of tears. Similarly, the parallel between R. Akiva and Imma Shalom as mediators (and Fonrobert allows, p. 74, that it may be unintentional) is limited since their mediations are very different.

[31] Greenwood, p. 319 notes how this is emphasized by the length of the sequel, considerably longer than the core story itself.

[32] R. Yosef Molcho, *Ohel Yosef, Baba Metzia* 59b, Maharal, *Netivot Olam, Netiv Ahahvat Reah,* 2, *Beeir HaGolah,* 4.

[33] For R. Akiva whom he taught miraculously the laws of cucumbers (*kishuin*) he predicts a more *severe* death (*Kashah*).

Eliezer from his prayer, calamity happens when she is herself distracted.[34]) *Maharal* sees the *olives, wheat, and barley* as the oil and grain that make up a loaf of bread, the afflicted elements of the world (*Hidushei Agadot*). *Maharsha* notes how each third is a *minority* in their combined form, the effects of the ban's separation and unification now integrated and unified. In other sources the sages come from Yavne to Lod where R. Eliezer, banished from the Beit Midrash, sits in the *store of bakers* to report the events in the *Beit Midrash*.[35]

The loaf of bread is the content, the product of, an oven in the narrative about the halachic status of the contents of an oven assembled from different pieces interpreted as, "symbolic of a question of unity within a diversity of opinions." Alternatively, there is an interpretation that without a majoritarian legal theory of which majority is the right majority, the majority will be an oven built of broken pieces held together by sand.[36] Alternatively, the oven is not just the subject of the debate but the debate itself in the first generation of the post-Destruction world, itself a shattered vessel re-created from the shards of destruction; the question is whether that world, the rebuilt oven, has the same mystical significance as the original when in that world the purity laws themselves lose significance in the Temple's absence.[37] In classic allegorical exegesis the oven stands for insult unatonable until conciliation is achieved with the aggrieved, or the oven's status is associated with the nature of the miracles.[38]

Ima Shalom's role is emblematic in this context. Structurally, she mediates between the the story's beginning and end. The dispute about the contents of an *oven* effects the "*dough in the hand of a woman*" and is resolved as she, a *woman,* goes to give *bread* to a poor man, causing R. Gamliel to die for invoking the ban. But in the narrative itself, Ima Shalom, R. Eliezer's wife and R. Gamliel's sister, mediates between them, the two modes of authority, the banner and the banned[39].

In one reading, Ima Shalom, "Mother Peace", mediates between peace and truth, between principles and relationships.[40] This is intriguing because some interpret the dispute as one between Hillelite and Shammaite modes of interpretation or authority.[41]

Indeed, A. Heiman points out that Ima Shalom, as sister of R. Gamliel (Beit Hillel) and wife of R. Eliezer (Beit Shamai), is the embodiment and referent of the Mishnaic tradition (m *Yevamot* 1:4): "Though Beit Hillel and Beit Shamai disagreed they did not desist from marrying each other."[42] Indeed the *Tosefta Yevamot* 1:10-11 version is: "Beit Shamai did not desist from marrying women from Beit Hillel nor Beit Hillel from Beit Shamai, but practiced the *truth and the peace* among each other, as it says (Zach. 8:19) *"the truth and the peace* you shall love." Strikingly, the Tosefta expands this: "Even though these forbid and these permit, *they did not desist from making their Toharot* [purities] *on top of each other.*" In this way Ima Shalom, personally embodies mediation between peace and truth.

Literary Symmetry: Form And Parallel

In the symmetry the debate is introduced as: "*On that day* R. Eliezer answered *all* the answers on earth and they didn't accept them." As a result: "*On that day* they burned *all* all pure things R. Eliezer had declared pure" (. As a result of that: "*On that day all* places R. Eliezer put his eyes were *burnt."* As a result R. Eliezer's question, "What is today from *all days*?" is redressed when R. Gamliel dies, and when R. Eliezer's wife "*on that day*" miscalculates the New Moon not realizing that day *is* different from *all days*.[43]

---

[34] Noted by Greenwood, "Akhnai", 318-319.

[35] *mYadayim* 2:16, *Tosefta Yadayim* 2:16.

[36] Greenwood,, p. 339.

[37] Greenwood, pp. 347-349. The "shattered vesels" metaphor is (anachronisticly) Lurianic, but interesting.

[38] R. Yosef b. Yaakov, *Rosh Yosef, Bava Metzia 59b.*

[39] See Greenwood, "Akhnai", p. 357, Rubenstein, *Talmudic Stories,* p. 45, Fonrobert , "When The Rabbi Weeps", p. 62-8.

[40] Greenwood, "Akhnai", p. 357. It is interesting if not convincing to note the *Bat Kol* as "*daughter* of a voice" (in *yMoed Katan* 3:3: "The law is according to Eliezer *my son*") and the tradition of "my *father's* house" and *Ima* Shalom="*mother* of peace", as mediating figure; see also Greenwood, "Akhnai" there. See also Fonrobert, "When The Rabbi Weeps", p. 68, who notes how Ima Shalom ("Mother of Peace") mediates between the rabbis ("my *sons* have defeated me").

[41] R. Margaliot, *Mehkarim BiDarchei HaTalmud,* p. 45, Gilat, *Mishnato Shel R. Eliezer ben Hyrcanus,* pp. 328-329, G. Allon,*The Jews in their Land,* 1980, 314-315.

[42] *Toledot Tanaim VeAmoraim, "R. Eliezer."* Gilat, *Mishnato Shel R. Eliezer,* p. 324, n. 62, reports hearing this idea from R. Ezra Zion Melamed.

[43] In b*Sanhedrin* 65b and *Gen. Rabah* 11:5 R. Akiva is asked this by Tornus Rufus who will later execute him as R. Eliezer

Since they reject *all* the answers *on earth* the ban could destroy *all the earth*. (R. Akiva *sits* four *Amot* away from R. Eliezer like the *carob* (*cheruv*) that moved away four hundred *Amot* to vindicate him because the ban's effects could *destroy* (*machriv*) all earth.) In the debate the *heavenly* voice supports R. Eliezer, "In *every place* the law is according to R. Eliezer,"—but because of the *earthly* ban the effects on earth are: "In *every place* R. Eliezer put his eyes it was burnt."

R. Eliezer's *eyes* drip tears when he is informed of the ban and as a result "every place he put *his eyes* was burnt". This motif is emblematic because in *Avot* 2:8 R. Eliezer is the student associated with "a good *eye*" as the best quality and "a bad *eye*" as the worst. In *Tosefta Yadayim* 2:16 *his eyes drip tears* when he hears they *voted* in his absence on a law he has by *tradition*.[44] In the b*Hagigah* 3b and *Midrash Tehilim* (Buber) 25:13 version the *eyes* of the student who reports it are removed until R. Eliezer prays and they return.

The sages not *accepting* (*kiblu*) R. Eliezer's traditions is redressed at the end when his wife says "So I *received* (*kibalti*) a tradition from my father's house, all gates are closed but those of oppression." For the ban made to reject the legal force of *traditions*[45] and "not for the honor *of my father's house*", R. Gamliel dies because of the *tradition of his father's house*. It was R. Eliezer who never said anything which was *not a tradition* from his teacher R. Yohanan b. Zakai.[46] He is banned for defending his teacher's traditions with a *heavenly voice* as R. Yehoshua argues that laws are decided not by heavenly voices but on earth. But R. Eliezer's wife/R. Gamliel's sister, knows of her brother's death *not* from an earthly *voice/sound*, that is, the ram's horn announcing his death, but from of a *tradition* of her father's house, a more privileged *spiritual* source on earth.

In the symmetry, the narrative on oppression ends with R. Eliezer's wife's saying, "All *gates* are locked but those of oppression" as she gives bread to a poor man *at the gate*, causing the death of R. Gamliel, the ban's initiator.

The issue of the heavenly gates of tears being locked is redressed at the gates of R. Eliezer's house on earth where they are opened. Moreover, in the etymology of וילענמ: *tying, closing,* a shoe, R. Eliezer's *untying* his shoes on earth, while sitting crying on the earth, directly unlocks the locked gates of tears of Heaven.[47]

The oppressed R. Eliezer removes, *unlocks, unties,* his shoes (*naalav*) when he hears of the ban and R. Gamliel dies because the *locked* (*ninaalu*) gates of oppression are opened at R. Eliezer's gate. The House of Study doors are locked before R. Eliezer because the torah is not in Heaven, whose rulings, too, are now locked out of there but they are unlocked at his house, and the effects are felt on earth.

R. Akiva tells R. Eliezer: "*It appears to me* your friends *separated* from you," counterpointed in the resulting danger at sea where R. Gamliel says, "*It appears to me* that this is because of R. Eliezer", arguing that he wanted to *prevent separation* in Israel. (It is reversed in y *Moed Katan* 3:3 as R. Eliezer says, "It *appears* that today my *friends are bringing me close* [rescinding the ban]").

But it does not really *appear* to R. Akiva; he *knows* it as fact but is only gently informing R. Eliezer who knows what happens in heaven but *not* what happened on earth.[48] R. Gamliel did *not* know of the ban's effects in heaven but *infers* it with earthly methodology rather than heavenly "tradition", to infer and *know* from earthly events what happened in heaven. Like R. Yehoshua who defeated heaven on earth he argues with heaven against the decree on earth and defeats it, saying, "It is *revealed* and *known to You*", that the ban was not for his honor.[49] *He* knows on earth what is *known and revealed* to

---

[47] *Aruch,* s.v. *"Naal",* see b *Beitzah* 15a.

[48] R. Akiva informs R. Eliezer of the ban; *both* were banned and disowned before at the beginning of their careers, *Nedarim* 60a, *Ketubot* 62b, *Pirkei DiR. Eliezer* 1.

[49] R. Gamliel's justification of the oppression, *"It is revealed and known to You,"* ironically mirrors the complaint of oppression at the beginning the discussion, of his ancestor King David (his "father's House"): *"It is revealed and known to You* that if they tore my flesh my blood would not flow on the ground."* His defense that the ban was not for his honor mirrors how the Beit Midrash walls did not fall nor straighten because of the *honors* of R. Yehoshua and R. Eliezer, which as C.E. Fonrobert, "When The Rabbi Weeps", p. 71, notes, mirrors the introductory legal *Sugya*: "A person should

---

predicted (b*Sanhedrin* 67b).

[44] And *Midrash Tehilim* (Buber) 25:13.

[45] See Gilat, *Mishnato Shel R. Eliezer ben Hyrcanus,* pp. 320-329.

[46] b*Yoma* 66a, b*Sukah* 27b, b*Berachot* 27a, y *Yoma* 6:3, *Tosefta Yevamot* 3:3.

Heaven: what is *not* known and revealed to R. Eliezer and must be revealed to him by his friends on earth.

What was known in heaven is *revealed* by Elijah to R. Natan on earth: that God laughed at earth's victory over heaven. Heaven's position, the law is as R. Eliezer *in every place*, is defeated by earth but its effects are felt *in every place,* even earth. But earth (R. Gamliel) defeats heaven as R. Yehoshua said, "The torah is not in Heaven." God laughs but R. Eliezer cries.

The Earthly Danger As Metaphor
Significantly, the earthly damage caused by the ban is read by a legal theorist as reflecting the inherent danger and tension in the victory of democratic majoritarian rule.[50] And within the levels of allegory even the narrative's *halachic* prooftexts are seen as a form of metaphor, possibly its central metaphor, depicting in narrative form, "the structural possibility which creates a space for Oral Torah."[51] The prooftexts for the torah not being in heaven are themselves "not in heaven." The *plain* contextual meaning of the verse, "The Torah is not in heaven" (Deut 30:12) is simply that fulfilling the torah is not beyond human reach, as the plain sense of "after the majority to incline" (Ex. 23:2) means not to incline to do evil after the many. The cited verses are "reinscribed" to *authoritatively* create space for innovative *interpretation.* The prooftexts for interpretation are themselves interpreted texts. Thus God says His sons, so to speak, have defeated him.

Additionally, D. Greenwood argues that since we cannot ignore the terrible punishment meted out to R. Gamliel for the ban, the *plain* meaning of the prooftext R. Yermiyah cites for majority rule, "Do not follow the many to do wrong" (Exod. 23:2), can be a metaphor for the ban's aftermath, or as Greenwood reads it, for the dangers and difficulties of majoritarian rule.[52] In fact, noting that the "act of interpretation justifies further interpretation [in] reading the Deuteronomic passage in a strikingly different way to allow strikingly different readings", he feels the story thus also expresses "the intense discomfort this indeterminacy must create."[53] (Actually, we

counter, in the story's classic interpretation, God, whose Torah it is, smilingly does not seem at all uncomfortable with this nor does Jewish law and the question has been raised if this is indeed indeterminacy.[54]) And in the narrative, just as interpreted verses are cited as prooftexts *for interpretation*, the principle of *majority rule* is upheld by *voting* to excommunicate R. Eliezer.

The conjectural interpretation,[55] that the editorial interweaving of the story within the discussion of hurtful wrongdoing suggests disapproval by the editors who emphasize the wrong done to R. Eliezer, itself creates a *deconstructing* paradox. The story teaches that heaven itself laughingly affirmed the right of the rabbis to disagree, "the structural possibility which creates a space for Oral Torah." Yet in the editorial "contextualizing" of the story to defend R. Eliezer against the rabbis, once more the rabbis (the *sugya's* editors) now argue with heaven, the same heaven that itself laughingly affirmed, "foregrounded", their right to disagree.[56] The paradox is deconstructing in invoking infinite regression.

The Unresolved Opposition of Standing/Sitting
Throughout the story *standing* and *sitting* are opposed; this is significant in a narrative interpreted to be about conflict between argued interpretation and received tradition[57]. "Studying *sitting*" and "studying *standing*" are Talmudic expressions for studying *logical* reasons or *traditions* without explanation, respectively (*b Hulin* 54a: "He studied before my teacher *sitting*, and I, *standing*").[58]

---

always be careful about his wife's *honor.*"

[50] Greenwood, "Akhnai", p. 351.

[51] Boyarin, *Intertextuality and Midrash,* pp. 34-37.

[52] "Akhnai" , pp. 351-352.

[53] Greenwood, "Akhnai, p. 355, note 154.

[54] D. Stern, "Midrash and Indeterminancy", 15 *Critical Inquiry* 132, 1988, pp.143, 153-56.

[55] Englard, "Majority Decision" p.139, "*Tanur shel Achnai*", p. 49, Greenwood, "Akhnai", p. 353, Stone, "In Pursuit of the Counter-Text", p. 857, Halivni, *Peshat and Derash,* 108-111, Rubenstein, *Talmudic Stories*, p. 40, no. 1, Fonrobert, "When The Rabbi Weeps", p.62.

[56] Englard, "*Tanur shel Achnai,* p. 56, closes his article noting that the lot of this Agadah which opened the gates of the right of interpretation has been to be interpreted in so many ways.

[57] See Gilat, *Mishnato shel R. Eliezer b. Hyrcanus,* pp. 328-329.

[58] See b*Berachot* 22a, *y Hagiga* 3:1, y*Shabbat* 10:5, y*Horayot* 3:5, *Gen. Rabah* 98:11. In b*Megilah* 21a Moses studied *sitting* and received traditions *standing*: "One verse says "And I *sat* on the mountain" (*Deut* 9:9), one says "And I *stood* on the mountain" (*Deut.* 10:10): Rava: he studied easy teachings standing, *difficult* teachings *sitting*"; Rav: he *received teaching* [Rashi: "directly from God" standing

Narrative tension between standing/sitting *becomes* the unresolved tension of interpretation and tradition.

R. Yehoshua *stands on his feet* to argue with the *Beit Midrash* walls—midpoint between heaven and earth—who mediate between R. Yehoshua (*interpretation* as authority) and R. Eliezer (*tradition* as authority) and mediate between heaven and earth.[59] They would *fall* to support R. Eliezer but do not, for R. Yehoshua's honor.[60] In the end they do not straighten but *stand*. R. Yehoshua *stands* on his feet to declare the torah is not in Heaven because of the principle of *inclining* after *majority rule* (*aharei rabim lehatot*); the walls "neither *fall* nor *stand* but still *incline*" (*matin*)[61]. Thus *despite* normative halachic process having voted to *incline* after the *majority* (*lehatot*), the debate is still unresolved just as the walls still *incline* (*matin*) until today. His scolding not to interfere as sages *argue* (*menatzhin*) is mirrored in the argument's result: God says His sons have *defeated* Him (*nitzhuni*).[62]

R. Eliezer, who invoked *heaven,* now *sits on the earth* because he is banned, but R. Akiva sits with him because the ban could destroy all the earth. Before the ban R. Yehoshua *stood on his feet* to argue the torah is *not in heaven,* after the ban R. Gamliel *stands on his feet* to argue *with heaven* about the resultant danger *on earth.* The *falling* or *standing* of the Beit Midrash walls to validate the positions is now reflected in fateful standing and falling *outside* the Beit Midrash walls, from which R. Eliezer is banned.

The walls did not *fall* to vindicate R. Eliezer's traditions when R. Yehoshua *stood on his feet* to scold them. They would fall for R. Eliezer's *honor* but do not, for R. Yehoshua's *honor.* Because of this conflict between argued interpretation and received tradition, a ban is initiated by R. Yehoshua *standing on his feet.* Because of it a storm at sea *stands* upon R. Gamliel who *stands on his feet in prayer* to argue that the ban wasn't for *his*

honor or that of *his father's house.* But he dies later as a result of R. Eliezer's *falling* upon his face *in prayer*, as the walls would to support his *traditions,* for the hurt to *his honor* and *traditions.* Thus R. Gamliel dies as R. Eliezer's wife brings out bread to a poor man *standing* at the gate and then says to R. Eliezer, "*Stand up,* you have killed my brother", because of her *tradition received* from *her father's house*—that is: *R. Gamliel's father's house.*[63]

Significantly in *Pirkei DiRabbi Eliezer* 1-2, R. Eliezer's first banning at the beginning of his career, disowned and banned[64] from his father's wealth for going to study, is directly resolved by *sitting and standing* in the Beit Midrash, his unwillingness to teach *sitting* while his father *stands.*[65] When he finishes teaching his father *stands on his feet* and announces that his ban is rescinded. (There is symmetry too between R. Eliezer sitting on the earth and crying here when informed of the ban, and his sitting on the earth and crying at the beginning of his career in *Pirkei DiRabbi Eliezer* 1, when he wished to go to study torah for which he was banned.)

In the same way, symmetrically, in b*Sanhedrin* 67b R. Yehoshua *stands on his feet* at R. Eliezer's death and announces that the (last) ban is rescinded, the ban he initiated by standing on his feet to argue that the torah is not in heaven. In this at least there is resolution and closure.

Parallels

This is all the more fascinating for its parallels to b*Berachot* 27-28 and b*Bechorot* 36a where R. Yehoshua himself is *made* to *stand on his feet* as R. Gamliel "*sat and expounded*" to punish and *isolate* him for *challenging his authority,* reflecting the subsequent deposings or bannings.[66] In the wordplay those in the Beit Midrash protest this by telling R. Gamliel's interpreter to *stop* the lecture: "*Stop*", Amod; in *Bechorot* 36b: *Amod, Amod.* And in fact R. Gamliel will soon be deposed as a result.

---

and *reviewed* [Rashi: "by himself" *sitting*." See R. Yaakov Reisher, *Iyun Yaakov, Menahot* 29b, R. Margoliot, *Mehkarim BiDarchei HaTalmud*, pp. 17-18.

[59] Some see them as the Beit Midrash students: Maharal, *Netivot Olam,* MaHaram Schiff, *Bava Metzia* 59b.

[60] See b*Hulin* 39b: "A case was in Ceasaria, they didn't forbid for the honor of the rabbis nor permit for the honor of R. Eliezer."

[61] Noted also by Greenwood, pp. 315 note 20.

[62] Noted also by Greenwood, "Akhnai", p. 316 ff 26.

---

[63] That is the traditions of Hillel, the debate reflecting Hillelite and Shamaite traditions and methods. And R. Gamliel's House goes back to the House of David, whose complaint of hurt introduces the Sugya. According to Rashi it is *that* tradition.

[64] Both terms appear in parallel versions in *Avot DiRabbi Natan* 6, ver. 2:13, *Gen. Rabah* 42:1, *Tanhuma LechLecha* 10.

[65] And *Avot DiRabbi Natan* 6.

[66] Noticed also by Greenwood, "Akhnai", 332 and 347.

The *Berachot* 27-28 parallels are noteworthy: the challenge of authority, the dissident's distancing and reinstatement, R. Akiva as mediator,[67] "Who will go inform him?", resolution for the honor of R. Gamliel's father, the danger of retaliation, halachic deliberations "on that day", resolution at R. Gamliel's *gate,* the *four hundred* added benches of students allowed into the Beit Midrash, etc. There R. Yehoshua is identified by *his walls* as R. Gamliel infers his trade as blacksmith from the walls of his house outside those of the Beit Midrash.[68] The post-ban phrase, *"And even R. Gamliel* [went on a ship]" appears in no other Tanaitic/Talmudic source but our narrative and *Berachot* 28b after R. Gamliel is deposed for distancing R. Yehoshua: *"And even R. Gamliel* [did not desist from the Beit Midrash]." Assuming this happened in the months after the ban, there is literary counterpoint in how R. Gamliel's relationship with R. Yehoshua inversely parallels his relationship with R. Eliezer as he himself is deposed for insulting R. Yehoshua.[69]

There too halachic discussion itself becomes metaphor for the debate in which it occurs. In *Berachot* 27b after R. Gamliel's deposing for making R. Yehoshua *stand,* all students were *permitted to enter* the house of study which until then R. Gamliel had *forbidden*. The m*Yadayim* 4:4 discussion of Amon and Moab, reported as occurring then, is presented *here:* Judah the Amonite convert asked if he was *permitted to enter* the congregation of Israel; R. Gamliel said he was *forbidden*; R. Yehoshua said he was *permitted*, arguing that Amon and Moab no longer *sit in their place*, they *immediately permitted him to enter.*

The inclusion of the Mishnah in the narrative makes its halachic issue a metaphor for its context. A discussion into which some are forbidden or permitted to enter is *itself* a debate about those who are forbidden or permitted to enter [the congregation], and its resolution becomes a resolving turning point. R. Gamliel had argued (*Bava Metzia* 59b) that he had excluded R. Eliezer from the Beit Midrash because he wished to create unity in the congregation of Israel: "Master of the world, it is revealed and known before You that not for my honor I did nor for the honor of my father's house but for Your honor that controversies not multiply in Israel."

And here the dispute is resolved when R. Gamliel asks R. Yehoshua to forgive the hurt, invoking the *honor* of his *father's house*. Similarly, in *Tosefta* and m*Yadayim* 2:16 when the students after the deliberations *"on that day"*, tell R. Eliezer they *voted* in the Beit Midrash on the status of [the lands of] *Amon and Moab* in his absence from those discussions, he cries, saying he has that law by *tradition* and there is no need to vote. Y. Fraenkel in fact notes how it is even possible to see this as an "positive" counter-image or resolution to the Achnai debate, as R. Eliezer has a ruling by *tradition* that *agrees* with what the sages have by *voting.* [70]

The aftermath may reflect cyclical dialectic. R. Gamliel banished R. Eliezer in the debate interpreted as about quality against quantity, with majority votes supporting majority ruling[71]. Yet when *he* is deposed it emerges that he had allowed only a *qualitative minority* into the Beit Midrash, *banning* the *majority* of students from there. When the Beit Midrash then fills with four hundred benches of students he feels badly, thinking he perhaps witheld torah from Israel, but is shown a vision (from *Heaven*) of containers of ash, the new students were not great. The Talmud concludes that the vision was not true; *Heaven* simply wished to protect R. Gamliel's feelings. Heaven thus defends R. Gamliel as it defended R. Eliezer and his feelings.

Additionally, Ima Shalom's miscalculating the New Moon's twenty-nine day cycle and her father's house's tradition ("So I *received a tradition* from my father's house") parallel the impetus for R. Gamliel's deposing in *Berachot* 27b: his disputes and traditions about the twenty-nine day lunar

---

[67] R. Akiva also mediates in b*Yevamot* 16b when the sages ask *who will go inform* R. Dostai b. Hyrkanus.

[68] In *Tosefta Sotah* 7:9, *Tosefta Hagiga* 3a, *Mechilta Bo* 15, *Avot DiRabbi Natan* 18, after R. Gamliel's deposing the students come to greet *R. Yehoshua* who asks what is new in the Beit Midrash, they avoid telling him, saying they are his students, he insists they tell *and he is overjoyed.* In b*Hagiga* 3b, after the ban students come to greet *R. Eliezer* who asks what is new in the Beit Midrash, they avoid telling him, saying they are his students, he insists they tell *and he cries.*

[69] Halevi, *Dorot Rishonim* Vol. III: ch. 25 argues that this happened in the months after the ban.

---

[70] Y. Fraenkel, *The Aggadic Story: Harmony of Form and Content* HaKibbutz Hameuchad: Tel Aviv, 2000, p. 361, no. 59.

[71] *Maharal, Beer HaGolah, Beer* 4, R. Reuven Margaliot, *Mehkarim BiDarchei HaTalmud,* pp. 34-45

calculation in *Rosh HaShanah* 25a (where *he* says: "So *I received a tradition* from my father's house").

Argumentation starts as R. Gamliel *accepts* the New Moon's witnesses against his colleagues' positions because of his father's house's *traditions* about the twenty-nine day cycle. In the argumentation the moon is compared to a woman; there too is conflict of R. Gamliel's and R. Yehoshua's authority with R. Akiva again acting as mediator.

Aftermath: The Tefillin
Other sources describe the aftermath and resolution. In *Sanhedrin* 66b-68a the sages come to R. Eliezer as he is close to death.[72] Having distanced him (*merachek*) they come on the eve of the Sabbath (like the day of the ban, called: "*That da*y", to rescind the *ban* sitting a *distance* (*merachok*) of four *Amot* from him. This counterpoints *Pirkei DiRebbi Eliezer* 1-2 where at the beginning of R. Eliezer's career his father Hyrkanos comes to Jerusalem on the eve of the Sabbath and waits for its onset to *ban* and *disown* (*leharchiko*) him but tension and conflict is resolved as he *sits* in R. Yohanan's Beit Midrash and R. Eliezer *stands* and *sits* and teaches.[73]

As the Sabbath approaches R. Eliezer's *son* Hyrkanos tries to remove R. Eliezer's *tefilin*. (In *Tanhuma* (Buber) *Lech Lecha* 10 R. Eliezer's father decides not to disown and ban him, seeing him *sitting in tefilin* teaching torah.) Yonah Frankel has discussed the dual temporal tensions here as the Sabbath approaches while R. Eliezer is close to death (the halachic requirements to remove the tefilin before the Sabbath and before death[74]) against the temporal tension of the sages anxious to rescind the ban before he dies.[75]

Here R. Eliezer rebukes his son who tells the sages *it appears* his father's mind is befuddled (*nitrafah*: "torn"); R. Eliezer replies it is Hyrkanos' mind that is befuddled, "How do we leave a prohibition liable with stoning [the need to light the candle before the Sabbath] and become involved in a rabbinic prohibition (*shevut*) [*tefilin*]?"[76] We add that this underscores the temporal tension as well as juxtaposing the elements of *death,* stoning, and the removal of the *tefilin*. There is temporal tension because if the ban is not rescinded within a few moments the sages will have to *stone* his coffin after his *death* as was done to R. Akaviah b. Mehalel and R. Eliezer b. Hanoch.[77]

This may be the son who in *m Eduyot* 5:7 cites the tension of his own status after his father's death if the ban is not rescinded. R. Eliezer answered him: "Your (own) actions will bring you close, your actions will *distance* you. The use of "It appears' recalls the informing of the original ban ("*It appears to me* your friends *separated* from you") and its possible rescinding (in y *Moed Katan* 3:3 R. Eliezer says, "It *appears* that today my *friends are bringing me close* [rescinding the ban]"). And when Hyrkanos tries to remove his father's *tefilin* R. Eliezer *scolds* him (*binezifah*); *nazaf* also means *excommunication* or *banning*.[78]

Wordplay underscores the tension here. Seeing from R. Eliezer's sharp *halachic* response (about a *shevut*) that his mind is lucid (*meyushevet*) they *sit* (*yoshvin*) and discuss with him *laws* of purity and impurity.[79] Having established that his mind is not befuddled ("*torn*") the sages ask about the status of leather objects that were *torn*. Though the b*Sanhedrin* 68a version doesn't mention the status of torn *tefilin,* all the other versions say R. Elazar b. Azariah reported asking the question as including (*torn*) tefilin and so the law is recorded in R. Elazar's name In *Tosefta Keilim Bava Batra* 2:6.[80] R. Eliezer replies they are impure and their contents are pure. They ask about the status of a *shoe* and he replies: "Pure!" as his soul departs in purity. R. Yehoshua *stands on his feet* as he did at the original ban and declares, "The ban is rescinded, the ban is rescinded." In the y *Shabbat* 2:5 version R. Yehoshua then removes R. Eliezer's *tefilin*.

---

[72] *Avot DiRabbi Natan*19, 25, *Sanhedrin* 68a, y *Shabbat* 2:7, *Derech Eretz Rabah, Pirkei Ben Azai* 1:5, *Kalah Rabati* 6:5.

[73] Parallel versions in *Avot DiRabbi Natan* 6, ver. 2, ch. 13, *Gen. Rabah* 42:1, *Tanhuma Lech Lecha* 10.

[74] b*Berachot* 18a.

[75] Y. Frankel, "Time and Its Shaping in Aggadic Narratives, *Studies in Aggadah* pp. 147-53.

[76] In y*Shabbat* 2:5: *Karet;* there (and in *Avot DiRabbi Natan* 26) the prohibitions are spelled out.

[77] *m Eduyot* 5:6, y*Berachot* 19a, y*Moed Katan* 3:1, *Sifrei Bamidbar* 7, *Num. Rabah* 9:28.

[78] b *Moed Katan* 16a, *Hulin* 133a, *Taanit* 12b, 24a, *Yevamot* 72a, *Shabbat* 115a, *Ex. Rabah* 41, *Tanhuma Tisa* 16.

[79] y *Shabbat* 2:5, *Avot DiRabbi Natatn* 6.

[80] *Avot DeRabbi Natan* 19,26, *Kalah Rabati* 6:4, *Derech Eretz Rabah, Pirkei Ben Azai* 1:5. See also *m Keilim* 23:7, *Mikvaot* 10:2 and *Dikdukei Soferim* to *Sanhedrin* 68b.

There is of course symmetry between R. Yehoshua *standing on his feet* as he did at the original ban and the beginning of R. Eliezer's career where his father Hyrkanos *stood on his feet* at the end of R. Eliezer's lecture to declare that he had come to excommunicate him from his properties but now retracts the ban.[81] (There is symmetry too between R. Eliezer sitting on the earth and crying when informed of the ban, and his sitting on the earth and crying at the beginning of his career in *Pirkei DiRabbi Eliezer* 1 when he wished to go to study torah, for which he was banned then by his father.)

The narrative's motifs describe its issues: they *sit* away *four Amot* from R. Eliezer [because he is under a ban] who *sits in tefilin,* he who, following the *tradition* of his teacher R. Yohanan, "never went *four Amot* without *torah or tefilin* but *sat* in study" (b*Sukah* 28a). The scene here at the ban's resolution is metaphoric of the tension created by R. Eliezer's faithfulness to his teacher's traditions that caused the ban. The original debate was created by his refusal to teach anything that was *not a tradition* from his teacher R. Yohanan b. Zakai; he was thus banned by the Sages for defending his teacher's traditions, to reject the legal force of *traditions* against interpretations.[82]

The motif of the *tefilin* becomes central, emblematic: they are the subject of the halachic discussion in the moments of extreme temporal tension as the sages wish to restore him to his former status and they are themselves the source, on two or three levels, of the tension itself. (In b *Moed Katan* 15a the question of whether or not an excommunicated person may wear *tefilin* is raised but left unsolved.[83])

The subject of the halachic discussion reflects narrative context to become a metaphor for the discussion. Eliezer Segal interprets as emblematic the halachic question, "about torn leather objects whether they may be restored to purity without emptying them of their contents."[84] Here, we add, in this case R. Eliezer renders a decision: "Pure!", the same ruling he made about the oven at the original ban. It becomes an interpretation of his own status as his soul departs in purity and the ban is thus rescinded, his ruling becoming self-referential upon himself and the effects of his previous ruling. We add that the questions of the ritual status of leather shoes and of torn leather tefilin reflect the removal of his *shoes* at the *banning* (and the *tearing* of his clothes), and the removal of his *tefilin* at *its cancellation* as he himself is restored to his former status.

As he is restored to his former status of purity at his passing at the culmination of his life and his career, his *tefilin* are removed. Elements of the story of the resolution reflect those of the story of the ban. Significantly in both, the halachic questions become metaphoric for the discussion itself, for dissolution and resolution respectively.

I have chosen to read the various sources as a composite whole. While it is perilous to ignore the differences between documents from different historical periods and different schools, reading them synchronically as of a whole piece reveals significant intertextual relationships and parallels. Debating whether the reconstructed fragments of the story, like the oven, have the status and strength of a unity itself re-creates the narrative's own metaphor. And when a text, reconstructed or deconstructed, on debate and interpretation engenders its own interpretive debate, the text and its reading again become its own allegory.

---

[81] *Pirkei DiRabbi Eliezer* 2, *Avot DiRabbi Natan* 6.

[82] b*Yoma* 66a, *Tosefta Yevamot* 3:3, b*Sukah* 27b, b*Berachot* 27a, y*Yoma* 6:3. See Gilat, *Mishnato shel R. Eliezer,* pp. 320-329.

[83] *Tosafot Nidah* 7b cites the question why the Talmud did not resolve it by citing this story of R. Eliezer; see also R. David Lurya, *Kuntres Emek Brachah* in his introduction to his commentary to *Pirkei DiRabi Eliezer.*

---

[84] E. Segal, "Law As Allegory:", pp. 245-246.

Lesson 4
Rabbi Akiva

Introduction

Langston Hughes asks, "What happens to a dream deferred?" Many of us have felt the sense of rage and loss that comes from laying a dream to rest. Rabbi Akiva, however, did not defer dreams, but embarked on the arduous path of making them come true.

At forty, an age when many people mourn lost opportunities, Rabbi Akiva began to pursue a dream. He invested more than twenty-five years of his life into the dream and lived to see it spring to life. When, in a few tragic weeks, the dream was destroyed, he did not despair. With tenacious optimism and perseverance, he began to rebuild. And the fruits of his efforts are still with us today.

רבי עקיבא

Historical Timeline

3776/16 CE	Birth of Rabbi Akiva
3810/50 CE	Rabban Yochanan ben Zakai is installed as *av bet din* in Yerushalayim
3716/56 CE	Rabbi Akiva departs for Yeshiva
3826/66 CE	Beginning of the Great War
3828/68 CE	Rabban Yochanan ben Zakai escapes siege of Yerushalayim to establish the academy at Yavneh
3829/69 CE	Second Temple is destroyed
3834/74 CE	Passing of Rabban Yochanan ben Zakai, succeeded as *av bet din* by Rabbi Yehoshua
3840/80 CE	Rabbi Akiva returns home with 24,000 students
3842/82 CE	Rabbi Eliezer is banned from the academy
3880/120 CE	Rabbi Akiva succeeds Rabbi Yehoshua as *av bet din*
3887/127 CE	Bar Kochba revolt begins in earnest (early resistance began in 123 CE)
3893/133 CE	The revolt is crushed, Beitar falls, and Rabbi Akiva is imprisoned
3896/136 CE	Passing of Rabbi Akiva and birth of Rabbi Yehudah

Roman Emperors

27 BCE–14 CE	**AUGUSTUS**
14–37 CE	**TIBERIUS**
37 – 41 CE	**CALIGULA**
41–54 CE	**CLAUDIUS**
54–68 CE	**NERO**
68 CE	**YEAR OF THE FOUR EMPERORS: GALBA, OTHO, VITELLIUS, AND VESPASIAN**
69–79 CE	**VESPASIAN**
79–81 CE	**TITUS**
81–96 CE	**DOMITIAN**
96–98 CE	**NERVA**
96–117 CE	**TRAJAN**
117–138 CE	**HADRIAN**

- Rabbi Akiva was born in the last year of the reign of Augustus.
- Rabbi Akiva came to Jerusalem in the last year of the reign of Claudius.
- Rabbi Akiva returned home during the reign of Vespasian.
- The Bar Kochba revolt and Rabbi Akiva's passing occurred during the reign of Hadrian.

Biographical Overview

The Talmud teaches that Adam was shown a glimpse of Rabbi Akiva's life story and he both rejoiced and mourned. He rejoiced over Rabbi Akiva's brilliant erudition and he mourned over Rabbi Akiva's tragic end.

Rabbi Akiva, a son of proselytes, was not born into a wealthy, illustrious family nor one that encouraged love of Torah. He met his wife, Rachel, when he was forty, and she inspired him to study. He departed for the academy, where he remained for twenty-four years. When he finally returned it was with twenty-four thousand students.

A famous scholar, Rabbi Akiva was now a man of influence and means. He directed his considerable resources to the teaching of Torah. Disaster struck when all of his students died in a plague. Undeterred despite his advanced age, Rabbi Akiva groomed five new students who would in turn disseminate Torah to the following generation.

Rabbi Akiva was a kabbalist of the highest order and the teacher of Rabbi Shimon bar Yochai, who authored the Zohar, the seminal text of the Kabbalah.

In the year 96, Rabbi Akiva was invited to join a rabbinic delegation to Rome to pay formal homage to the newly appointed Emperor Nerva. Nerva lifted many of the repressive edicts against the Jews. Unfortunately, Nerva reigned for only two years and was followed in 98 by the Emperor Trajan.

Trajan drafted a series of repressive acts against the Jews reactivating many of his predecessors' discriminatory and oppressive policies. The reign of Trajan was a difficult time for the Jewish people and especially for its rabbinate. The *sanhedrin* was forced to temporarily disband and its leaders were forced into hiding.

Trajan died in battle in the year 122 and was succeeded by Hadrian, who at first appeared tolerant of the Jews and sympathetic to their cause. But later Hadrian turned against the Jews. New laws were promulgated forbidding the practice of circumcision and Torah study. Moreover, Hadrian built a Greek temple on the site where the *Beit HaMikdash* had stood. These new restrictions, coupled with unyielding repression, sparked a rebellion led by Bar Kochba.

Rabbi Akiva was very optimistic at first that the Bar Kochba uprising would bring respite to the Jewish people. But his hopes were to be sorely disappointed. The rebellion succeeded initially—Jerusalem was freed of Roman legions and an independent Jewish government was established. However, this government was short lived—it lasted only two and a half years. Then Rome sent reinforcements, forced the Jewish army into the Beitar fortress, and crushed the rebellion in 134.

Although Rabbi Akiva lived to be 120, the end of his life was tragic. Following the defeat of Bar Kochba, the harshness of the Roman rule worsened, and a series of draconian decrees was enforced. Despite a Roman ban on teaching Torah publicly, Rabbi Akiva continued to teach his students. For this crime, he was imprisoned and cruelly executed.

From Shepherd to Scholar

Text 1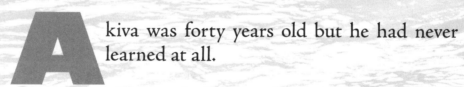

בן ארבעים שנה היה ולא שנה כלום

פעם אחת היה עומד על פי הבאר

אמר: מי חקק את אבן זו

אמרו: לא המים שתדיר נופלים עליה בכל יום

אמרו לו: עקיבא אי אתה קורא אבנים שחקו מים (איוב יד,יט)

מיד היה רבי עקיבא דן קל וחומר בעצמו

מה רך פסל את הקשה

דברי תורה שקשה כברזל

על אחת כמה וכמה

שיחקקו את לבי שהוא בשר ודם

אבות דרבי נתן ו,ב

Akiva was forty years old but he had never learned at all.

One day standing near a well, [Rabbi Akiva noticed a hollowed out stone].

He asked, "Who hollowed out this stone?"

They replied, "It has been hollowed out by drippings that fall on it each day."

[Rabbi Akiva was surprised at this.] They then asked him, "Have you not read the passage 'as waters wear away stones?'" (Job 14:19)

Rabbi Akiva immediately applied the analogy to himself. "Just as these soft drippings can carve hard rock, how much more so can the words of Torah, which are strong as bronze, shape my heart of human flesh?"

AVOT DeREBBI NATAN 6:2

Text 2a

רבי עקיבא רעיא דבן כלבא שבוע הוה

חזיתיה ברתיה דהוה צניע ומעלי

אמרה ליה: אי מקדשנא לך אזלת לבי רב

אמר לה: אין

תלמוד בבלי כתובות סב,ב

Rabbi Akiva was a shepherd of Ben Kalba Savua. The latter's daughter, seeing how modest and noble [the shepherd] was, said to him, "If I were to be betrothed to you, would you leave home to [study Torah at] the academy?"

"Yes," he replied.

TALMUD KETUBOT 62B

Text 2b

שמע בר כלבא שבוע אדרה הנאה מכל נכסיה

אזלא ואיתנסיבה ליה בסיתוא

הוה גנו בי תיבנא

הוה קא מנקיט ליה תיבנא מן מזייה

אמר לה: אי הואי לי, רמינא ליך ירושלים דדהבא

אתא אליהו אידמי להון כאנשא וקא קרי אבבא

אמר להו: הבו לי פורתא דתיבנא, דילדת אתתי ולית לי מידעם לאגונה

אמר לה רבי עקיבא לאנתתיה: חזי גברא דאפילו תיבנא לא אית ליה

אמרה ליה: זיל הוי בי רב

אזל תרתי סרי שנין קמי דרבי אליעזר ורבי יהושע

תלמוד בבלי נדרים נ,א

When her father was informed, he vowed that [because she married a man ignorant of Torah] she would not benefit from his property. She [subsequently] went and married him during the winter. They slept on straw, and [in the mornings] he would pick the straw from his hair.

"If only I could afford it," he would tell her, "I would present you with a golden [tiara on which would be engraved the image of] Jerusalem."

[One day] Elijah appeared in the guise of a mortal and cried out at the door, "Give me some straw, for my wife is in labor and I have nothing for her to lie on."

"See!" Rabbi Akiva observed to his wife, "[we are fortunate compared to] this man who lacks even straw."

[Subsequently] she counseled him, "Go, and become a scholar." So he went and spent twelve years [studying] under Rabbi Eliezer and Rabbi Yehoshua.

TALMUD NEDARIM 50A

Text 3a

כי אתא, אייתי בהדיה תרי סרי אלפי תלמידי

שמעיה להההוא סבא דקאמר לה: עד כמה קא מדברת אלמנות חיים

אמרה ליה: אי לדידי ציי"ת, יתיב תרי סרי שני אחריני

אמר: ברשות קא עבידנא, הדר אזיל ויתיב תרי סרי שני אחריני בבי רב

כי אתא, אייתי בהדיה עשרין וארבעה אלפי תלמידי

שמעה דביתהו הות קא נפקא לאפיה

אמרו לה שיבבתא: שאילי מאני לבוש ואיכסאי

אמרה להו: יודע צדיק נפש בהמתו (משלי יב,י)

תלמוד בבלי כתובות סב,ב

When he returned home he brought with him twelve thousand disciples. [As he approached his home] he overheard an old man saying to her, "How long will you lead the life of a living widow?"

"If [my husband] would listen to me," she replied, "he would spend another twelve years [in study]."

Rabbi Akiva observed, "I will indeed return to the Academy for it is with her consent that I am acting."

He departed again and spent another twelve years at the academy. When he finally returned, he brought with him twenty-four thousand disciples. His wife heard [of his arrival] and went out to meet him.

Her neighbor counseled her, "Borrow some respectable clothes to wear [when you greet this great man]."

She replied, "A righteous shepherd regards the [inner] character of his flock" (Proverbs 12:10).

TALMUD KETUBOT 62B

Text 3b

אתת לאיתחזויי ליה, קא מדחן לה רבנן
אמר להון: הניחו לה, שלי ושלכם שלה הוא
תלמוד בבלי נדרים נ,א

So she went to see him, but the disciples wished to repulse her. "Make way for her," he told them, "for my [learning] and yours are hers."

TALMUD NEDARIM 50A

Text 3c 📖

שמע אבוה דאתא גברא רבה למתא

אמר: איזיל לגביה, אפשר דמפר נדראי

אתא לגביה, אמר ליה: אדעתא דגברא רבה מי נדרת

אמר ליה: אפילו פרק אחד ואפילו הלכה אחת

אמר ליה: אנא הוא

נפל על אפיה ונשקיה על כרעיה, ויהיב ליה פלגא ממוניה

תלמוד בבלי כתובות סב,ב

[About this time, Rachel's father regretted his vow against his suffering daughter and sought to have it annulled.]

U pon hearing that a great man had come to visit, he said, "I shall visit him; perhaps he will annul my vow."

When he came to him [he did not recognize his son-in-law. He asked Rabbi Akiva to annul his vow.] Rabbi Akiva asked, "Would you have made your vow if you had known that your son-in-law was a great [Torah Scholar]?"

"Had he known even one chapter or even one single *halachah* [I would not have made the vow]," he replied.

Rabbi Akiva [revealed his identity and] said, "I am the man."

Kalba Savua fell upon his face and kissed Rabbi Akiva's feet. He then presented Rabbi Akiva with half his wealth.

TALMUD KETUBOT 62B

Text 3d 📜

אמרו: לא נפטר מן העולם עד שהיו לו שולחנות של כסף ושל זהב

ועד שעלה למטתו בסולמות של זהב

היתה אשתו יוצאה בקרדמין ובעיר של זהב

אמרו לו תלמידיו: רבי ביישתנו ממה שעשית לה

אמר להם: הרבה צער נצטערה עמי בתורה

אבות דרבי נתן ו,ב

It was said that Rabbi Akiva passed away a wealthy man; his tables were of silver and gold, and he climbed to his bed on ladders of gold. His wife [Rachel] dressed in garments befitting a princess and [wore] a golden [tiara upon which was engraved the image of the] city [Jerusalem].

His students complained, "Rabbi you shame us [in that we cannot provide the same for our wives]."

Said Rabbi Akiva, "She has suffered greatly alongside me for the sake of Torah."

AVOT DeRebbi Natan 6:2

Text 4

אמר ליה: ומי הוא

עקיבא בן יוסף

אמר ליה: אתה הוא עקיבא בן יוסף, ששמך הולך מסוף העולם ועד סופו

שב בני שב, כמותך ירבו בישראל

תלמוד בבלי יבמות טז,א

"Who is he?" [Dosa ben Horkinas] asked.

"Akiva the son of Yosef," [he was told].

[Dosa ben Horkinas exclaimed,] "Are you, Akiva, son of Yosef, whose reputation travels from one end of the world to the other? Sit down, my son, sit down. May men like you multiply in Israel."

Talmud Yevamot 16a

Resilience

Text 5 📜

שנים עשר אלף זוגים תלמידים היו לו לרבי עקיבא . . .

. . . וכולן מתו בפרק אחד מפני שלא נהגו כבוד זה לזה

תנא: כולם מתו מפסח ועד עצרת

אמר רב חמא בר אבא, ואיתימא רבי חייא בר אבין: כולם מתו מיתה רעה

מאי היא אמר רב נחמן: אסכרה

תלמוד בבלי יבמות סב,ב

Rabbi Akiva had twelve thousand pairs of disciples . . . all of whom perished within a short period because they did not treat each other with respect . . .

A sage taught, "They all perished between Passover and Shavuot."

Rav Chama ben Abba said (some attribute this saying to Rabbi Chiya ben Avin),

"They suffered a cruel death."

What was it?

Rav Nachman replied, "Croup."

TALMUD YEVAMOT 62B

Text 6a 📜

והיה העולם שמם עד שבא רבי עקיבא אצל רבותינו שבדרום ושנאה להם
רבי מאיר ורבי יהודה ורבי יוסי ורבי שמעון ורבי אלעזר בן שמוע
והם הם העמידו תורה אותה שעה

תלמוד בבלי יבמות סב,ב

The world remained spiritually desolate [after his students perished] until Rabbi Akiva came to our masters in the South [of Israel] and taught the Torah to them. These were Rabbi Meir, Rabbi Yehudah, Rabbi Yose, Rabbi Shimon, and Rabbi Elazar ben Shamua. It was they who revived the Torah at that time.

Talmud Yevamot 62b

Text 6b 📜

דאמר רבי יוחנן
סתם מתניתין רבי מאיר, סתם תוספתא רבי נחמיה
סתם ספרא רבי יהודה, סתם ספרי רבי שמעון
וכולהו אליבא דרבי עקיבא

תלמוד בבלי סנהדרין פו,א

Rabban Yochanan said: [The statements of] an unattributed Mishnah is Rabbi Meir; of an unattributed Tosefta is Rabbi Nechemiah; of an unattributed [dictum in the] Sifra is Rabbi Yehudah; in the Sifri, Rabbi Shimon. All taught according to the teachings of [their master] Rabbi Akiva.

Talmud Sanhedrin 86a

Text 7 📖

רבי עקיבא אומר: למד תורה בילדותו ילמוד תורה בזקנותו

היו לו תלמידים בילדותו יהיו לו תלמידים בזקנותו

שנאמר (קהלת יא,ו): בבקר זרע את זרעך וגו'

תלמוד בבלי יבמות סב,ב

Rabbi Akiva said, "If a man studied Torah in his youth, he should continue to study it in his old age; if he had disciples in his youth, he should have more disciples in his old age. For it is said (Ecclesiastes 11:6), 'In the morning plant your seed [and in the evening do not withhold your hand].'"

TALMUD YEVAMOT 62B

Text 8 📖

דרבי עקיבא דהוה קאזיל באורחא, מטא לההיא מתא

בעא אושפיזא לא יהבי ליה, אמר: כל דעביד רחמנא לטב

אזל ובת בדברא, והוה בהדיה תרנגולא וחמרא ושרגא

אתא זיקא כבייה לשרגא, אתא שונרא אכליה לתרנגולא

אתא אריה אכלא לחמרא

אמר: כל דעביד רחמנא לטב

ביה בליליא אתא גייסא, שבייה למתא

אמר להו: לאו אמרי לכו כל מה שעושה הקדוש ברוך הוא הכל לטובה

תלמוד בבלי ברכות ס,ב

Rabbi Akiva was once going along the road and he came to a certain town and looked for lodgings, but he was everywhere refused.

He said, "Everything God does is for the best," and he went and spent the night in the open field.

He had with him a rooster, a donkey, and a lamp. A gust of wind came and blew out the lamp, a weasel came and ate the rooster, and a lion came and ate the donkey.

He said, "Everything God does is for the best."

That same night, some bandits came and carried off the inhabitants of the town.

He said, "Did I not say, 'Whatever the All-Merciful does is for the best?'"

TALMUD BERACHOT 60B

וכבר היה רבן גמליאל ורבי אלעזר בן עזריה ורבי יהושע ורבי עקיבא מהלכין בדרך
ושמעו קול המונה של רומי מפלטה ברחוק מאה ועשרים מיל
והתחילו בוכין, ורבי עקיבא משחק
אמרו לו: מפני מה אתה משחק, אמר להם: ואתם מפני מה אתם בוכים
אמרו לו: הללו כושיים שמשתחוים לעצבים ומקטרים לעבודת כוכבים
יושבין בטח והשקט
ואנו בית הדום רגלי אלהינו שרוף באש ולא נבכה
אמר להן: לכך אני מצחק, ומה לעוברי רצונו כך
לעושי רצונו על אחת כמה וכמה

שוב פעם אחת היו עולין לירושלים
כיון שהגיעו להר הצופים קרעו בגדיהם
כיון שהגיעו להר הבית, ראו שועל שיצא מבית קדשי הקדשים
התחילו הן בוכין ורבי עקיבא מצחק
אמרו לו: מפני מה אתה מצחק, אמר להם: מפני מה אתם בוכים
אמרו לו: מקום שכתוב בו (במדבר א,נא) והזר הקרב יומת
ועכשיו שועלים הלכו בו ולא נבכה
אמר להן: לכך אני מצחק
דכתיב (ישעיהו ח,ב) ואעידה לי עדים נאמנים
את אוריה הכהן ואת זכריה בן יברכיהו
וכי מה ענין אוריה אצל זכריה, אוריה במקדש ראשון וזכריה במקדש שני
אלא תלה הכתוב נבואתו של זכריה בנבואתו של אוריה
באוריה כתיב (מיכה ג,יב) לכן בגללכם ציון שדה תחרש
בזכריה כתיב (זכריה ח,ד) עוד ישבו זקנים וזקנות ברחובות ירושלם
עד שלא נתקיימה נבואתו של אוריה
הייתי מתיירא שלא תתקיים נבואתו של זכריה
עכשיו שנתקיימה נבואתו של אוריה בידוע שנבואתו של זכריה מתקיימת
בלשון הזה אמרו לו: עקיבא ניחמתנו, עקיבא ניחמתנו
תלמוד בבלי מכות כד,א

Once, as Rabban Gamliel, Rabbi Elazar ben Azariah, Rabbi Yehoshua, and Rabbi Akiva were walking on the road, they heard the noise of the crowds in Rome from a distance of a hundred and twenty *mil*. They started to weep, but Rabbi Akiva laughed.

"Why are you laughing?" they demanded.

"Why are you weeping?" he replied.

They lamented, "These heathens who bow down to images and burn incense to idols live in safety and ease, whereas our Temple, the footstool of our God, is destroyed by fire; should we not weep?"

He replied, "This is precisely why I am laughing. If those who transgress God's will enjoy such prosperity, how much better those who obey Him shall fare!"

Yet again they were ascending to Jerusalem. As they crested Mount Scopus, they rent their garments. As they reached the Temple Mount, they saw a fox emerging from [where] the Holy of Holies [had once stood]. They started to weep, but Rabbi Akiva laughed.

"Why are you laughing?" they demanded.

"Why are you weeping?" he replied.

They lamented, "A place of which it is said (Numbers 1:51) 'And the common man that draws near shall be put to death,' has now become the haunt of foxes, should we not weep?"

He replied, "This is precisely why I am laughing; for it is written 'And I will take to Me faithful witnesses to record, Uriah the priest and Zechariah the son of Yeberechiah' (Isaiah 8:2). Now what is the connection between Uriah the priest and Zechariah? Uriah lived during the times of the first Temple, whereas Zechariah lived during the second Temple, but the Holy Writings linked the [later] prophecy of Zechariah with the [earlier] prophecy of Uriah. In the [earlier] prophecy of Uriah it is written, 'Therefore, because of you, Zion shall be ploughed as a field' (Micah 3:12). In Zechariah (8:4) it is written, 'There shall yet be a time when old men and old women will sit in the promenades of Jerusalem.' So long as Uriah's prophecy had not been fulfilled, I had misgivings lest Zechariah's prophecy might [also] not be fulfilled [literally]; now that Uriah's prophecy has been [literally] fulfilled, it is certain that Zechariah's prophecy will also find its [literal] fulfilment."

They replied with the following words, "Akiva, you have comforted us! Akiva, you have comforted us!"

Talmud, Makot 24a

When Rabbi Akiva [lost his candle, rooster, and donkey and] declared, "All that God does is for the best," he meant that his present circumstances were negative, but their purpose was good. Sleeping in the fields and losing his possessions caused him anxiety and damage, but what came of it was good—it was for a good purpose—it saved his life.

The episode with the fox in the Holy of Holies was different in that Rabbi Akiva did not only view what would come of it as good; he viewed the episode itself as an initiation, a part of the process, of the good outcome. Hence his citation of the prophecy "Therefore Zion shall be ploughed as a field." Ploughing a field does not destroy the soil; on the contrary, it is the first step one takes to develop the soil's potential and to cultivate the crop. The more thorough the ploughing is, the more successful the crop will be. The destruction of the Temple is similar to ploughing in that the destruction itself augured the blessing of redemption. Therefore, when Rabbi Akiva saw that the destruction was complete, whereby even the Holy of Holies was desecrated, he knew that the groundwork had been laid for the redemption to be complete.

RABBI MENACHEM MENDEL SCHNEERSON, LIKUTEI SICHOT VOL. 19 P. 72

The End

Text 11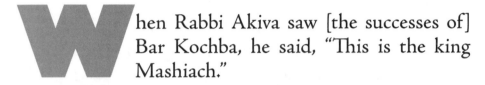

רבי עקיבא כד הוה חמי ליה להדין בר כוזיבא

הוה אמר היינו מלכא משיחא

אמר ליה רבי יוחנן בן תורתא: עקיבא, יעלו עשבים בלחייך ועדיין אינו בא

איכה רבה ב,ד

hen Rabbi Akiva saw [the successes of] Bar Kochba, he said, "This is the king Mashiach."

Rabbi Yochanan ben Turta said to him, "Akiva, grass will grow on your cheeks before the [Mashiach] comes."

E I C H A   R A B A H   2 : 4

Text 12a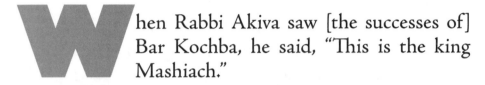

תנו רבנן: פעם אחת גזרה מלכות הרשעה שלא יעסקו ישראל בתורה

בא פפוס בן יהודה ומצאו לרבי עקיבא שהיה מקהיל קהלות ברבים ועוסק בתורה

אמר ליה: עקיבא, אי אתה מתירא מפני מלכות

אמר לו: אמשול לך משל, למה הדבר דומה לשועל שהיה מהלך על גב הנהר

וראה דגים שהיו מתקבצים ממקום למקום

אמר להם: מפני מה אתם בורחים

אמרו לו: מפני רשתות שמביאין עלינו בני אדם

אמר להם: רצונכם שתעלו ליבשה

ונדור אני ואתם כשם שדרו אבותי עם אבותיכם

אמרו לו: אתה הוא שאומרים עליך פקח שבחיות, לא פקח אתה, אלא טפש אתה

ומה במקום חיותנו אנו מתיראין, במקום מיתתנו על אחת כמה וכמה

אף אנחנו, עכשיו שאנו יושבים ועוסקים בתורה

שכתוב בה (דברים ל,כ) כי הוא חייך ואורך ימיך, כך

אם אנו הולכים ומבטלים ממנה, על אחת כמה וכמה

אמרו: לא היו ימים מועטים עד שתפסוהו לרבי עקיבא וחבשוהו בבית האסורים

ותפסו לפפוס בן יהודה וחבשוהו אצלו

אמר לו: פפוס, מי הביאך לכאן

אמר ליה: אשריך רבי עקיבא שנתפסת על דברי תורה

אוי לו לפפוס שנתפס על דברים בטלים

תלמוד בבלי ברכות סא,ב

ur Rabbis taught: Once the wicked government [of Rome] issued a decree forbidding the Jews to study the Torah. Pappus ben Yehudah found Rabbi Akiva teaching the Torah to public gatherings. Said Pappus, "Akiva, are you not afraid of the government?" He replied, "I will explain with a parable. A fox was once walking alongside a river and saw fish swimming in swarms [from one side of the river to the other]. Said the fox, 'From whom are you fleeing?' They replied, 'From nets cast for us by the men.' The fox replied, 'Would you like to come up on to dry land so that you and I can live together in the way that my ancestors lived with your ancestors?' They replied, 'Are you the one that they call the cleverest of animals? You are not clever, but foolish. If we are afraid in the waters in which we [can hope for a chance to] live, how much more [should we fear] dry land on which we would [certainly] die!' So it is with us [concluded Rabbi Akiva]. If such is our condition when we sit and study the Torah, of which it is written (Deuteronomy 30:20), 'For that

[Torah] is your life and the length of your days,' if we neglect the Torah how much worse off will we be!"

It is related that soon after this exchange Rabbi Akiva was imprisoned. Pappus ben Yehudah was also arrested and imprisoned next to him. Rabbi Akiva asked, "Pappus, who brought you here?" He replied, "Fortunate are you, Rabbi Akiva, that you have been seized for busying yourself with the Torah! Woe to Pappus who has been seized for busying himself with idle things!"

TALMUD BERACHOT 61B

Text 12b

בשעה שהוציאו את רבי עקיבא להריגה זמן קריאת שמע היה

והיו סורקים את בשרו במסרקות של ברזל

והיה מקבל עליו עול מלכות שמים

אמרו לו תלמידיו: רבינו, עד כאן

אמר להם: כל ימי הייתי מצטער על פסוק זה

בכל נפשך (דברים ו,ה) אפילו נוטל את נשמתך

אמרתי: מתי יבא לידי ואקיימנו, ועכשיו שבא לידי לא אקיימנו

היה מאריך באחד עד שיצתה נשמתו באחד

יצתה בת קול ואמרה: אשריך רבי עקיבא שיצאה נשמתך באחד

אמרו מלאכי השרת לפני הקדוש ברוך הוא

זו תורה וזו שכרה, ממתים ידך ה' ממתים וגו' (תהלים יז,יד)

אמר להם: חלקם בחיים

יצתה בת קול ואמרה: אשריך רבי עקיבא שאתה מזומן לחיי העולם הבא

תלמוד בבלי ברכות סא,ב

When Rabbi Akiva was led out to his execution, it was the hour for the recital of the *shema*. [Even as the Romans] combed his flesh with iron combs, he was accepting the kingdom of heaven upon himself. His disciples asked, "Our teacher, even to this extent?" [i.e., even as you are tortured, you think of God?]

He replied, "All my days I have been troubled by the verse (Deuteronomy 6:5), '[Love God] with all your soul,' [which is interpreted to mean 'one must love God] even if He takes your soul.' I said, when shall I have the opportunity to fulfill this? And now that I have the opportunity, shall I not fulfill it?"

He prolonged the word *echad* [the last word of the *shema* that proclaims the absolute unity of God] until his breath left him and he died with the word *echad* upon his lips. A heavenly voice went forth and proclaimed, "Fortunate are you, Akiva that your soul has departed with the word *echad*!"

The ministering angels said before the Holy One, blessed be He, "Such is Torah, and such is its reward? [He should have been] 'from those who die by Your hand, O Lord'" (Psalms 17:14).

God replied to them, "The portion [of the righteous] is [eternal] life."

A heavenly voice went forth and proclaimed, "Fortunate are you, Rabbi Akiva, that you are destined for the life of the world to come."

Talmud Berachot 61b

Key Points

1. Rachel, daughter of the rich Kalba Savua, was impressed by the unschooled but noble Akiva and against the will of her father, agreed to marry him provided he study Torah.

2. The now-disowned Rachel endured poverty and loneliness, sending her husband away to study for twenty-four long years.

3. When Akiva returned after twenty-four years with twenty-four thousand students, he proclaimed that all that he and they had was due to her.

4. Rabbi Akiva's students all perished due to the fact that they did not show sufficient respect to one another.

5. Despite his advanced age, Rabbi Akiva nurtured additional students who preserved the oral tradition.

6. Rabbi Akiva's life is marked with extraordinary optimism and resilience.

7. As a result of the failure of the Bar Kochba rebellion, Roman rule became harsher, and Rabbi Akiva was imprisoned and eventually executed for teaching Torah.

8. Rabbi Akiva died as he lived, with the *shema* on his lips, thankful for the opportunity to give his life for God.

Additional Readings

The Child and the Slave

Talmud, Bava Batra 10a

Turnusrufus asked Rabbi Akiva: "If your G-d loves the poor, why doesn't He feed them?"

Said Rabbi Akiva to him: "So that we should be saved from purgatory (in the merit of the charity we give)."

Said he to him: "On the contrary: for this you deserve to be punished."

"I'll give you an analogy. This is analogous to a king who got angry at his slave and locked him away in a dungeon, and commanded 'If your G-d loves the poor, why doesn't He feed them?' that he not be given to eat or to drink; and a person came along and gave him to eat and to drink. When the king hears of this, is he not angry at that person? And you are called slaves, as it is written (Leviticus 25:55) 'The Children of Israel are My slaves.'"

Said Rabbi Akiva to him: "I'll give you an analogy.

"This is analogous to a king who got angry at his child and locked him away in a dungeon, and commanded that he not be given to eat or to drink; and a person came along and gave him to eat and to drink. When the king hears of this, does he not reward that person?

"And we are G-d's children, as it is written (Deuteronomy 14:1) 'You are children of the L-rd your G-d.'"

Talmud, Bava Batra 10a

Reprinted with permission from chabad.org.

The Mystery of Lag Ba'Omer

By **Rabbi Pinchas Stolper**

Thirty-three days following the first day of Passover, Jews celebrate a "minor" holiday called Lag Ba'Omer, the thirty third day of the Omer. It is an oasis of joy in the midst of the sad Sefirah period which is almost unnoticed by most contemporary Jews. Yet it contains historic lessons of such great severity—that this generation must not only unravel the mystery of Lag Ba'Omer but will discover that its own fate is wrapped in the crevices of its secrets.

The seven weeks between Passover and Shavuot are the days of the "Counting of the Omer," the harvest festivities which were observed in Eretz-Israel when the Temple stood on Mt. Moriah in Jerusalem.

This fifty day period should have been a time of joyful anticipation. Having experienced the Exodus from Egypt on Pesach, every Jew literally "counts the days" from the first night of Passover until *Mattan Torah*—the revelation of Torah at Mt. Sinai which took place on Shavuot, exactly fifty days after the Exodus. While the Exodus marks the physical birth of the Jewish nation—the Giving of Torah completes the process through the spiritual birth of the Jewish nation.

Each year, as we celebrate the Seder on Passover, we are commanded to "see ourselves as though each of us actually experienced the Exodus." It therefore follows that we must prepare ourselves during the Sefirah period (counting of the Omer), to once again accept the Torah on Shavuot—to make our freedom spiritually complete.

Clearly then, the Sefirah days should have been days of joy, but instead, they are observed as a period of semi-mourning. Weddings, music, and haircuts are not permitted, some do not shave during this entire period. It is on the sad side of Sefirah that we come across the holiday of Lag Ba'Omer, the one day during this sad period when our mourning is halted, when sadness is forbidden.

What is the reason for sadness during what should have been a period of joyful anticipation? The reason, the Babylonian Talmud tells us, [Yevamot:62:2] is that during this period, Rabbi Akiva's 24,000 students, who lived 1,850 years ago in the Roman dominated Land of Israel, died from a mysterious G-d sent plague. Why did they die? Because the Talmud teaches, "they did not show proper respect to one another." Lag Ba'Omer is celebrated on the thirty-third day because on that day the plague ended and Rabbi Akiva's students stopped dying.

This explanation leaves us with a number of difficulties and still more unanswered questions.

Why does this event, the death of Rabbi Akiva's students, tragic as it was, merit thirty-two days of mourning when greater tragedies in Jewish history, such as the destruction of both Temples or the breaking of the Stone Tablets of the Covenant by Moses, are marked by a single day of mourning. In terms of numbers, the massacres of the Spanish Inquisition, the Crusades, the Chemelnitsky pogroms, and the Holocaust, which destroyed European Jewry and cost six-million Jewish lives far overshadow the death of Rabbi Akiva's students. Yet, these tragic events are not commemorated by even one special day of mourning. Why is the death of Rabbi Akiva's students given so much more weight?

Every event in the Jewish calendar was placed there by the Divine hand because it conforms to a pre-set notion of the significance of the seasons and of history. Nature and events correspond and intermesh, certain days and periods are most suited to joy or sadness. Why does the Sefirah mourning coincide with the joyous holidays of Passover and Shavuot, which in turn coincide with the period of harvest festivities?

There also appear to be glaring inconsistencies in the story itself. What were Rabbi Akiva's students guilty of that they deserved to die? If Rabbi Akiva's students died as a result of G-d's punishment for their sins, why should we mourn them? Didn't they deserve their punishment?

Why is Lag Ba'Omer a day of "celebration"? If all that happened on Lag Ba'Omer was but a temporary halt in the dying, wouldn't it be more fitting to set it aside as a memorial day for the twenty-four thousand scholars who died?

What is the connection between Lag Ba'Omer and the revolt against the Romans by Bar Kochba and his army? And how does all of this relate to Rabbi Shimon Bar Yochai, author of the mystical books of the 'Zohar' who lived in the same era, about whom we sing on Lag Ba'Omer.

And finally, why are all these questions never discussed in the open, as are for example the Four Questions of the Passover Seder?

The answers to these and other questions lie shrouded in the history of a turbulent age and in the mysteries of the Jewish concept of the Messianic era.

First, we must understand that much of the material in the Talmud that deals with political matters was written with a keen sensitivity to the Roman censor. The Talmud could not speak openly concerning the political ramifications of events. In order to obtain a true picture of what happened, we must piece together the story from various historical sources and Talmudic hints. What we discover goes something like this:

The Second Temple was destroyed by the Romans in the year 70 C.E. Jerusalem and the surrounding countryside lay in ruins from border to border. Scores of thousands died in the fierce fighting and subsequently from persecution and starvation; thousands more were sold as slaves and forced into exile. The Romans considered the Jewish nation defeated, obliterated and done for. The Roman General Titus erected a grand victory monument in Rome which stands to this day that says just that—the famous Arch of Titus on which is inscribed Judea Capita—Judea is kaput, finished—done for.

But even in defeat the spiritual leaders of the Jewish people struggled to rebuild Jewish life and recreate Jewish institutions. They were so successful that around 135 C.E. a Jewish military leader named Bar Kosiba succeeded in organizing a fighting force to rid the Land of

Israel of the hated Romans. Thousands rallied to his cause, including the greatest Talmudic scholar of all times, the Tanna Rabbi Akiva ben Yosef, whose insights and brilliant decisions fill the Mishnah.

Many of Rabbi Akiva's contemporaries felt that a new revolt against the Romans was doomed to failure and urged the avoidance of bloodshed. But Bar Kosiba persisted and succeeded in organizing and training a superb military force of 200,000 men. The Talmud relates that Bar Kosiba demanded that each recruit demonstrate his bravery by cutting off a finger—when the Rabbis protested he substituted a new test, each recruit was expected to uproot a young tree while riding a horse. Such was the level of their bravery and readiness.

Rabbi Akiva disagreed with his Rabbinic colleagues and won over a majority to his point of view. From the military point of view, he felt that a successful revolt was feasible. It is said by some historians that twenty percent of the population of the Roman Empire between Rome and Jerusalem was Jewish.

The pagan foundations of Rome were crumbling. Many Romans were in search of a religious alternative—which many of them subsequently found in a mitzvah-less Christianity in the following two centuries. Many Romans were attracted to Judaism, and significant numbers converted. There were thousands—tens of thousands of sympathizers. Some members of the Roman Senate converted to Judaism. If the large numbers of Jews who lived throughout the Roman Empire could be inspired into coordinated anti-Roman revolts, many historians believe that the prospects for toppling Rome were very real.

And if the revolts succeeded and Jews from all over the world united to return and rebuild their homeland, Rabbi Akiva believed that they could bring about the Messianic Era—the great era of spirituality and universal peace foretold by Israel's Prophets—the great millennia during which all Jews would return to the land of Israel, the Jerusalem Temple would be rebuilt and Israel would lead the world into an era of justice, spiritual revival, and fulfillment.

In his Laws of Kings, (Chapter 11:3) Maimonides, in discussing the Messianic era says, "Do not think that the King Messiah must work miracles and signs, create new natural phenomena, restore the dead to life or perform similar miracles. This is not so. For Rabbi Akiva was the wisest of the scholars of the Mishna and was the armor bearer of Bar Kosiba (the actual family name of Bar Kochba) the King. He said concerning Ben Kosiba that he is the King Messiah. Both he and the sages of his generation believed that Bar Kosiba was the King Messiah, until (Bar Kosiba) was killed because of his sins. Once he was killed, it became evident to them that he was not the messiah."

To Bar Kochba and his officers, all seemed to be in readiness; Rome was rotten and corrupt—many captive nations strained at the yoke—rebellion was in the air. Rabbi Akiva (Jerusalem Talmud: Ta'anit 4:15) gave Bar Kosiba a new name, "Bar Kochba"—Son of the Star—in fulfillment of the prophecy—"a star will go forth from Jacob." Bar Kochba trained an army capable of igniting the powder keg of rebellion and Rabbi Akiva lit it with one of the most dramatic proclamations in Jewish history—he proclaimed that Bar Kochba was the long awaited Messiah.

One of the greatest Torah teachers and leaders of all time, Rabbi Akiva could not have made this crucial and radical declaration unless he was certain. He would never have proclaimed a man Messiah unless he knew. Rabbi Akiva added a new, spiritual dimension to the war of liberation. He attempted to merge the soldiers of the sword with the soldiers of the book—his twenty- four thousand students—each a great Torah scholar and leader.

These outstanding scholars would become the real "army" of the Jewish people, a spiritual and moral force that would bring Torah to the entire world, overcoming anguish, suffering, and the cruel boot of the corrupt Roman Empire. They would soon inaugurate a new era of peace, righteousness, and justice, an era in which "the Knowledge of G-d would cover the earth as water covers the seas." The fact that the Jews were able to unite around a single leader separates this event from the great revolt of the previous century when bitterly divided factions warred with each other inside the walls of Jerusalem even as the Roman army stormed the gates.

The rebellion raged for six years. Bar Kochba's army achieved many initial victories. Many non Jews joined

Bar Kochba's army—it is reported that it grew to 350,000 men—more men than the Roman Army. Bar Kochba was so successful that Hadrian called in all of his best troops from England and Gaul. Rome felt threatened as never before. On Lag Ba'Omer, it is believed by some, Bar Kochba's army reconquered Jerusalem, and we celebrate that great event today. For four years Jewish independence was restored. Many believe that Bar Kochba actually began to rebuild the Bait Hamikdash, the Temple. Some even believe that he completed the building of the Third Temple.

There were two Roman legions in the country when the uprising began, one in Jerusalem and one near Megido. Both were decimated by Bar Kochba's men. Reinforcements were dispatched from Trans-Jordan, Syria and Egypt but these, too, were mauled. The legion sent from Egypt, the 22nd, disappeared from the listings of military units published in Rome, and scholars speculate that it was cut up so badly, probably around Lachish, that it ceased to exist as an organized force. The Jews apparently employed guerilla tactics—foraying from their underground lairs, ambushing convoys and striking at night.

In desperation, Hadrian sent for his best commander, Julius Severus, who was then engaged in battle at the hills of far off Wales. Severus imported legions from the lands of Britain, Switzerland, Austria, Hungary and Bulgaria. So badly had the Romans been hurt in the bruising campaign that Severus, upon returning to Rome to report to the Senate on his success, omitted the customary formula "I and my army are well."

This was total war. In the middle of the effort to rebuild the Bait Hamikdash the tide turned and Bar Kochba lost the support of Rabbi Akiva and the Sages who backed him. What happened? Bar Kochba had murdered the Tannah Rabbi Elazar. He accused the great Rabbi of revealing the secret entrances of the fortress city of Betar to the Romans. It is now believed that this betrayal was the work of the Jewish Christians who wanted to undermine Bar Kochba. Rabbi Akiva then realized that Bar Kochba no longer possessed the qualities which initially led him to believe that he was the Messiah.

There was an additional spiritual dimension to the failure of the Messiah-ship of Bar Kochba as well; whether the spiritual failure of Rabbi Akiva's students was the cause—or whether it was the failure of Bar Kochba to rise to the spiritual heights expected of the Messiah is beyond our knowledge. For then—out of the blue, the great plague Askera descended and struck. The dream collapsed. For reasons that will probably forever remain obscure, the students of Rabbi Akiva were not considered by Heaven to have reached the supreme spiritual heights necessary to bring about the Messianic Age. As great as they were, an important factor was missing.

The Talmud tells us that "Rabbi Akiva's students didn't show proper respect one for the other." Precisely what this phrase refers to we do not know. With greatness comes heightened responsibility and with greatness comes a magnification of reward and punishment. For their failure and deficiencies—which would certainly be counted as minor in a generation such as ours, but which were crucial for great men on their high spiritual level—their mission was cancelled and they died a mysterious death.

With them died the Messianic hope of that era and for thousands of years to come. Bar Kochba was not a false messiah but a failed messiah. In the terrible war which followed, Bar Kochba and his army were destroyed in the great battles defending the fortress city of Betar. The war had been a catastrophe. Dodio Cassius reports the death of 580,000 Jews by Roman swords in addition to those who died of hunger and disease. Some scholars think that the bulk of the Jewish population of Judea was destroyed in battle and in subsequent massacres. One historian believes that the Jews lost a third of their number in the war, perhaps more fatalities than in the Great Revolt of the year 70.

For the survivors, the Bar Kochba uprising marked the great divide between the hope for national independence and dispersal in the Diaspora. The trauma of Betar coming after the fall of Jerusalem effected deep changes in the Jewish people. The stiff necked, stubborn, fanatically independent people that did not hesitate to make repeated suicidal lunges at the mightiest superpower of antiquity lost its warlike instincts. It would be 2,000 years before there would be a Jewish fighting force. As a result, the hope of the Jew for redemption was to be delayed for at least two thousand years. In the great and tragic defeat not only were between half a million to six hundred thousand Jews killed but the Romans were determined, once and for all to uproot the Jewish religion and the Jewish people—to bring an end to their hopes and their dreams.

It is for this reason that we mourn today. The mourning of Sefirah is not for the students alone, but for the failure of the Jewish people to bring about the Messianic Age, for the fall of the curtain on Jewish independence, Jewish hopes and Jewish Messianic ambitions. Every anti-Semitic outbreak for which Jews suffered since that day, every pogrom, massacre, crusade, Holocaust, and banishment that took the toll of so many millions during the two thousand year long and bitter night of exile, wandering and persecution, must be traced directly to the failure of Bar Kochba—but ultimately to the failure of the students of Rabbi Akiva. This was a tragedy of inestimable proportions to a war-ravaged world suffering under the bitter yoke of Rome as well as to the Jewish people. Rome did not fall at that time, but its fury and rage led to the exile and dismemberment of the Jewish people.

Yet, on that very Lag Ba'Omer day two thousand years ago, a new hidden light of hope emerged. In the midst of defeat, the Tannah, Rabbi Shimon Bar Yochai revealed to a small number of students the secrets of the mystical Zohar. In the Zohar, in its formulas, disciplines and spirituality, lie the secrets whose seed will bring about the coming of the Messiah. The Zohar's living tradition has kept that hope alive down to this very day. On Lag Ba'Omer the plague stopped, the dream was delayed, but it was not destroyed. It was to be nurtured through the generations—the stirrings of its realization enliven us today.

Because Lag Ba'Omer deals with the secrets of the future Messianic Age, it cannot be discussed openly or understood as clearly as can the Exodus or other events of the past. Whenever we stand between Passover and Shavuot—between our physical liberation from Egypt and our spiritual elevation during the Revelation at Sinai we recall those chilling events. For today we are also able to celebrate the liberation of Jerusalem and the site of our destroyed Temple. History is bringing together so many crucial events—the history of our ancient past is once again coming alive in the land of our fathers.

There are frightening parallels between our own age and the age of Rabbi Akiva and Bar Kochba. Following a frightful Holocaust which many believed would spell the end of the Jewish people, we experienced a restoration of Jewish independence—once more did a Jewish army score miraculous victories against overwhelming odds. Following the destruction of the great European centers of Torah scholarship, we witnessed the rebuilding of yeshivot in America and in Israel. We experienced a great revival of Torah study. The teshuva movement has brought about a return to Torah for so many who strayed. Jerusalem and the Temple Mount are in our hands.

All around us world empires are tottering while despair and corruption rages. Once again, the Jewish people have been entrusted with a great and frightful opportunity. Once again we have been given the potential to recreate a Jewish civilization of Torah greatness in our own land. Will we succeed or will our efforts be aborted because of our own failures, our own inability to respect the differences within the Torah community and unite the Jewish people to our cause?

The personality of Rabbi Akiva itself offers frightful lessons and opportunities. It was Rabbi Akiva who understood that "love your fellow as you love yourself" is the over-riding principle which the Torah people must internalize if it is to achieve its goals. Rabbi Akiva, too, is the quintessential ba'al teshuva—it was he who was forty years old and was unable to distinguish between an aleph and a bet—it was he who rose to be Jewry's greatest Torah scholar.

Hundreds of thousands of Jews; Americans, Israelis, and Russians are today's potential Rabbi Akivas. The fate of Jewry and the achievement of Heaven's greatest goals are in the hands of this generation. Will we attempt to achieve them or will we withdraw into our own selfish cocoons by refusing to shoulder the responsibilities which history and history's God has set before us?

It is not enough to wait for the Messiah's coming; we must toil to perfect our Torah lives if we are to bring about his speedy arrival. Only if we learn from the lesson of Rabbi Akiva's students will we understand that the coming of the Messiah depends on us.

Reprinted with permission from ou.org.

The Gift of Speech

Refining the way we speak:
An inspiring blend of stories, laws, and insights.

By **Rabbi Shimon Finkelman**

From Chapter 4: The Benefit of the Doubt
A Special Worker

Our Sages relate the following amazing story:

A Jew from Upper Galilee in northern Israel hired himself out for three years to a landowner in the south. At the end of the three years, the day before Yom Kippur, the worker asked for his wages so that he could return home and feed his family.

His employer responded: "I have no money."

"Then pay me with fruit, " said the worker.

"I have none," came the reply.

"Pay me with land."

"I have none."

"Pay me with livestock."

"I have none."

"Pay me with pillows and blankets."

"I have none."

The worker slung his pack over his shoulder and headed home, deeply disappointed.

When Succos ended, the landowner appeared at his worker's door with full payment for the three years of work, along with three donkeys laden with food, drink and delicacies. The food was brought inside and the two enjoyed a hearty meal together.

When the meal was over and the worker had received his money, the landowner asked him, "When you asked for your earnings and I replied that I had no money, what did you think?"

The worker replied, "I thought that perhaps a deal that you could not pass up had come along and you had used all your cash for that."

"And when I said that I had no land?"

"I thought that perhaps all your land had been leased to others."

"And when I said that I had no fruit?"

"I thought that perhaps you had not had an opportunity to separate *terumos* and *maasros* from your fruits."

"And when I said that I had no pillows and blankets?"

"I thought that perhaps you had dedicated all your possessions to the *Beis HaMikdash*."

The landowner exclaimed, "I make an oath that that is exactly what happened! ... Just as you judged me favorably, so too should Hashem judge you favorably."

Who was this wonderful worker and who was his employer? Our Sages say that the worker was Rabbi Akiva and his employer was Rabbi Eliezer ben Hurkanos. Rabbi Akiva began to study Torah at age forty; this story took place when he was still ignorant of Torah knowledge. As the Chasam Sofer points out, we see from this story that even before he began to study Torah, Rabbi Akiva possessed exceptional *midos*. No doubt, Rabbi Akiva's sterling character had a lot to do with his becoming the greatest Torah sage of his generation and one of the greatest of all time. Good character is the foundation upon which one can grow in Torah. In Pirkei Avos, the Sages list forty-eight qualities which one needs

to make Torah a part of his being. In the words of R'
Aharon Kotler, "To attempt to acquire Torah without
these qualities ...accomplishes nothing."

Surprise

As we saw in the above story, judging others favorably is not always easy. Many would have found it
hard to believe that the landowner, Rabbi Eliezer ben
Hurkanos, had actually used up his available cash,
leased all his property, dedicated his possessions to
the *Beis HaMikdash* and been unable to separate *terumos* and *maasros* from his fruits and vegetables. But
that is exactly what had happened and his worker, Akiva
ben Yosef, passed a great test in accepting his claims
as truth.

We should always bear in mind that in the course of
life, the strangest and most unlikely things can sometimes happen.

Reprinted with permission from ArtScroll Mesorah Publications
and TheJewishEye.com.

Lesson 5
Rabbi Meir
Introduction

What will Rabbi Meir do when his primary teacher of Torah, Elisha ben Avuyah, turns heretic and colludes with the Romans in oppressing his own people?

The rabbis refuse to even speak his name. Reviled and ostracized, Elisha is left alone in a private hell of his own making. He may be able to flee his past but he cannot flee himself.

And now Rabbi Meir must choose his own response. Will Rabbi Meir side with his colleagues and turn away from Elisha? Or, knowing Elisha as no one else knows him, does his conscience dictate another decision?

Historical Timeline

3880/120 CE	Rabbi Akiva succeeds Rabbi Yehoshua as *av beit din*
3887/127 CE	Bar Kochba revolt begins in earnest (early resistance began in 123 CE)
3893/133 CE	The revolt is crushed, Beitar falls, and Rabbi Akiva is imprisoned
3896/136 CE	Passing of Rabbi Akiva and birth of Rabbi Yehudah
3909/149 CE	*Sanhedrin* established in Usha with Rabban Shimon II as nasi, Rabbi Natan as *av bet din,* and Rabbi Meir as *chacham*
3926/166 CE	Rabbi Yehudah succeeds his father and is appointed *nasi*
3949/189 CE	Writing of the Mishnah and passing of Rabbi Yehudah

ROMAN EMPERORS

96–117 CE	TRAJAN
117–138 CE	HADRIAN
138–161 CE	ANTONINUS PIUS
161–180 CE	MARCUS AURELIUS ANTONINUS AUGUSTUS
180–192 CE	LUCIUS AURELIUS COMMODUS ANTONINUS

• Rabbi Meir was a student under the reign of Hadrian.
• Rabbi Meir risked his life to liberate his sister-in-law under the reign of Hadrian.
• Rabbi Meir was appointed chacham under the reign of Antoninus Pius.

Brief Biographical Overview

Rabbi Meir is the most brilliant of the *tana'im.* Despite his acknowledged erudition, his colleagues often disagreed with him. They revered him, but they did not understand him. Those who see what others cannot see often walk a lonely path. Yet Rabbi Meir persisted in his vision. He suffered many setbacks but also scored many triumphs.

In his youth, he experienced the Bar Kochba revolt, and in its aftermath, suffered terribly. His teachers, Rabbi Akiva, Rabbi Yishmael, and Rabbi Yehudah, who ordained him, were executed by the Romans. During this period, Rabbi Meir's father-in-law and mother-in-law were also executed. His sister-in-law was imprisoned and forced into a brothel. His brother-in-law was murdered by bandits. He lost two sons whom he loved deeply. His wife also passed away under tragic circumstances. His mentor Elisha ben Avuyah turned heretic. Rabbi Meir himself once went down in a shipwreck and nearly drowned, but was saved by a miracle. Yet, Rabbi Meir never complained. Like his teacher Rabbi Akiva, he believed that "everything that God does is for the best."

During this time, many great Torah scholars were persecuted by Rome, and in order to escape a similar fate, many scholars fled to Babylonia (where Rabbi Yehudah ben Beteira taught Torah in Netzivin). Rabbi Meir, who was sought by Rome for rescuing his sister-in-law from the brothel, fled to Babylonia as well.

In 148, fifteen years after the revolt was crushed, Rome, under the reign of Antonius Pius, began to normalize relations with Judea. The *sanhedrin* convened in Usha under the leadership of Rabban Shimon ben Gamliel and many scholars (such as Rabbi Natan Habavli, who was appointed *av beit din*) arrived from Babylonia. The *sanhedrin* continued to organize the oral tradition, a task begun in Yavneh after the destruction of the Temple and picked up in earnest by Rabbi Akiva when he realized that the oral law would soon need to be documented. Recognizing the quality of his erudition, the sages appointed Rabbi Meir to the office of *chacham,* supreme scholar.

Rabbi Meir continued in this role for a time, but due to his differences with the *nasi*, he was forced to resign his position. He asked that his body be taken to Israel for burial. Rabbi Meir passed away while in Asia Minor but was buried in Tiberias, overlooking the Kineret.

Ancient synagogue mosaic floor in Hammat Tiberias

In a Class of His Own

Text 1 📜

שפעם אחת גזרה מלכות הרשעה שמד על ישראל

שכל הסומך יהרג, וכל הנסמך יהרג, ועיר שסומכין בה תיחרב

ותחומין שסומכין בהן יעקרו

מה עשה יהודה בן בבא, הלך וישב לו בין שני הרים גדולים

ובין שתי עיירות גדולות, ובין שני תחומי שבת, בין אושא לשפרעם

וסמך שם חמשה זקנים

ואלו הן: רבי מאיר, ורבי יהודה, ורבי שמעון, ורבי יוסי, ורבי אלעזר בן שמוע . . .

כיון שהכירו אויביהם בהן אמר להן: בניי, רוצו

אמרו לו: רבי, מה תהא עליך

אמר להן: הריני מוטל לפניהם כאבן שאין לה הופכים

אמרו: לא זזו משם עד שנעצו בו שלש מאות לונביאות של ברזל

ועשאוהו ככברה

תלמוד בבלי סנהדרין יד,א

Once, [Hadrian's] wicked government decreed that whoever performed an ordination should be put to death, and whoever received ordination should be put to death, the city in which the ordination took place demolished, and the boundaries wherein it had been performed, uprooted. What did Rabbi Yehudah ben Bava do? He went and sat between two great mountains [that lay] between two large cities; between the Sabbath boundaries of the cities of Usha and Shefaram, and there he ordained five elders: Rabbi

Meir, Rabbi Yehudah, Rabbi Shimon, Rabbi Yose and Rabbi Eliezer ben Shamu'a. . . .

As soon as their enemies discovered them, [Rabbi Yehudah ben Bava] urged them, "My children, flee."

They said to him, "What will become of you, Rabbi?"

"I lie before them like a stone which none [is concerned to] overturn," he replied.

It was said that the enemy did not stir from the spot until they had driven three hundred iron spear-heads into his body, making it like a sieve.

TALMUD SANHEDRIN 14A

Text 2

אמר רבי אחא בר חנינא
גלוי וידוע לפני מי שאמר והיה העולם שאין בדורו של רבי מאיר כמותו
ומפני מה לא קבעו הלכה כמותו, שלא יכלו חביריו לעמוד על סוף דעתו. . .
תנא, לא רבי מאיר שמו אלא רבי נהוראי שמו
ולמה נקרא שמו רבי מאיר שהוא מאיר עיני חכמים בהלכה
תלמוד בבלי עירובין יג,ב

Rabbi Acha ben Chanina said: "It is manifestly known before God, that in the generation of Rabbi Meir there was none equal to him; why was not the *Halachah* fixed in agreement with his views? Because his colleagues could not fathom the depths of his mind. . . ."

One sage taught: His name was not Rabbi Meir but Rabbi Nehorai. Why was he called Rabbi Meir? Because he enlightened the sages in *Halachah*.

TALMUD ERUVIN 13B

Rabbi Meir and Beruria

Text 3

רבי שמלאי אתא לקמיה דרבי יוחנן

אמר ליה: ניתני לי מר ספר יוחסין . . . ניתנייה בשלשה ירחי . . .

אמר ליה: ומה ברוריה דביתהו דרבי מאיר, ברתיה דרבי חנניה בן תרדיון

דתניא תלת מאה שמעתתא ביומא משלש מאה רבוותא

ואפילו הכי לא יצתה ידי חובתה בתלת שנין

ואת אמרת בתלתא ירחי

תלמוד בבלי פסחים סב,ב

Rabbi Simlai came before Rabbi Yochanan and proposed, "Let the Master teach me the Book of Genealogies. . . but let us learn it in three months." . . . Rabbi Yochanan replied, "Beruria, the wife of Rabbi Meir, daughter of Rabbi Chanina ben Teradyon, who studied three hundred laws from three hundred teachers in a day, could not master [the Book of Genealogies] in three years, yet you propose to accomplish this feat in three months!"

TALMUD PESACHIM 62B

Text 4

הנהו בריוני דהוו בשבבותיה דרבי מאיר והוו קא מצערו ליה טובא

הוה קא בעי רבי מאיר רחמי עליהו כי היכי דלימותו

אמרה ליה ברוריא דביתהו:

מאי דעתך משום דכתיב (תהלים קד,לה) יתמו חטאים

מי כתיב חוטאים, חטאים כתיב . . .

אלא, בעי רחמי עליהו דלהדרו בתשובה ורשעים עוד אינם

בעא רחמי עליהו והדרו בתשובה

A group of bandits that lived in Rabbi Meir's neighborhood vexed him greatly. Rabbi Meir prayed that they should die.

His wife Beruria remarked, "How do you justify [this prayer for the death of the sinner]? For it is written (Psalms 104:35) 'May sin cease?' David did not pray for the sinner to cease, just that the sins should cease. . . . [Rather than for their death] pray for their repentance, and then the wickedness shall cease."

He did pray for them, and they repented.

TALMUD BERACHOT 10A

מעשה היה ברבי מאיר שהיה יושב במנחה בשבת ודורש ומתו שני בניו

מה עשתה אמן, הניחה שניהם על המטה ופירשה סדין עליהם

במוצאי שבת בא רבי מאיר מבית המדרש אמר לה: היכן שני בני

אמרה לו: לבית המדרש הלכו, אמרו לה: צפיתי בבית המדרש ולא ראיתים

נתנה לו הכוס של הבדלה והבדיל וחזר ואמר לה: היכן שני בני

אמרה לו פעמים שהלכו למקום פלוני ועכשו הם באים

הקריבה לפניו לאכול, לאחר שאכל אמרה לו: רבי שאלה יש לי לשאול . . .

קודם היום בא אחד ונתן לי פקדון ועכשו בא ליטול אחזיר לו או לאו

אמר לה: בתי מי שיש לו פקדון אינו צריך להחזיר לרבו

אמרה לו: חוץ מדעתך לא הייתי מחזרת אותו . . .

תפשה אותו בידו והעלהו לחדר והקריבה אותו למטה

נטלה הסדין מעליהם וראה שניהם מתים מונחים על המטה

התחיל בוכה ואומר: בני בני רבי רבי

בני בדרך ארץ ורבי שהיו מאירין עיני בתורתן

באותה שעה אמרה ליה: רבי לא כך אמרת לי

שאנו צריכין להחזיר פקדון לרבו

כך ה' נתן וה' לקח יהי שם ה' מבורך (איוב א,כא)

אמר רבי חנינא: בדבר זה נחמתו ונתישבה דעתו

לכך נאמר (משלי לא,י) אשת חיל מי ימצא

ילקוט שמעוני משלי תתקסד

ne Shabbat afternoon, while Rabbi Meir was lecturing [at the academy], two of his sons died. What did their mother do? She laid them on the bed and covered them with a sheet.

When Rabbi Meir arrived home, after Shabbat, he asked, "Where are my sons?"

"They went to the lecture hall," she replied.

"But I looked in the study hall and didn't see them," he said.

She handed him a glass of wine for *havdalah.*

He recited *havdalah* and asked, "Where are my sons?"

"They went to a particular place and will soon return," she replied and then served dinner.

After he ate she said, "My teacher, I have a question to ask . . . Before today a man left an item with me for safekeeping and he has now come to collect it. Shall I return the item or not?"

"My daughter," Rabbi Meir replied, "Is not a custodian required to return the deposit to its master?"

"My teacher," she replied, "If not for your words I could not [have brought myself to] return it."

. . . She took his hand and led him to the bedroom. She approached the bed, drew back the sheet and he saw his two children lying dead.

"My sons, my sons, my teachers, my teachers," he cried. "They were my sons in the ways of the world, but my teachers for they enlightened my eyes with words of Torah."

At that moment she interjected, "My master, did you not tell me that we are required to return our deposit to their master? 'G-d has given and God has taken May the name of G-d be blessed for eternity'" (Job 1:21).

Said Rabbi Chanina, "With these words she offered him solace and relief [from the intensity of his grief]. Of her it is written 'A woman of valor who can find'" (Proverbs 31:10).

YALKUT SHIMONI MISHLEI 964

Text 6

אזל לגבי שומר דידה, אמר ליה: הבה ניהלה

אמר ליה: מיסתפינא ממלכותא

אמר ליה: שקול תרקבא דדינרא, פלגא פלח ופלגא להוי לך

אמר ליה: וכי שלמי מאי איעביד, אמר ליה:

אימא אלהא דמאיר ענני ומתצלת

אמר ליה: ומי יימר דהכי איכא, אמר ליה השתא חזית

הוו הנהו כלבי דהוו קא אכלי אינשי, שקל קלא שדא בהו

הוו קאתו למיכליה, אמר: אלהא דמאיר ענני, שבקוה, ויהבה ליה

לסוף אשתמע מילתא בי מלכא, אתיוה אסקוה לזקיפה

אמר: אלהא דמאיר ענני, אחתוה. אמרו ליה: מאי האי

אמר להו: הכי הוה מעשה

אתו חקקו לדמותיה דרבי מאיר אפיתחא דרומי

אמרי: כל דחזי לפרצופא הדין לייתיה

יומא חדא חזיוהי, רהט אבתריה, רהט מקמייהו . . .

בשולי עובדי כוכבים חזא, טמש בהא ומתק בהא . . .

אמרי: חס ושלום, אי רבי מאיר הוה לא הוה עביד הכי

קם ערק

תלמוד בבלי עבודה זרה יח,א

He went to her warden and said, "Release her to me."

He replied, "I am afraid of the government [who will punish me for releasing their charge]."

"Take this basket of dinars," said Rabbi Meir. "One half can be used for the distribution [of bribes and] the other half shall be for you."

"And what shall I do when these are used up?" he asked.

"Then," he replied, "say [the following prayer:] 'O God of Meir, answer me!' and you will be saved."

"But," said the warden, "who can assure me that that this prayer is effective?"

Rabbi Meir replied, "You will see."

There were several dogs [in the compound] that would bite anyone [who incited them]. Rabbi Meir took a stone and threw it at them, and when they were about to bite him, he exclaimed, "O God of Meir answer me!" and they left him alone. The warden then handed her over to him.

Eventually, the matter [of her disappearance] became known to the government, and [the warden] on being brought [for judgment] was taken up to the gallows, whereupon he exclaimed, "O God of Meir answer me."

[Try as they might, they failed to affix him to the gallows.] They took him down and asked him to explain the meaning of his prayer. He told them about the incident that had happened. They then engraved Rabbi Meir's likeness on the [city gates] and proclaimed that anyone seeing a person resembling that picture should bring him [to justice].

One day [some Romans] saw him and chased him, but he eluded them . . . . He happened just then to see [non-kosher] food cooked by non-Jews and he dipped in one finger and then sucked the other [creating the impression that he had partaken of their soup. They seized Rabbi Meir, but pointing to the fact that he had eaten non-kosher food, he denied that he was Rabbi Meir] . . .

"Impossible," agreed the Romans. "Were this Rabbi Meir, he would not have acted this way," [and they left him]. Rabbi Meir then arose and ran away [for fear of being apprehended].

TALMUD AVODAH ZARAH 18A

Learning Activity One

Based on the stories we have discussed so far, how would you characterize Beruria and Rabbi Meir? Bring evidence from the stories to support your characterization.

Rabbi Meir and Elisha
A Scholar Turned Heretic

Text 7a

תנו רבנן: ארבעה נכנסו בפרדס

ואלו הן: בן עזאי, ובן זומא, אחר, ורבי עקיבא

תלמוד בבלי חגיגה יד,ב

ur rabbis taught: Four entered the *Pardes*; ben Azai, ben Zoma, Acher, and Rabbi Akiva.

T A L M U D   C H A G I G A H   1 4 B

Text 7b

אחר הציץ וקיצץ בנטיעות

מני אחר, אלישע בן אבויה שהיה הורג רבי תורה

אמרין: כל תלמיד דהוה חמי ליה משכח באוריתא הוה קטיל ליה

ולא עוד, אלא דהוה עליל לבית וועדא והוה חמי טלייא קומי ספרא

והוה אמר: מה אילין יתבין עבדין הכא

אומנותיה דהן בנאי, אומנותיה דהן נגר, אומנותיה דהן צייד, אומנותיה דהן חייט

וכיון דהוון שמעין כן הוון שבקין ליה ואזלין לון

תלמוד ירושלמי חגיגה ב,א

cher peered into the *Pardes* and ended up cutting down the shoots. Who is Acher? Elisha ben Avuyah, who would kill the

teachers of Torah. They say that he would kill any student whom he saw succeeding in Torah.

Moreover, he would enter the schools and would see children studying from books and he would say, "What are they doing sitting here? This one would do better to work as a builder, this one would do better to work as a smith, this one would do better would he work as a hunter, this one would do better would he work as a tailor."

When the students would hear this, they would abandon their studies and leave the academy.

JERUSALEM TALMUD CHAGIGAH 2:1

Text 8a

רבי מאיר הוה יתיב דרש בבית מדרשא דטיבריה

עבר אלישע רביה רכיב על סוסייא ביום שובתא

אתון ואמרון ליה הא רבך לבר

פסק ליה מן דרשה ונפק לגביה

תלמוד ירושלמי חגיגה ב,א

Rabbi Meir was lecturing in the academy of Tiberias when Elisha his [former] teacher rode by on a horse on Shabbat. They came and told Rabbi Meir, "Your teacher is outside." Rabbi Meir paused and stepped out.

JERUSALEM TALMUD CHAGIGAH 2:1

Text 8b

שאל אחר את רבי מאיר . . .

מאי דכתיב (איוב כח,יז) לא יערכנה זהב וזכוכית ותמורתה כלי פז

אמר לו: אלו דברי תורה, שקשין לקנותן ככלי זהב וכלי פז

ונוחין לאבדן ככלי זכוכית

אמר לו: רבי עקיבא רבך לא אמר כך

אלא: מה כלי זהב וכלי זכוכית, אף על פי שנשברו יש להם תקנה

אף תלמיד חכם, אף על פי שסרח יש לו תקנה

תלמוד בבלי חגיגה טו,א

Acher asked Rabbi Meir, " . . . What is the meaning of the verse, 'Crystal and gold cannot equal it?'"(Job 28:17)

Rabbi Meir said to him, "These are the words of Torah that are hard to acquire like vessels of gold and fine gold, but as easy to lose as vessels of crystal."

Acher said to him, "Akiva your teacher did not explain it so. Rather, he said, 'Just as vessels of gold and crystal, even after they have broken, can be repaired, so a Torah scholar, even after he has been disgraced, can be redeemed.'"

TALMUD CHAGIGAH 15A

Text 8c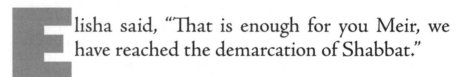

אמר ליה: דייך מאיר עד כאן תחום שבת

אמר ליה: מן הן את ידע

אמר ליה: מן טלפי דסוסיי דהוינא מני והולך אלפיים אמה

אמר ליה: וכל הדא חכמתא אית בך ולית את חזר בך

אמר ליה: לית אנא יכיל

אמר ליה: למה

אמר ליה: שפעם אחת הייתי עובר לפני בית קודש הקדשים

רכוב על סוסי ביום הכיפורים שחל להיות בשבת

ושמעתי בת קול יוצאת מבית קודש הקדשים

ואומרת: שובו בנים חוץ מאלישע בן אבויה שידע כחי ומרד בי

תלמוד ירושלמי חגיגה ב,א

Elisha said, "That is enough for you Meir, we have reached the demarcation of Shabbat."

Rabbi Meir asked, "How do you know?"

Elisha replied, "I counted the hoof beats of my horse and know that we have walked two thousand cubits."

Rabbi Meir said, "There is so much wisdom in you, will you not return yourself?"

Elisha replied, "I cannot."

Rabbi Meir asked, "But why?"

Elisha replied, "I once rode my horse past the Holy of Holies on Yom Kippur that fell on Shabbat and I heard a voice from heaven emerging from the Holy of Holies saying, 'Return errant children, return, except for Elisha son of Avuyah, who knew how awesome I am and rebelled against Me.'"

JERUSALEM TALMUD CHAGIGAH 2:1

For the Sake of His Torah

Text 9

אמרון לרבי מאיר: אין אמרין לך בההוא עלמא

למאן את בעי למבקרא לאבוך או לרבך

אמר לון: אנא מיקרב לרבי קדמיי ובתר כן לאבא

אמרין ליה: ושמעין לך

אמר לון: ולא כן תנינן מצילין תיק הספר עם הספר תיק תפילין עם התפילין

מצילין לאלישע אחר בזכות תורתו

תלמוד ירושלמי חגיגה ב,א

They asked Rabbi Meir, "If, in the world to come, you are offered a choice to visit your father or your [former] teacher, [whom would you choose?]"

Rabbi Meir replied, "I would approach my teacher first and then my father." They said to him, "Would [the hosts of heaven] honor your wishes?"

He said to them, "Have we not learned that we salvage the Torah cover along with the Torah, the Tefilin Bag along with the Tefilin? We save Elisha in the merit of his Torah."

JERUSALEM TALMUD CHAGIGAH 2:1

Text 10

רבי מאיר אומר: כל העוסק בתורה לשמה זוכה לדברים הרבה
ולא עוד אלא שכל העולם כלו כדי הוא לו
נקרא ריע אהוב אוהב את המקום אוהב את הבריות
משמח את המקום משמח את הבריות

פרקי אבות ו,א

Rabbi Meir would say, "Whoever studies Torah for Torah's sake alone, merits many things; not only that, but [the creation of] the entire world is worthwhile for him alone. He is called friend, beloved, lover of G-d, lover of humanity, rejoicer of G-d, rejoicer of humanity. . . ."

PIRKEI AVOT 6:1

For the Sake of His Repentance

Text 11

אתון ואמרון לרבי מאיר הא רבך באיש

אזל בעי מבקרתיה ואשכחיה באיש

אמר ליה: לית את חזר בך

אמר ליה: ואין חזרין מתקבלין

אמר ליה: ולא כן כתיב (תהלים צ,ג) תשב אנוש עד דכא

עד דיכדוכה של נפש מקבלין

באותה שעה בכה אלישע ונפטר ומת

והיה רבי מאיר שמח בלבו ואומר דומה שמתוך תשובה נפטר רבי

תלמוד ירושלמי חגיגה ב,א

They told Rabbi Meir, "Your Rabbi is ill." Rabbi Meir went to visit and found him ill [on his death bed]. Rabbi Meir said, "Will you not repent?" Elisha replied, "Are returnees accepted?" Rabbi Meir replied, "Doesn't it say, (Psalms 90:3) 'You return man [to you] till he is crushed,' meaning repentance is possible until the moment the soul has completely expired?" At that moment, Elisha wept and [soon thereafter] expired. Rabbi Meir rejoiced, saying, "It appears to me that my teacher passed away as a penitent."

JERUSALEM TALMUD CHAGIGAH 2:1

For the Sake of His Essence

Text 12

בנים אתם לה׳ אלהיכם (דברים יד,א)

בזמן שאתם נוהגים מנהג בנים אתם קרוים בנים

אין אתם נוהגים מנהג בנים אין אתם קרוים בנים, דברי רבי יהודה

רבי מאיר אומר: בין כך ובין כך אתם קרוים בנים

תלמוד בבלי קידושין לו,א

"Y ou are sons of the Lord your God" (Deuteronomy 14:1).

When you behave as G-d's sons, you are called sons; but when you do not behave as sons, you are not called sons; this is Rabbi Yehudah's view.

Rabbi Meir said, "In both cases, you are called sons."

TALMUD KIDDUSHIN 36A

Text 13a

אשכחיה רבה בר שילא לאליהו, אמר ליה: מאי קא עביד הקדוש ברוך הוא

אמר ליה: קאמר שמעתא מפומייהו דכולהו רבנן

ומפומיה דרבי מאיר לא קאמר

אמר ליה: אמאי, משום דקא גמר שמעתא מפומיה דאחר

תלמוד בבלי חגיגה טו,ב

abah bar Shila once met Elijah and said to him, "What is the Holy One, blessed be He, doing?" He answered, "He is reviewing the teachings of all the sages, with the exception of Rabbi Meir." Rabah asked, "Why [does he ignore Rabbi Meir]?" Elijah replied, "Because he studied from Acher."

TALMUD CHAGIGAH 15B

Text 13b

אמר ליה: אמאי, רבי מאיר רמון מצא, תוכו אכל, קליפתו זרק

תלמוד בבלי חגיגה טו,ב

aid Rabah to Elijah, "Rabbi Meir found a pomegranate; he ate the inside and threw away the peel!"

TALMUD CHAGIGAH 15B

Text 13c

אמר ליה: השתא קאמר, מאיר בני אומר

בזמן שאדם מצטער שכינה מה לשון אומרת: קלני מראשי, קלני מזרועי

תלמוד בבלי חגיגה טו,ב

lijah replied, "Now [God, satisfied with your argument] is saying: Meir my son says, When a man suffers, what does the *Shechinah* (divine presence) say? 'My head is heavy, my arm is heavy.'"

TALMUD CHAGIGAH 15B

Text 14

לאחר ימים באו בנותיו ותובעות צדקה אצל רבינו

אמר: אל יהי לו מושך חסד ואל יהי חונן ליתומיו (תהלים קט,יב)

אמרין: רבי לא תסתכל בעובדוהי תסתכל לאורייתיה

באותה שעה בכה רבי וגזר עליהון שיתפרנסו

אמר: מי שלא היתה תורתו לשם שמים כך העמיד

מי שתורתו לשם שמים על אחת כמה וכמה

רות רבה ו

After Acher's passing, his daughters came to Rebbi asking for charity. Rebbi said, "[Does it not say regarding a case such as this] 'He should not draw kindness towards him nor should he show grace to his orphans?'" (Psalms 109:12).

They said, "Rebbi, do not look at his actions; look at his Torah."

Then Rebbi began to weep and declared that they should be supported. He said, "If one who did not study for the sake of Heaven had children such as these, how much more so one who studies for the sake of Heaven."

Rut Rabah 6

Key Points

1. Rabbi Meir was a student of Rabbi Akiva and arguably the most brilliant of the sages. He was frequently misunderstood by his peers.

2. He endured many losses and great suffering in his life, but like his teacher Rabbi Akiva, bore suffering with grace and optimism.

3. His wife, Beruria, was a brilliant scholar in her own right and shared with him the qualities of bold thinking and deep compassion.

4. Elisha was a noted Talmudic scholar who suffered a crisis of faith and ended up betraying his own community.

5. Though the other scholars shunned Elisha, Rabbi Meir continued to study with him and to encourage his return.

6. Rabbi Meir's actions were motivated by his love of Torah, his hope to inspire Elisha to repentance, and his belief in the essential goodness of every Jew, even those who have not yet repented of their wrongdoing.

7. Ultimately, Rabbi Meir's view of Elisha was vindicated. Elisha repented on his death bed and his righteous daughters were accepted with compassion.

Additional Readings

R' Meir Ba'al Hanes: His Life

The *gemorah* tells us (Gittin 56) that when the Roman Caesar Nero led his army into battle against Yerushalayim he wanted to determine if he would be successful in destroying her. He therefore shot arrows in all four directions and they all fell towards Yerushalayim. He took this as a heavenly sign that he would be victorious. He then found a young boy and asked him to expound upon a posuk. The child read him the verse "and I will take revenge of Edom, through the Jewish people." He thereupon said to himself, "G-d wants me to destroy His House and later avenge Himself in me?" He immediately decided to convert and become a Jew, and it was from him that the great Tanna Rebbi Meir descended.

His actual name was Rebbi Nehora'i (which is the Aramaic equivalent for "light") and so he was called Rebbi Meir because "he lit up the eyes of the *chachomim* with his *Halacha*" (Eruvin 13:).

While he was a student of the famed Rebbi Akiva, from whom he received his *semicha* at a very young age, he also studied Torah under the tutelage of Rabbi Yishmoel and Elisha ben Avuya (usually referred to as "Acher").

When he was much older, he was ordained once again by Rebbi Bava ben Buta who was riddled to death by more than three hundred spears by Roman soldiers for defying the Roman decree forbidding rabbinical ordination. Rebbi Meir as well as Rebbi Yehudah, Rebbi Yossi, Rebbi Elozar bar Rebbi Shimon and Rebbi Nechemiah where able to escape with their lives and it was through them that the unbroken chain of the oral tradition was passed on to all oncoming generations.

He was married to Bruriah the daughter of Rebbi Chaninah ben Tradyon, who is the only woman quoted in the *gemorah* for her great brilliance and wisdom.

When Rabbi Meir once prayed that the wicked people who where constantly harassing and annoying him should die, she told him that he should rather pray that they do *teshuvah*. He took her advice and, sure enough, they repented and became G-d fearing Jews.

When she saw a student studying silently, she scolded him by saying that only by studying out loud does one remember his learning.

She mocked the words of the *chachomim* that said that women were "light-minded" and are easily influenced. Rabbi Meir wanted to prove her wrong, so he put up one of his students to test her. He kept on trying to seduce her to sin with him until she finally consented. Rebbi Meir thereupon disguised himself as the student and now proved to her that *chazal* were right on target when they said that "*noshim daatom kalos*." The entire episode backfired when she committed suicide out of great shame. Rabbi Meir now left the country in terrible embarrassment on account of what happened.

He lived right after the destruction of the *Bais Ha'mikdosh*, a time of terrible Roman persecution. He saw twenty four thousand students of Rebbi Akiva die in a devastating plague between Pesach and Shevuos. Both his father-in-law and his Rebbi where brutally murdered by the hated and evil Roman government for defying their decree not to teach or study the Torah. Rebbi Chaninah ben Tradyon was burned at the stake wrapped in a Sefer Torah, while Rebbi Akiva was tortured to death with metal scrapers that tore at his skin mercilessly.

His wife's sister was jailed in a prison filled with harlots and immorality. Upon the pleas of his wife, Rebbi Meir set out to see if he would be able to rescue her. "If she is not guilty of an immoral act then I'm sure that a miracle will occur and I will be able to set her free" he said. He dressed himself up as a distinguished Roman nobleman and bribed his way into the prison compound and tried to seduce her to see if she was truly righteous. When she resisted all his attempts, he realized that she merited a miracle. He bribed the guard to let her out, but the guard was afraid that his superiors would hold him responsible if she would be found missing. Rebbi Meir assured him that if he ever gets caught, all he has to do is cry out "May the G-d of Meir answer me" and he would immediately be saved. As proof that this incantation would really work, the guard untied some of the ferocious dogs which began to attack Rebbi Meir. The moment Rebbi Meir uttered these words, the dogs turned into little puppies. Upon seeing this miracle, the guard released her. Sure enough, her escape was soon found out and the warden was taken out to be hung. As they began pulling upon the rope he cried out "May the G-d of Meir answer me" whereupon the rope snapped and he fell to the ground. When they questioned him as to what he had said, he told them the entire story. Rebbi Meir was immediately placed on the most wanted list and a handsome reward for his arrest was offered. A large bust of his face was put up at the entrance gate so that he could be easily recognized.

One day as he was walking down the street, someone recognized him and gave chase. One version of the story goes that Eliyahu Ha'novi disguised himself as a beautiful harlot and he ran into her arms and embraced her. Realizing that this couldn't be Rebbi Meir, for such a holy man would never act in such a manner, they let him go.

Rebbi Meir was a *Sofer* and earned but three *selo'im* a day. One he used for food, the other for clothing and the third he gave to poor scholars. His Rebbi, Rebbi Yishmoel once warned him to be extremely careful when writing a *Sefer Torah* for even a single mistake can destroy worlds. (Eruvin).

He encouraged parents to teach their children a clean, simple and easy trade. "Wealth and poverty depends on G-d and not on one's profession," he would tell them. He advises us to lessen the time we occupy with business and rather use it for Torah study. (Avos perek 4, mishnah 12). "One must be extremely humble before any man. If one wastes even a single moment of precious Torah study time, then he will eventually be burdened with many other things that will occupy his time. Those who learn with great effort will be richly rewarded," he would constantly tell his students. "Don't judge the contents of a jug by its outside looks," he would often say.

He was a very tall man and reached to the shoulders of Rebbi Tarfon who was the tallest man of his generation.

One Friday night a woman came home very late because she enjoyed listening to Rebbi Meir's Friday night lectures. Her husband was furious and demanded that she go to *Shul* and spit into Rebbi Meir's eye. Rebbi Meir, in his great holiness, realized the problem and made believe that his eye ached him. 'Please," he said to the woman, "I need you to spit in my eye seven times so that it will be cured of my great pain," he asked of her. After finally convincing her to do so, he told her to go back and tell her husband that not only did you spit once but you spit seven times in all. He would do absolutely anything to bring peace between man and wife no matter how he would have to degrade himself.

He suffered great personal tragedy. When his two dearest sons passed away on the holy day of Shabbos, his wife covered them up and didn't tell him anything about it so as not to sadden him on this joyful day. When he came home and asked her if she had seen them, she brushed his question aside and said that they were probably in the study hall. After *Havdala* she asked him, "What if someone gave me a great treasure to hold for him and he now demands that I return it, must I give it back?" "Why of course," was his reply, not understanding what the question was all about. She now took his hand and led him into the room where the two dead children lay. When she removed the cover and he realized the great tragedy he began to cry. "Didn't you just say that we must return the treasure to its owner?" she consoled him. "G-d gave them to us and now G-d took them back. May His name be blessed," -for didn't Rebbi Meir teach us that "one is required to bless G-d for the bad just like for the good." (Berochos 48:) And like his Rebbi, Rebbi Akiva, he was always in the habit of saying that "all Hashem does is for the good." (Berochos 60:) It was only with such faith and trust in Hashem that life could go on during those terrible times.

His arguments were so brilliant that even his own contemporaries could not get to the very depths of his thoughts and therefore the halacha did not follow his opinion. His arguments were so fierce that it would seem as if he "would uproot giant mountains and crush them against one another." One could learn even from seeing Rebbi Meir's cane. He was a master at giving *mosholim*—fables—in order to get his point across. Any *mishnah* left nameless usually means that it follows the opinion of Rebbi Meir—for the rule is "*stam mishneh* Rebbi Meir."

He had an amazing insight into people's names. Once when he and some of his friends stayed at an inn, he suspected that the innkeeper was a thief and therefore hid his money in a nearby cemetery. Sure enough, his friend's monies were all stolen and his was the only money not taken. When they asked him what it was that had tipped him off as to the innkeeper's dishonesty, he replied that he had recognized him by his name which was Kiddor. There is a *posuk* which reads "*Ki dor tapuchos haymoh*," which shows that the name is related to dishonest people.

He once stayed at an inn where the owner would wake the guests at night and tell them to go on their way. In fact, the owner himself would offer to escort the guests and was in cahoots with a band of robbers who would then rob the guests of all they owned. When the owner asked Rebbi Meir to leave in the middle of the night, he replied that he had to wait for his brother to arrive. He told the owner that his brother's name was Ki Tov and that he was staying at a nearby *shul*. The owner went there at once and called out his name but no one answered. He waited there all night and kept calling "Ki Tov, Ki Tov," but no one arrived.

In the morning when Rabbi Meir began to leave, the innkeeper asked him where his brother was and why he doesn't wait for him? He replied "the light of the day is my brother and it is for him that I have waited!" (Medrash)

When he saw his Rebbi, Elisha ben Avuya (referred to as Acher) going astray, he tried his very best to reason with him so that he does Teshuvah but his rebbi refused to listen. "I've heard a heavenly voice call out that I'm too far gone and my *Teshuvah*, will not be accepted," he replied. Little did his Rebbi realize that this was only being done in order to deter him from doing *Teshuvah*. Yet as we all know, the doors of *Teshuvah* are never closed! When "Acher" died, the heavenly court refused him entry into *Gan Eden* because of his many sins and saw it unfit for him to be put into *gehenom* because of his greatness in Torah learning. Thereupon Rabbi Meir prayed that he be put into *gehenom* so that he will eventually be able to enter *Gan Eden*. Upon Rebbi Meir's death, one could see smoke rising from "Acher's" grave. When Rebbi Yochanan died the smoke stopped; a heavenly sign that his punishment was over.

Rebbi Meir taught his students that Torah was the most important thing in life and that anyone who learns Torah for its own sake—*lishmoh*—would be greatly rewarded. (See the first *mishnah* in Mesechta Avos perek 6, for all the good things one merits by learning Torah *lishmoh*.)

Being such a great and holy man, he simply couldn't understand how someone could succumb to the *yetzer horah's* temptations until he was taught a powerful lesson. While walking along the banks of a river he suddenly saw the most beautiful woman standing on the opposite side. He lost all control of himself and tried everything in his power to cross over to the other side. It was only then that the woman vanished and he shamefully realized that it was just a mirage and that he nearly failed the test. This taught him that no matter how holy a person can be, one can never trust himself until the day of his death. One must forever be on guard lest the *yetzer horah* get the better of him. Never challenge Hashem to test you. In fact, the greater the person, the stronger and more powerful is his *yetzer horah*. (see Mesechta Sukka). If it weren't for Hashem's constant help, man would not be able to fight the *yetzer horah* on his own. And so a person is led along the path he himself chooses. The decision is ours-so we had better wisen up. When we open up our hearts even as much as the size of a pin hole to serve Hashem , then Hashem will help us along by opening our hearts to the size of the entrance to the *Ulam*.

While Rebbi Meir died someplace in Asia, he asked that he be buried in Eretz Yisroel. And so he lies buried on the shores of the Kinneret only a short distance from the city of Tveryah. Thousands of people flock to his holy grave site and pray "may the G-d of Meir answer me." It has become a worldwide custom to give *tzedokah* to *kollelim* in Eretz Yisroel in which people are immersed in Torah day and night and pray that in their great *zchus* one's prayers be answered. These *tzedokos* are called Rebbi Meir *Ba'al Ha'nes*. Many people claim that they have been helped on account of it.

Reprinted with permission from campsci.com.

Lesson 6
Rabbi Yehudah HaNasi
Introduction

The book of Genesis speaks of the epic struggle between the twin brothers, Jacob and Esau, from whom would descend, respectively, the Jewish people and Rome. Jacob bequeathed his children the mandate of teaching the world about G-d; Esau fathered a people that would conquer nations and build the infrastructure of modern civilization. At times, these worldviews have clashed, with terrible results. But what would happen if peace could exist between brothers, with each benefiting from what the other could provide? Rabbi Yehudah HaNasi lived in such an era, providing a glimpse of the possibility of idyllic co-existence, a glimmer of a perfect time.

מאימתי קורין את שמע בערבית משעה שהכהנים נכנסים לאכול בתרומתן
סוף האשמורה הראשונה דברי ר׳ אליעזר וחכמים אומרים עד חצות
גמליאל אומר עד שיעלה עמוד השחר מעשה שבאו בניו מבית המשתה אמרו לו לא קרינו את ש
אמר להם אם לא עלה עמוד השחר חייבין אתם לקרות
לא זו בלבד אלא כל מה שאמרו חכמים עד חצות עמוד השחר הקטר חל

Historical Timeline

3896/136 CE Passing of Rabbi Akiva and birth of Rabbi Yehudah

3909/149 CE *Sanhedrin* established in Usha with Rabban Shimon II as *nasi*, Rabbi Natan as *av bet din*, and Rabbi Meir as *chacham*

3926/166 CE Rebbi succeeds his father and is appointed *nasi*

3949/189 CE Writing of the Mishnah and passing of Rabbi Yehudah

ROMAN EMPERORS

117–138 CE	**HADRIAN**
138–161 CE	**ANTONINUS PIUS**
161–180 CE	**MARCUS AURELIUS ANTONINUS AUGUSTUS**
180–192 CE	**LUCIUS AURELIUS COMMODUS ANTONINUS**

- Rabbi Yehudah was born during the reign of Hadrian.
- He was a student during the reign of Antoninus Pius.
- He was appointed *nasi* during the reign of Marcus Aurelius Antoninus.
- He wrote the Mishnah and passed away during the reign of Lucius Aurelius Commodus Antoninus.

Born for Greatness

Text 1

כשמת רבי עקיבא נולד רבי . . .

ללמדך, שאין צדיק נפטר מן העולם עד שנברא צדיק כמותו

שנאמר (קהלת א,ה): וזרח השמש ובא השמש

תלמוד בבלי קידושין עב,ב

On the day that Rabbi Akiva died, Rebbi was born . . . . This teaches you that a righteous person does not pass away from this world until another one just as righteous has been born. As it states (Ecclesiastes 1:5), "The sun shines and the sun sets."

TALMUD KIDUSHIN 72B

Text 2

כשנולד רבי גזרו שלא למול, ואביו ואמו מלוהו

שלח קיסר והביאו לרבי ואמו לפניו

והחליפתו אמו באנטונינוס והניקתו עד שהביאתו לפני קיסר

ומצאוהו ערל ופטרום לשלום

ואמר אותו הגמון: אני ראיתי שמלו את זה

אלא הקדוש ברוך הוא עושה להם נסים בכל עת

ובטלו הגזרה

תוספות, עבודה זרה י,ב

When Rebbi was born, there was a [Roman] decree against circumcision. The procurator summoned Rebbi and his mother [to inspect whether the baby was circumcised, but] his mother exchanged her son with [the Roman baby] Antoninus [whose mother she had befriended]. She nursed Antoninus [as if he were her own son] and brought him before the procurator. When they saw that he was uncircumcised they set him free in peace.

The officer said, "I saw them circumcise him, but G-d does miracles for the [Jewish people] all the time."

[As a result of this incident,] the decree [banning circumcision] was annulled.

Tosafot (quoting Midrash), Talmud Avodah Zarah 10b

Text 3

דכי הוו יתבי רבן שמעון בן גמליאל ורבי יהושע בן קרחה אספסלי

יתבי קמייהו רבי אלעזר ברבי שמעון ורבי אארעא, מקשו ומפרקו

אמרי: מימיהן אנו שותים והם יושבים על גבי קרקע

עבדו להו ספסלי, אסקינהו

אמר להן רבן שמעון בן גמליאל: פרידה אחת יש לי ביניכם

ואתם מבקשים לאבדה הימני, אחתוהו לרבי

אמר להן רבי יהושע בן קרחה: מי שיש לו אב יחיה, ומי שאין לו אב ימות

אחתוהו נמי לרבי אלעזר ברבי שמעון

חלש דעתיה אמר: קא חשביתו ליה כוותי

עד ההוא יומא, כי הוה אמר רבי מילתא

הוה מסייע ליה רבי אלעזר ברבי שמעון

מכאן ואילך, כי הוה אמר רבי יש לי להשיב

אמר ליה רבי אלעזר ברבי שמעון: כך וכך יש לך להשיב, זו היא תשובתך

השתא היקפתנו תשובות חבילות שאין בהן ממש

חלש דעתיה דרבי, אתא אמר ליה לאבוה

אמר ליה: בני, אל ירע שהוא ארי בן ארי, ואתה ארי בן שועל

תלמוד בבלי בבא מציעא פד,ב

The teachers of the academy, among them Rabban Shimon ben Gamliel and Rabbi Yehoshua ben Karchah sat on chairs, [while the students] Rabbi Elazar ben Rabbi Shimon [bar Yochai] and Rebbi sat before them on the ground.

[These two students] raised questions [that their teachers could not answer] and proceeded to answer [their own questions].

The teachers remarked, "We drink their water [i.e., benefit from their learning], yet they sit on the ground; let seats be brought in for them!" So they were promoted.

Rabban Shimon ben Gamliel protested, "I have a pigeon amongst you, and you wish to destroy it!" [i.e., by casting an evil eye upon him.] So Rebbi was put down [i.e., seated on the ground].

Thereupon Rabbi Yehoshua ben Karchah said, "Should he, who has a father, live, and he who has no father die!" [i.e., should Rabbi Elazar be imperiled by the evil eye because his father was not present to protest?] So Rabbi Elazar was also put down. [Rabbi Elazar] felt hurt and remarked, "You have made him equal to me!"

Now, until that day, whenever Rebbi made a statement, Rabbi Elazar supported him. But from then onward, when Rebbi would say, "I have an objection," Rabbi Elazar [would preempt the objection and say], "If you have such and such an objection, this is your answer; now you have encompassed us with loads of questions to which there is no substance."

Rebbi, thus humiliated, went and complained to his father. "Let it not grieve you," his father replied, "for he is a lion, the son of a lion, whereas you are a lion, the son of a fox[i.e., his wisdom is greater than yours because his father is greater than your father]."

TALMUD BAVA METSIA 84B

Rebbi and Rome

Text 4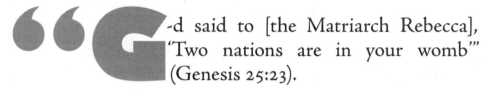

וַיֹּאמֶר ה' לָהּ שְׁנֵי גוֹיִם בְּבִטְנֵךְ (בראשית כה,כג)

אמר רב יהודה אמר רב . . . זה אנטונינוס ורבי

שלא פסקו מעל שולחנם לא חזרת ולא קישות ולא צנון

לא בימות החמה ולא בימות הגשמים

תלמוד בבלי עבודה זרה יא,א

G-d said to [the Matriarch Rebecca], "Two nations are in your womb'" (Genesis 25:23).

Rav Yehuda said in the name of Rav, ". . . This refers to Antoninus and Rebbi [one a descendant of Esau, the other of Jacob], whose tables never lacked radish, lettuce, or cucumbers, either in summer or winter!"

TALMUD AVODAH ZARAH 11A

Text 5

בשעת פטירתו של רבי

זקף עשר אצבעותיו כלפי מעלה

אמר: רבונו של עולם, גלוי וידוע לפניך שיגעתי בעשר אצבעותי בתורה

ולא נהניתי אפילו באצבע קטנה

תלמוד בבלי כתובות קד,א

Rebbi, at the time of his passing, raised ten fingers heavenward and proclaimed: "Sovereign of the Universe, it is revealed and known to you that I have labored in the study of the Torah with my ten fingers and that I did not enjoy [any worldly] benefits even with my little finger."

TALMUD KETUBOT 104A

Text 6

כל יומא הוה שדר ליה דהבא פריכא במטראתא וחיטי אפומייהו

אמר להו: אמטיו חיטי לרבי

אמר ליה רבי: לא צריכנא, אית לי טובא

אמר: ליהוו למאן דבתרך דיהבי לבתראי

דאתו בתרך ודאתי מינייהו ניפוק עלייהו

תלמוד בבלי עבודה זרה י,ב

Every day Antoninus sent Rebbi gold in a leather bag filled with wheat at the top, saying [to his servants], "Carry the wheat to Rebbi."

Rebbi sent word to Antoninus, "I have no need for it; I have quite enough of my own."

Antoninus answered, "Leave it to those who will come after you so they might give it to those who will come after me, for your descendants and those who will follow them will hand it over to my descendants."

TALMUD AVODAH ZARAH 10B

Recording the Mishnah

Text 7

דברים שבכתב אי אתה רשאי לאומרן על פה
דברים שבעל פה אי אתה רשאי לאומרן בכתב
תלמוד בבלי גיטין ס,ב

You are not at liberty to quote from memory those words that were transcribed [by God in the Torah], and you are not at liberty to recite from writing those words that were transmitted orally [by God to Moses at Sinai].

TALMUD GITIN 60B

Text 8

וכבר ידעת שאפילו התלמוד המקובל לא היה מחובר בספר מקדם
לענין המתפשט באומה, דברים שאמרתי לך על פה
אי אתה רשאי לאומרם בכתב
והיה זה תכלית החכמה בדת, שהוא ברח ממה שנפל בו באחרונה
רצוני לומר, רוב הדעות והשתרגם
וספקות נופלות בלשון המחובר בספר, ושגגה תתחבר לו
ותתחדש המחלוקת בין האנשים, ושובם חבורות
והתחדש הבלבול במעשים
מורה הנבוכים א,עא

ven the traditional Talmud, as you are well aware, was not originally committed to writing, in conformity with the rule to which our nation adhered, "things which I have communicated to you orally, you must not communicate in writing." This rule was the epitome of wisdom; for while it remained in force it averted the disadvantages which happened subsequently, namely, great diversity of opinion, doubts as to the meaning of written words, slips of the pen, dissensions among the people and the formation of sects, and confused notions about practical subjects.

GUIDE TO THE PERPLEXED VOL. I, 71

Text 9

ולמה עשה רבינו הקדוש כך ולא הניח הדבר כמות שהיה

לפי שראה שתלמידים מתמעטין והולכין

והצרות מתחדשות ובאות, ומלכות רומי פושטת בעולם ומתגברת

וישראל מתגלגלין והולכין לקצוות

חיבר חיבור אחד להיות ביד כולם כדי שילמדוהו במהרה ולא ישכח

רמב״ם, הקדמה למשנה תורה

nd why did Rebbi do this and did not leave matters as they were? He saw that the number of students was waning, while the instances of Jewish suffering were increasing. The Roman Empire was gaining might and expanding while Jews were scattered across the world. He therefore wrote [the oral law into] one book, so that everyone could learn it quickly and it should not be forgotten.

MAIMONIDES, INTRODUCTION TO MISHNAH TORAH

Text 10 📖

ושלח וקבץ כל תלמידי ארץ ישראל

ועד ימיו לא היו מסכתות סדורות

אלא כל תלמיד ששמע דבר מפי גדול הימנו גרסה

ונתן סימנים, הלכה פלונית ופלונית שמעתי משם פלוני

וכשנתקבצו אמר כל אחד מה ששמע

ונתנו לב לברר טעמי המחלוקת דברי מי ראוין לקיים

וסידרו המסכתות, דברי נזיקין לבדם, ודברי יבמות לבדם ודברי קדשים לבדם

רש״י, בבא מציעא לג,ב

He sent for and convened all the scholars of the land of Israel. Until his day [the oral tradition] was not organized along ordered tractates. Students would hear traditions from their teachers and incorporate it into their study. They would form mnemonics [as memory aids] "this and that *Halachah* I heard from this master," etc.

When they gathered [in the times of Rebbi], each shared what he had learned. They labored to understand the underlying reasons for the disputes and determined the traditions that should be preserved. They then organized the tractates: laws of damages and injury in one tractate, laws of levirate marriages in another tractate, and laws related to the sacrificial rite in another.

RASHI, TALMUD BAVA METSIA 33B

A Beloved Leader

Text 11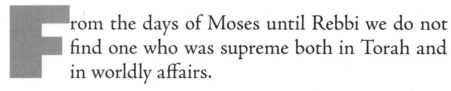

מימות משה ועד רבי לא מצינו תורה וגדולה במקום אחד

תלמוד בבלי גיטין נט,א

From the days of Moses until Rebbi we do not find one who was supreme both in Torah and in worldly affairs.

TALMUD GITIN 59A

Text 12

הרבה תורה למדתי מרבותי, ומחבירי יותר מהם, ומתלמידי יותר מכולן

תלמוד בבלי מכות י,א

Much have I learned from my teachers, more from my colleagues, but from my students, most of all.

TALMUD MAKOT 10A

Text 13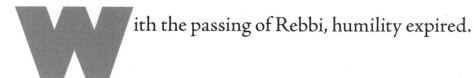

משמת רבי בטלה ענוה
תלמוד בבלי סוטה מט,ב

With the passing of Rebbi, humility expired.

Talmud Sotah 49b

Text 14

כשחלה רבי, נכנס רבי חייא אצלו ומצאו שהוא בוכה

אמר לו: רבי, מפני מה אתה בוכה . . .

אמר ליה: אנא אתורה ומצות קא בכינא
תלמוד בבלי כתובות קג,ב

When Rebbi fell ill, Rabbi Chiya entered into his presence and found him weeping.

"Master," he said to him, "Why are you weeping . . . ?"

Rebbi replied, "On account of the Torah and *mitzvot* I weep [for I will soon be separated from them]."

Talmud Ketubot 103b

ההוא יומא דנח נפשיה דרבי גזרו רבנן תעניתא ובעו רחמי

ואמרי: כל מאן דאמר נח נפשיה דרבי, ידקר בחרב

סליקא אמתיה דרבי לאיגרא

אמרה: עליונים מבקשין את רבי והתחתונים מבקשין את רבי

יהי רצון שיכופו תחתונים את העליונים

כיון דחזאי . . . וקמצטער

אמרה: יהי רצון שיכופו עליונים את התחתונים

ולא הוו שתקי רבנן מלמיבעי רחמי

שקלה כוזא שדייא מאיגרא לארעא

אישתיקו מרחמי ונח נפשיה דרבי

אמרו ליה רבנן לבר קפרא: זיל עיין

אזל אשכחיה דנח נפשיה, קרעיה ללבושיה ואהדריה לקרעיה לאחוריה

פתח ואמר: אראלים ומצוקים אחזו בארון הקדש

נצחו אראלים את המצוקים ונשבה ארון הקדש

אמרו ליה: נח נפשיה, אמר להו: אתון קאמריתו ואנא לא קאמינא

תלמוד בבלי כתובות קד,א

On the day of Rebbi's passing, the sages decreed a public fast and offered prayers for heavenly mercy. They furthermore announced that whoever said that Rebbi was dead would be severely punished.

Rebbi's handmaid climbed to the roof and prayed, "The immortals desire Rebbi [to join them] and the mortals desire Rebbi [to remain with them]; may it be the will [of the Almighty] that the mortals overpower the immortals."

However, when she saw . . . how much Rebbi suffered, she prayed, "May it be the will [of the Almighty] that the immortals overpower the mortals."

As the sages incessantly continued their prayers for [heavenly] mercy [thus preventing his death], she took a glass jar up to the roof and threw it to the ground. [Startled by the noise,] they ceased praying [for a moment], and the soul of Rebbi departed to its eternal rest.

"Go," said the sages to Bar Kappara, "and see what happened."

He went and found that Rebbi had passed on. He tore his cloak and turned the tear backwards [so it would not be seen. On returning to the rabbis] he cried, "The angels and the mortals have taken hold of the holy ark. The angels overpowered the mortals and the holy ark has been captured."

They asked him, "Has he gone to his eternal rest?"

"You said it," he replied. "I did not say it."

TALMUD KETUBOT 104A

Text 16

מעשה ניסין נעשו באותו היום
ערב שבת היתה, ונתכנסו כל העיירות להספידו
ואשירוניה תמני עשרה כנישן, ואחתוניה לבית שריי
ותלה לון יומא עד שהיה כל אחד ואחד מגיע לביתו
וממלא לו חבית של מים ומדליק לו את הנר
כיון ששקעה החמה קרא הגבר
שרון מציקין אמרין: דילמא דחללינן שבתא
יצתה בת קול ואמרה להן
כל מי שלא נתעצל בהספידו של רבי
יהא מבושר מחיי העולם הבא
תלמוד ירושלמי כלאים ט,ג

Beit She'arim

Great miracles happened on the day [of Rebbi's funeral]. It was a Friday and all the communities gathered to eulogize him. They [eulogized him in] eighteen separate gatherings and brought him [to his resting place in] Beit She'arim. The sun did not set for them until each returned home, filled a basin of water, and lit the Shabbat candle. As soon as the sun set, the rooster crowed.

They said to themselves, "Perhaps we have desecrated the Shabbat."

A heavenly voice echoed forth, "All who were not lax in the eulogy of Rebbi are destined for the world to come."

JERUSALEM TALMUD KILAYIM 9:3

Course Conclusion

Text 17

רבי הוה משלח לרבי אסי ולרבי אמי דיפקון ויתקנון קרייתא דארעא דישראל

והוון עלין לקרייתא ואמרין להון: אייתו לן נטורי קרתא

והוון מייתו להון ריש מטרתא וסנטרא

והוון אמרין להון אלין נטורי קרתא, אלין חרובי קרתא

אמרו להון: ומאן אינון נטורי קרתא

אמרו להם: אלו סופרים ומשנים

שהם הוגים ומשנים ומשמרין את התורה ביום ובלילה

איכה רבה פתיחתא ב

Rebbi sent [his disciples] Rabbi Ami and Rabbi Asi to travel and assist Jewish communities across the land of Israel.

When the two would arrive to a city they would say, "Bring forth the city's guardians!"

The citizens would usher in the sentries and the commanders of the city's guard [to which the rabbis] would respond, "Are these the city's guardians? These are its destroyers!"

The townspeople would then inquire, "Who are the city's guardians?"

The rabbis would reply, "The scribes and the teachers, who study, teach and preserve the Torah day and night."

EICHAH RABAH, PETICHTA 2

Key Points

1. Rebbi was born on the day that Rabbi Akiva was executed and was saved from death upon his circumcision when his mother exchanged him with the Roman baby, Antoninus, who would eventually become his lifelong friend.

2. Rebbi studied with at least four of Rabbi Akiva's five major students and was himself an outstanding student.

3. Despite the stature of being a scion of the house of Hillel, Rebbi was unassuming and received no special privileges in the academy.

4. As *nasi*, Rebbi was incredibly wealthy but did not use his wealth and position for personal benefit.

5. Rebbi used his influence with Roman notables, including the emperor Antoninus, in order to create a tranquil environment for the Jews of his time.

6. Rebbi took advantage of this period of calm to record the oral tradition so that there would never again be a danger of it being lost.

7. Rebbi convened gatherings to collect and transcribe the students' body of knowledge, to clarify any points of disagreement, and to organize the knowledge into tractates.

8. The life of Rebbi demonstrates that although we must not neglect political and practical means of protecting our people, these efforts can only succeed when they are rooted in the vision provided in the Torah, which gives purpose to our survival.

Course Summary

Leader	Unique Contribution
Hillel	
Rabban Yochanan ben Zakai	
Rabbi Eliezer	

Leader	Unique Contribution
Rabbi Akiva	
Rabbi Meir	
Rabbi Yehudah HaNasi	

Additional Readings

Gallery of Our Great: Rabbi Judah the Prince

By **Nissan Mindel**

I. Rabbi Judah was the son of Rabbi Simeon ben Gamliel and was elected "Prince" (*Nassi*) after the death of his father. He was born on the very day that Rabbi Akiba died in the hands of the Romans. In the *Mishnah*, Rabbi Judah the Prince is called, simply, "Rabbi," for he was so famous that he needed no other name by which to identify him.

"Rabbi" was very wealthy, which was not the case with most other Rabbis, and it was believed that in his stables there was more wealth than in the treasury of the King of Persia! Yet, in spite of his great wisdom and wealth and the great honor in which he was held, "Rabbi" was a modest person and showed respect to all the great Rabbis, even those amongst his own student He was fond of saying: "I have learned much from my teachers, even more from my friends and fellow students, but most of all I learned from my pupils."

"Rabbi" used his wealth to support the poor and needy. When a famine broke out in the land, Rabbi Judah the Prince opened his orchards and stores of food to feed the hungry.

Because of his high moral character and teachings, because of his refusal to enjoy selfishly his own great wealth, and because of his great personal qualities and piety, he was recognized everywhere as a holy person, and everyone called him "our saintly teacher" (*Rabbenu Hakadosh*). Our Sages used to say that all noble virtues were united in him and that even Elijah the Prophet, invisible though he was, sat among the students of "Rabbi" to listen to his teaching of the Torah.

II. Rabbi Judah the Prince said many things that could serve as a guide to others. "When a Jew performs a Mitzvah," he used to say, "he should not rejoice merely over that commandment alone, for one Mitzvah brings others after it. Likewise, when a Jew commits a sin, he should not regret merely that one sin, for other sins will surely follow that sin."

That a person should never consider himself too great to learn from someone younger or more humble than himself, "Rabbi" showed through the following example. The Torah is likened to water. Just as, with water, an older person is not ashamed to ask someone younger to give him a drink, so should he not be ashamed to ask a younger person to quench his thirst for knowledge. And also, just as no one is too lazy to seek a drink when he is thirsty, so too, no student should be too lazy to seek after Torah in a Yeshiva.

A person who does not wish to study or pray was regarded by "Rabbi" just like a dumb beast. Indeed, he once declared that he who occupies himself with the study of the Torah may eat the flesh of an animal or bird, but he who refuses to engage in the study of the Torah is not justified in eating the flesh of the lower creatures, of whom he is one.

III. There are many stories related in the Talmud and Midrash of the great friendship that existed between Rabbi Judah the Prince and the Roman Emperor Antoninus. The Emperor used to visit "Rabbi's" house secretly in order to learn from him something of the wisdom of the Torah and to consult him about various difficult problems concerning the government of his Empire, for he greatly valued the good advice he received from the Jewish Sage.

In order that others should not suspect that he was asking the Rabbi for his counsel concerning matters of state, they often disguised questions or answers by means of a code or some action which the other alone understood. On one occasion Antoninus sent a messenger to "Rabbi" with the question: "The Imperial Treasury is empty. What shall I do?" Rabbi Judah called the messenger into his garden, where he uprooted some plants and replaced them with others. The messenger from the palace watched in amazement and then asked: "What reply shall I give to my royal master?" "Rabbi" replied that no answer was required. The puzzled Roman returned to the Emperor, informing him that the Rabbi had refused to answer the Emperor's question. Antoninus, however, asked the messenger whether Rabbi Judah had not performed any action in his presence. Thereupon the messenger described to the Emperor how the Jewish Rabbi had pulled up some plants in his garden and had put others in their place. The Emperor understood the message hidden in this action of the Rabbi. He dismissed several of his officials, whom "Rabbi" had suspected of being dishonest, and appointed others in their place. Soon the royal treasury was full again.

Later the friendship between the Emperor and the Rabbi was displayed openly. They began to visit each other and argued and discussed regarding G-d and His Torah. Once Antoninus asked "Rabbi": "How can the human soul be punished in the next world? The soul will be able to say: 'How can I be held to blame? I am a spiritual creation. It was the body that sinned, not I . . . .' On the other hand, the body will be able to say: 'How can I be guilty? Without the soul I could not have sinned, for it is the soul which gives life to the body.'"

To this question of the Emperor, "Rabbi" replied with a clever parable (example), as follows: A man once owned an orchard, over which he set two servants to guard it. One of the watchers was blind; the other was lame: The lame man, tempted by the sight of the ripe fruit which he could not reach, said to his blind companion: "Carry me on your shoulders and lead me to that tree, laden with rich fruit, to which I shall guide you. In this way both of us will enjoy the fruit"

When the owner, noticing the loss of his fruit, later accused his two servants of the theft of his choicest fruit, the blind man protested his innocence. "How could I have seen where the fruit was growing?" And the lame servant said: "How could I have reached the fruit?"

How did the owner act? He placed the lame man on the shoulders of the blind man and then punished them together.

So, too, replied the Rabbi, does G-d with the human body and soul when each falsely tries to avoid punishment for its guilt.

IV. "Rabbi" was sick for many years but he was cured, as he had become ill, through a strange happening.

"Rabbi" was once walking to the *Beth Hamidrash* (the House of Study), when a calf, which was being driven to *shechita* (slaughter), broke loose and came up to the Rabbi, appearing to plead with him to save it from death. "Rabbi" said to the calf: "Go to your fate, for to this end you were created." At this, a Heavenly Voice (a *Bath Kol*) proclaimed from Heaven that, as "Rabbi" had not had pity on one of G-d's creatures, he should be punished with physical suffering.

For thirteen years this holy Rabbi suffered, and then one day he was healed just as suddenly. It happened like this:

A maidservant in the Rabbi's house was once cleaning a room when she found some newly-born kittens. She wanted to put them out of the house, but "Rabbi" restrained her. "G-d has pity on all His creatures," he said, "and human beings must follow His example. Leave the kittens in the house." A *Bath Kol* at once proclaimed that, just as "Rabbi" had had pity on G-d's lowly creatures, so should pity be taken on him. He was immediately cured.

When Rabbi Judah the Prince became seriously ill and near to death, the Rabbis prayed to G-d for him. Later they sent a Rabbi, called Bar Kappara, to see how "Rabbi" was progressing, but when he arrived he learned that the holy scholar had died. Bar Kappara rent his clothes as a sign of mourning and, returned to the Rabbis. He broke the sad news to them with this remark: "The angels have struggled with us human beings for 'the Holy Ark!' The angels have been victorious and have captured 'the Holy Ark. . . .'" The Rabbis asked: "Is he dead?" Bar Kappara replied: "You have spoken it. I did not want to let my lips utter the words."

V. The most important achievement for which Rabbi Judah Hanassi is famous is his edition of the *Mishnah*. The Torah, given to us by G-d on Mount Sinai, consists of two parts—the Written Law (known, as TaNaKh, the initials of which stand for Torah, *Neviim* and *Ketuvim*, that is, the Five Books of the Torah, the Prophets and the Holy Writings) and the Oral Law, the explanation of the Torah given by word of mouth to Moses, as well as the Laws of Israel (*Halacha L'Moshe Mi-Sinai*).

This Oral Law was handed down from generation to generation by word of mouth from Moses to Joshua, from Joshua to the Seventy Elders, from the Elders to the Prophets, from the Prophets to the Men of the Great Synagogue, and from them to the greatest scholars of every generation. All these laws, traditions and customs were learned by heart and memorized. They were not allowed to be written down.

Rabbi Judah the Prince saw, however, that as a result of the difficulties of the Exile which the Jewish nation had to endure and would have to suffer for many centuries until the coming of the Messiah, there was a strong probability that many of these sacred laws would be forgotten or accidentally changed, G-d forbid. He therefore decided to gather together the laws and write them down, so that they might remain permanently recorded in what was called the "*Mishnah*" (the meaning of which is "learning by repetition").

This was, of course, a tremendous task, but "Rabbi" succeeded in his great undertaking. He not only assembled the laws of the Oral Law, but he also arranged them in a logical order in six volumes, or "*Sedarim*," known by the abbreviation, "*Shass*." The order of the "*Shass*" is as follows: (1) *Zeraim*—consisting of the laws of agriculture and the commandments concerned with the land; (2) *Moed*—consisting of the laws of the Sabbath, Festivals and. Fasts; (3) *Nashim*—consisting of the laws concerned with family life, marriage, etc.; (4) *Nezikin*—consisting of the laws concerned with injuries done to others, compensation, business and money matters, etc.; (5) *Kodoshim*—consisting of the laws concerned with the sacrifices; (6) *Taharot*—consisting of the laws concerned with purity and impurity.

The *Mishnah* is written in Hebrew.

The later Rabbis, who discussed and expanded the *Mishnah*, were no longer called by the title of *Tarxim* (as the earlier Rabbis had been called), but were called *Amoraim*. The volumes which contain their learned discussions are called the *Gemara*, an Aramaic word which means "completion," or "explanation," and these are mainly written in Aramaic. About three centuries of such Rabbinic discussions passed by after the *Mishnah* had been written down, before the *Gemara* also was put down in writing. The *Mishnah* and *Gemara* together are known as the Talmud, for whose existence we owe a tremendous debt of gratitude to Rabbi Judah the Prince.

Published and copyrighted by Kehot Publication Society. Reprinted with permission from chabad.org.

Acknowledgments

Many of us have encountered various stories about the sages of the Talmud and have thoroughly enjoyed these vignettes of Jewish wisdom. But over the past two years, the **JLI** editorial team has grappled with what might be accomplished when these stories are brought together in a coherent whole, with six sequential biographies arrayed across a historical expanse. The result is an unforgettable epic of Jewish resilience and survival.

It has been a great pleasure to work with **Rabbi Eliezer Gurkow**, who has thoroughly researched the lives of the six sages upon which this course is based, and has woven a breathtakingly beautiful tapestry from the strands of information he has gathered. With scholarly precision and painstaking thoroughness, he has indeed created for us portraits in leadership, a rare glimpse into the lives of the figures who continue to shape our Jewish lives today.

A **JLI** course is always a vast collaborative effort, but it is the course author who stands at the helm, skillfully steering us through uncharted waters with a vision that only he possesses. On behalf of our staff, our affiliates, and our **JLI** students, we thank Rabbi Gurkow, and wish him much success in all his future endeavors.

We are greatly indebted to **Rabbi Mordechai Dinerman**, our dedicated research associate, for his extensive contributions to the course. Rabbi Dinerman carefully reviewed the manuscript, making many valuable editorial suggestions that enhanced the accuracy and teachability of the course content. His breadth of knowledge and formidable research skills are a real treasure. Rabbi Dinerman also prepared and proofed our Hebrew sources and references with great precision. We are indeed fortunate to have him as a member of our **JLI** editorial team.

The **JLI** Editorial Board has provided invaluable assistance that has guided the development of the course, providing many valuable suggestions along the way. Our thanks to **Rabbi Shalom Adler, Rabbi Yaakov Latowicz**, and **Rabbi Aryeh Weinstein** for providing feedback on lesson drafts and piloting the course.

Many thanks to our production team: **Sarah A. Kass,** our copyeditor; **Nachman Levine**, our layout designer; **Shimon Leib Jacobs**, our printer; **Spotlight Design** for cover design; and **Rabbi Mendel Sirota**, who oversees production and shipping.

We warmly welcome **Rabbi Zalman Abraham**, our new director of marketing, to the **JLI** family. Our thanks as well to the members of our marketing board, **Rabbi Simcha Backman, Rabbi Ronnie Fine, Rabbi Ovadiah Goldman**, and **Rabbi Yehudah Shemtov,** as well as **Rabbi Shraga Sherman**, who reveiws our marketing materials.

Special thanks to **Chabad.org,** an invaluable online resource of Jewish learning and information, for providing many of the articles for our additional readings.

The hardworking support staff at **JLI** Central is critical to the success of every project.

We thank **Mrs. Rivka Sternberg**, administrator of our flagship courses, for her conscientious attention to the smooth coordination of our process, from the inception stage to coordination. **Rabbi Mendel Sirota** provides the prompt and courteous customer support for which **JLI** is famous with warmth and efficiency. **Rabbi Benny Rapoport** designs the powerpoints that enhance the teaching of every lesson, both visually and conceptually. **Rabbi Dr. Shmuel Klatzkin** and **Mrs. Chana Lightstone** develop our multimedia scripts and provide editorial review for the powerpoint slides. The weekly videos are produced by the talented and creative hand of **Rabbi Levi Teldon**. Rabbi **Mendel Bell** ensures the integrity of our online environment. **Rabbi Levi Kaplan's** keen assessment and practical approach have been helpful on many occasions. Our devoted affiliate liaisons, **Mrs. Mindy Wallach** and **Mrs. Musie Kesselman**, coordinate the many details that hone our professional edge to perfection. **Mrs. Shaina Basha Mintz , Mrs. Shainy Weinberg,** and **Mrs. Nechama Shmotkin** oversee our accounts. A special welcome to **Rabbi Mendel Popack**, director of our newly-formed **JLI** Academy.

We are immensely grateful for the encouragement of our principal patron, vice chairman of *Merkosh Le'Inyonei Chinuch*—Lubavitch World Headquarters, **Rabbi Moshe Kotlarsky**, as well as for the unwavering support of **JLI**'s principal patron, **Mr. George Rohr**, who has been instrumental in the monumental growth of the organization.

The constant progress in **JLI** is a testament to the visionary leadership of our director, **Rabbi Efraim Mintz**, who is never content to rest on his laurels and who boldly encourages continued innovation and change.

JLI's devoted executive board—**Rabbi Chaim Block, Rabbi Hesh Epstein, Rabbi Yosef Gansburg, Rabbi Shmuel Kaplan, Rabbi Avremel Sternberg**, and **Rabbi Yisrael Rice**—devote countless hours to the development of **JLI**. Their dedicated commitment and sage direction have helped **JLI** continue to grow and flourish.

Finally, **JLI** represents an incredible partnership of more than 300 *shluchim* giving of their time and talent to further Jewish education. We thank them for generously sharing their thoughts, feedback, questions, and teaching experiences. They are our most valuable critics, and our most helpful contributors.

Inspired by the call of the Lubavitcher Rebbe of righteous memory, it is the mandate of the Rohr **JLI** to assist all Jews in experiencing their Torah heritage. It is my hope that this course succeeds in small measure in fulfilling that charge.

Chana Silberstein
Course Editor
Ithaca, New York
24 Tevet, 5770

The Rohr Jewish Learning Institute

An affiliate of
Merkos L'Inyonei Chinuch
The Educational Arm of
The Chabad Lubavitch Movement
822 Eastern Parkway, Brooklyn, NY 11213

Chairman
Rabbi Moshe Kotlarsky
Lubavitch World Headquarters
Brooklyn, NY

Principal Benefactor
Mr. George Rohr
New York, NY

Executive Director
Rabbi Efraim Mintz
Brooklyn, NY

Executive Committee
Rabbi Chaim Block
S. Antonio, TX

Rabbi Hesh Epstein
Columbia, SC

Rabbi Yosef Gansburg
Toronto, ON

Rabbi Shmuel Kaplan
Potomac, MD

Rabbi Yisrael Rice
S. Rafael, CA

Rabbi Avrohom Sternberg
New London, CT

Rabbinic Consultant
Rabbi Dr. J. Immanuel Shochet
Toronto, ON

Advisory Board
Rabbi Shmuel Kaplan
Chairman
Potomac, MD

Rabbi Dovid Eliezrie
Yorba Linda, CA

Rabbi Yosef Gopin
West Hartford, CT

Rabbi Shalom D. Lipskar
Bal Harbour, FL

Dr. Stephen F. Serbin
Columbia, SC

Educational Consultants
Dr. Andrew Effrat
Professor, School of Education
University of Massachusetts, Amherst
Amherst, MA

Dr. Nechie King
Towson State University
Towson, MD

Dr. David Pelcovitz
Professor of Education and Psychology
Yeshiva University
New York, NY

Professor Andrew Warshaw
Marymount Manhattan College
New York, NY

Mr. Michael Brandwein
Speech and Communication Expert
Lincolnshire, IL

Authors
Rabbi Yitschak M. Kagan
Of blessed memory

Rabbi Berel Bell
Montreal, QC

Rabbi Tzvi Freeman
Toronto, ON

Rabbi Eliezer Gurkow
London, ON

Rabbi Aaron Herman
Raleigh, NC

Rabbi Dr. Shmuel Klatzkin
Dayton, OH

Rabbi Dr. Chaim D. Kagan
Monsey, NY

Rabbi Chaim Zalman Levy
New Rochelle, NY

Rabbi Moshe Miller
Chicago, IL

Rabbi Yisrael Rice
S. Rafael, CA

Rabbi Eli Silberstein
Ithaca, NY

Rabbi Shais Taub
Milwaukee, WI

Editorial Board
Rabbi Yisrael Rice
Chairman
S. Rafael, CA

Rabbi Shalom Adler
Palm Harbour, FL

Rabbi Yisroel Altein
Pittsburgh, PA

Rabbi Berel Bell
Montreal, QC

Rabbi Hesh Epstein
Colombia, SC

Rabbi Zalman Aaron Kantor
Mission Viejo, CA

Rabbi Levi Kaplan
Brooklyn, NY

Rabbi Dr. Shmuel Klatzkin
Dayton, OH

Rabbi Yakov Latowicz
Ventura, CA

Rabbi Yosef Loschak
Goleta, CA

Rabbi Levi Mendelow
Stamford, CT

Rabbi Yossi Nemes
Metairie, LA

Rabbi Reuven New
Boca Raton, FL

Rabbi Dr. Shlomo Pereira
Richmond, VA

Rabbi Shalom Raichik
Gaithersburg, MD

Rabbi Benny Rapoport
Clarks Summit, PA

Rabbi Nochum Schapiro
Sydney, Australia

Rabbi Shraga Sherman
Merion Station, PA

Rabbi Avrohom Sternberg
New London, CT

Rabbi Aryeh Weinstein
Newton, PA

Editors

Rabbi Dr. Shmuel Klatzkin
Dayton, OH

Mr. Yaakov Ort
Jerusalem, Israel

Dr. Chana Silberstein
Ithaca, NY

Multimedia Development

Rabbi Chesky Edelman
Rabbi Dr. Shmuel Klatzkin
Mrs. Chana Lightstone
Rabbi Benny Rapoport
Rabbi Levi Teldon

Research Staff

Rabbi Mordechai Dinerman
Rabbi Shaul Goldman
Rabbi Yehuda Shurpin

Administration

Rabbi Mendel Sirota
Mrs. Mindy Wallach
Rabbi Mendy Weg

Affiliate Support

Rabbi Mendel Sirota

Online Division

Rabbi Mendel Bell
Rabbi Mendel Sirota
Rabbi Schneur Weingarten

Affiliate Liaisons

Mrs. Musie Kesselman
Mrs. Nechama Shmotkin
Mrs. Rivka Sternberg
Mrs. Mindy Wallach

Marketing Committee

Rabbi Zalman Abraham
Director

Rabbi Mendy Halberstam
Miami Beach, FL

Rabbi Simcha Backman
Glendale, CA

Rabbi Ronnie Fine
Montreal, QC

Rabbi Ovadiah Goldman
Oklahoma City, OK

Rabbi Yehuda Shemtov
Yardley, PA

Marketing Consultants

Tzvi Freeman
Toronto, ON

J.J. Gross
Blowdart Advertising & Marketing
New York, NY

Warren Modlin
MednetPro, Inc.
Alpharetta, GA

Alan Rosenspan
Alan Rosenspan & Associates
Sharon, MA

Alan M. Shafer
Alliant Marketing Solutions
Stamford, CT

Gary Wexler
Passion Marketing
Los Angeles, CA

Graphic Design

Spotlight Design
Brooklyn, New York

Friedman Advertising
Los Angeles, CA

Publication Design

Nachman Levine
Detroit, MI

Printing

Shimon Leib Jacobs
Point One Communications
Montreal, CA

Accounting

Mrs. Shaina B. Mintz
Mrs. Nechama Shmotkin

JLI Departments
JLI Flagship

Rabbi Yisrael Rice
Chairman
S. Rafael, CA

Dr. Chana Silberstein
Director of Curriculum
Ithaca, NY

Mrs. Rivka Sternberg
Administrator
Brooklyn, NY

Mrs. Chana Lightstone
Research Associate
Brooklyn, NY

Ms. Sarah A. Kass
Copy Editor
Brooklyn, NY

Nachman Levine
Research Editor
Detroit, MI

Dr. Michael Akerman, MD
Consultant
Continuing Medical Education
Associate Professor of Medicine,
SUNY–Downstate Medical Center

Bernard Kanstoroom, Esq.
Consultant
Continuing Legal Education
Bethesda, MD

JLI For Teens
in partnership with
CTeeN: Chabad Teen Network

Rabbi Chaim Block
Chairman
San Antonio, TX

Rabbi Benny Rapoport
Director
Clarks Summit, PA

Rabbi Beryl Frankel
Director, CTeeN
Yardley, PA

JLI International Desk

Rabbi Avrohom Sternberg
Chairman
New London, CT

Rabbi Moshe Heber
Coordinator

JLI Supplementary Courses

Rabbi Levi Kaplan
Director
Brooklyn, NY

Authors

Mrs. Chani Abehsera
Los Angeles, CA

Rabbi Zalman Abraham
Brooklyn, NY

Rabbi Levi Jacobson
Toronto, ON

Mrs. Malka Touger
Jerusalem, Israel

Mrs. Shimonah Tzukernik
Brooklyn, NY

JLI Teacher Training

Rabbi Berel Bell
Director
Montreal, QC

myShiur:
Advanced Learning Initiative

Rabbi Shmuel Kaplan
Chairman
Potomac, MD

Rabbi Levi Kaplan
Director

National Jewish Retreat

Rabbi Hesh Epstein
Chairman
Columbia, SC

Bruce Backman
Coordinator

Rabbi Avrumy Epstein
Liaison

Sinai Scholars Society
in partnership with
Chabad on Campus

Rabbi Menachem Schmidt
Chairman
Philadelphia, PA

Rabbi Moshe Chaim Dubrowski
Chabad on Campus

Rabbi Yitzchok Dubov
Director

Torah Café Online Learning

Rabbi Levi Kaplan
Director

Rabbi Simcha Backman
Consultant

Rabbi Mendel Bell
Webmaster

Getzy Raskin
Filming and Editing

Rabbi Mendy Elishevitz
Website Design

Moshe Raskin
Video Editing

Mrs. Miri Birk
Adminisrator

Torah Studies

Rabbi Yossi Gansburg
Chairman
Toronto, ON

Rabbi Meir Hecht
Director

Rabbi Yechezkel Deitsch
Mrs. Nechama Shmotkin
Administrators

JLI Academy

Rabbi Hesh Epstein
Chairman

Rabbi Mendel Popack
Director

Beis Medrosh L'Shluchim
in partnership with
Shluchim Exchange

Steering Committee

Rabbi Simcha Backman
Rabbi Mendy Kotlarsky
Rabbi Efraim Mintz

Rabbi Sholom Zirkind
Administrator

Rabbi Yitzchok Steiner
Coordinator

Rabbi Mendel Margolin
Producer

Advisory Board

Rabbi Yisroel Altein
Pittsburgh, PA

Rabbi Mendel Cohen
Sacramento, CA

Rabbi Mordechai Farkash
Bellevue, WA

Rabbi Mendel Lipsker
Sherman Oaks, CA

JLI Central
Founding Department Heads

Rabbi Zalman Charytan
Acworth, GA

Rabbi Mendel Druk
Cancun, Mexico

Rabbi Menachem Gansburg
Toronto, ON

Rabbi Chaim Zalman Levy
New Rochelle, NY

Rabbi Elchonon Tenenbaum
Napa Valley, CA

Rohr **JLI** Affiliates

Share the **Rohr JLI** experience with friends and relatives worldwide

ALABAMA
BIRMINGHAM
Rabbi Yossi Friedman
205.970.0100

ARIZONA
CHANDLER
Rabbi Mendel Deitsch
480.855.4333

FLAGSTAFF
Rabbi Dovie Shapiro
928.255.5756

GLENDALE
Rabbi Sholom Lew
602.375.2422

PHOENIX
Rabbi Zalman Levertov
Rabbi Yossi Friedman
602.944.2753

SCOTTSDALE
Rabbi Yossi Levertov
Rabbi Yossi Bryski
480.998.1410

ARKANSAS
LITTLE ROCK
Rabbi Pinchus Ciment
501.217.0053

CALIFORNIA
AGOURA HILLS
Rabbi Moshe Bryski
Rabbi Yisroel Levin
Rabbi Shlomo Bistritzky
818.991.0991

BAKERSFIELD
Rabbi Shmuel Schlanger
661.835.8381

BEL AIR
Rabbi Chaim Mentz
310.475.5311

BRENTWOOD
Rabbi Boruch Hecht
Rabbi Mordechai Zaetz
310.826.4453

BURBANK
Rabbi Shmuly Kornfeld
818.954.0070

CALABASAS
Rabbi Eliyahu Friedman
818.585.1888

CARLSBAD
Rabbi Yeruchem Eilfort
Rabbi Michoel Shapiro
760.943.8891

CENTURY CITY
Rabbi Tzemach Cunin
310.859.6060

CHATSWORTH
Rabbi Yossi Spritzer
818.718.0777

GLENDALE
Rabbi Simcha Backman
818.240.2750

HUNTINGTON BEACH
Rabbi Aron Berkowitz
714.846.2285

IRVINE
Rabbi Alter Tenenbaum
Rabbi Elly Andrusier
949.786.5000

LAGUNA BEACH
Rabbi Elimelech Gurevitch
949.499.0770

LOMITA
Rabbi Eli Hecht
Rabbi Sholom Pinson
310.326.8234

LONG BEACH
Rabbi Abba Perelmuter
562.621.9828

LOS FELIZ
Rabbi Leibel Korf
323.660.5177

MALIBU
Rabbi Levi Cunin
310.456.6588

MARINA DEL REY
Rabbi Danny Yiftach
Rabbi Mendy Avtzon
310.859.0770

MILL VALLEY
Rabbi Hillel Scop
415.381.3794

MISSION VIEJO
Rabbi Zalman Aron Kantor
949.770.1270

MONTEREY
Rabbi Dovid Holtzberg
831.643.2770

MT. OLYMPUS
Rabbi Sholom Ber Rodal
323.650.1444

NEWHALL
Rabbi Elchonon Marosov
661.254.3434

NEWPORT BEACH
Rabbi Reuven Mintz
949.721.9800

NORTH HOLLYWOOD
Rabbi Nachman Abend
818.989.9539

NORTHRIDGE
Rabbi Eli Rivkin
818.368.3937

PACIFIC PALISADES
Rabbi Zushe Cunin
310.454.7783

PASADENA
Rabbi Chaim Hanoka
626.564.8820

RANCHO CUCAMONGA
Rabbi Sholom B. Harlig
909.949.4553

RANCHO PALOS VERDES
Rabbi Yitzchok Magalnic
310.544.5544

REDONDO BEACH
Rabbi Dovid Lisbon
310.214.4999

ROSEVILLE
Rabbi Yossi Korik
916.677.9960

SACRAMENTO
Rabbi Mendy Cohen
916.455.1400

S. BARBARA
Rabbi Yosef Loschak
805.683.1544

S. CLEMENTE
Rabbi Menachem M. Slavin
949.489.0723

S. CRUZ
Rabbi Yochanan Friedman
831.454.0101

S. DIEGO
Rabbi Motte Fradkin
858.547.0076

S. FRANCISCO
Rabbi Peretz Mochkin
415.571.8770

S. MONICA
Rabbi Boruch Rabinowitz
310.394.5699

S. RAFAEL
Rabbi Yisrael Rice
415.492.1666

S. ROSA
Rabbi Mendel Wolvovsky
707.577.0277

SIMI VALLEY
Rabbi Nosson Gurary
805.577.0573

STOCKTON
Rabbi Avremel Brod
209.952.2081

STUDIO CITY
Rabbi Yossi Baitelman
818.508.6633

TEMECULA
Rabbi Yitzchok Hurwitz
951.303.9576

THOUSAND OAKS
Rabbi Chaim Bryski
805.493.7776

TUSTIN
Rabbi Yehoshua Eliezrie
714.508.2150

VENTURA
Rabbi Yakov Latowicz
Mrs. Sarah Latowicz
805.658.7441

WEST HILLS
Rabbi Avrahom Yitzchak Rabin
818.337.4544

YORBA LINDA
Rabbi Dovid Eliezrie
714.693.0770

COLORADO
ASPEN
Rabbi Mendel Mintz
970.544.3770

BOULDER
Rabbi Pesach Scheiner
303.494.1638

COLORADO SPRINGS
Rabbi Moshe Liberow
719.634.2345

DENVER
Rabbi Yossi Serebryanski
303.744.9699

HIGHLANDS RANCH
Rabbi Avraham Mintz
303.694.9119

LONGMONT
Rabbi Yaakov Dovid Borenstein
303.678.7595

VAIL
Rabbi Dovid Mintz
970.476.7887

WESTMINSTER
Rabbi Benjy Brackman
303.429.5177

CONNECTICUT
BRANFORD
Rabbi Yossi Yaffe
203.488.2263

GLASTONBURY
Rabbi Yosef Wolvovsky
860.659.2422

GREENWICH
Rabbi Yossi Deren
Rabbi Menachem Feldman
203.629.9059

LITCHFIELD
Rabbi Yoseph Eisenbach
860.567.3609

NEW LONDON
Rabbi Avrohom Sternberg
860.437.8000

ORANGE
Rabbi Sheya Hecht
Rabbi Adam Haston
203.795.5261

RIDGEFIELD
Rabbi Sholom Y. Deitsch
203.748.4421

SIMSBURY
Rabbi Mendel Samuels
860.658.4903

STAMFORD
Rabbi Yisrael Deren
Rabbi Levi Mendelow
203.3.CHABAD

WESTPORT
Rabbi Yehuda L. Kantor
Mrs. Dina Kantor
203.226.8584

WEST HARTFORD
Rabbi Yosef Gopin
Rabbi Shaya Gopin
860.659.2422

DELAWARE
WILMINGTON
Rabbi Chuni Vogel
302.529.9900

FLORIDA
AVENTURA
Rabbi Laivi Forta
Rabbi Chaim I. Drizin
305.933.0770

BAL HARBOUR
Rabbi Mendy Levy
305.868.1411

BOCA RATON
Rabbi Moishe Denberg
Rabbi Zalman Bukiet
561.417.7797

EAST BOCA RATON
Rabbi Ruvi New
561.417.7797

BOYNTON BEACH
Rabbi Yosef Yitzchok Raichik
561.732.4633

BRADENTON
Rabbi Menachem Bukiet
941.388.9656

BRANDON
Rabbi Mendel Rubashkin
813.657.9393

COCONUT CREEK
Rabbi Yossi Gansburg
954.422.1987

CORAL GABLES
Rabbi Avrohom Stolik
305.490.7572

DEERFIELD BEACH
Rabbi Yossi Goldblatt
954.422.1735

DELRAY BEACH
Rabbi Sholom Ber Korf
561.496.6228

FORT LAUDERDALE
Rabbi Yitzchok Naparstek
954.568.1190

FORT MYERS
Rabbi Yitzchok Minkowicz
Mrs. Nechama Minkowicz
239.433.7708

HOLLYWOOD
Rabbi Leizer Barash
954.965.9933

Rabbi Zalman Korf
Rabbi Yakov Garfinkel
954.374.8370

KENDALL
Rabbi Yossi Harlig
305.234.5654

KEY BISCAYNE
Rabbi Yoel Caroline
305.365.6744

KEY WEST
Rabbi Yaakov Zucker
305.295.0013

MIAMI BEACH
Rabbi Zev Katz
305.672.6613

Rabbi Aron Rabin
Rabbi Mendy Halberstam
305.535.0094

NAPLES
Rabbi Fishel Zaklos
239.262.4474

NORTH MIAMI BEACH
Rabbi Moishe Kievman
305.770.1919

ORLANDO
Rabbi Yosef Konikov
407.354.3660

PALM BEACH GARDENS
Rabbi Dovid Vigler
561.215.0404

PARKLAND
Rabbi Mendy Gutnik
954.796.7330

PINELLAS COUNTY
Rabbi Shalom Adler
727.789.0408

S. PETERSBURG
Rabbi Alter Korf
727.344.4900

SARASOTA
Rabbi Chaim Shaul Steinmetz
941.925.0770

SOUTH PALM BEACH
Rabbi Leibel Stolik
561.889.3499

SUNNY ISLES BEACH
Rabbi Yisrael Baron
CLASSES IN ENGLISH
305.792.4770

Rabbi Alexander Kaller
CLASSES IN RUSSIAN
305.803.5315

TALLAHASSEE
Rabbi Schneur Zalmen Oirechman
850.523.9294

VENICE
Rabbi Sholom Ber Schmerling
941.493.2770

WALNUT CREEK
Rabbi Zalman Korf
954.374.8370

WESTON
Rabbi Yisroel Spalter
Rabbi Yechezkel Unsdorfer
954.349.6565

WEST PALM BEACH
Rabbi Yoel Gancz
561.659.7770

GEORGIA
ALPHARETTA
Rabbi Hirshy Minkowicz
770.410.9000

ATLANTA
Rabbi Yossi New
Rabbi Isser New
404.843.2464

ATLANTA: INTOWN
Rabbi Eliyahu Schusterman
Rabbi Ari Sollish
404.898.0434

GWINNETT
Rabbi Yossi Lerman
678.595.0196

MARIETTA
Rabbi Ephraim Silverman
Rabbi Zalman Charytan
770.565.4412

IDAHO
BOISE
Rabbi Mendel Lifshitz
208.853.9200

ILLINOIS
CHICAGO
Rabbi Meir Hecht
312.714.4655

GURNEE
Rabbi Sholom Ber Tenenbaum
847.782.1800

GLENVIEW
Rabbi Yishaya Benjaminson
847.998.9896

HIGHLAND PARK
Mrs. Michla Schanowitz
847.266.0770

NAPERVILLE
Rabbi Mendy Goldstein
630.778.9770

NORTHBROOK
Rabbi Meir Moscowitz
847.564.8770

PEORIA
Rabbi Eli Langsam
309.692.2250

SKOKIE
Rabbi Yochanan Posner
847.677.1770

WILMETTE
Rabbi Dovid Flinkenstein
847.251.7707

INDIANA
INDIANAPOLIS
Rabbi Mendel Schusterman
317.251.5573

KANSAS
OVERLAND PARK
Rabbi Mendy Wineberg
913.649.4852

LOUISIANA
METAIRIE
Rabbi Yossi Nemes
504.454.2910

MARYLAND
BETHESDA
Rabbi Bentzion Geisinsky
Rabbi Sender Geisinsky
301.913.9777

BALTIMORE
Rabbi Elchonon Lisbon
410.358.4787

Rabbi Velvel Belinsky
CLASSES IN RUSSIAN
410.764.5000

BALTIMORE DOWNTOWN
Rabbi Levi Druk
410.605.0505

COLUMBIA
Rabbi Hillel Baron
410.740.2424

GAITHERSBURG
Rabbi Sholom Raichik
301.926.3632

POTOMAC
Rabbi Mendel Bluming
301.983.4200

SILVER SPRING
Rabbi Berel Wolvovsky
301.593.1117

MASSACHUSETTS
HYANNIS
Rabbi Yekusiel Alperowitz
508.775.2324

LONGMEADOW
Rabbi Yakov Wolff
413.567.8665

NATICK
Rabbi Levi Fogelman
508.650.1499

SHARON
Rabbi Chaim Wolosow
Rabbi Ilan Meyers
781.784.4269

SUDBURY
Rabbi Yisroel Freeman
978.443.3691

SWAMPSCOTT
Mrs. Layah Lipsker
781.581.3833

MICHIGAN
ANN ARBOR
Rabbi Aharon Goldstein
734.995.3276

NOVI
Rabbi Avrohom Susskind
248.790.6075

WEST BLOOMFIELD
Rabbi Kasriel Shemtov
248.788.4000

Rabbi Elimelech Silberberg
Rabbi Avrohom Wineberg
248.855.6170

MINNESOTA
MINNETONKA
Rabbi Mordechai Grossbaum
952.929.9922

ROCHESTER
Rabbi Dovid Greene
507.288.7500

MISSOURI
S. LOUIS
Rabbi Yosef Landa
314.725.0400

MONTANA
BOZEMAN
Rabbi Chaim Shaul Bruk
406.585.8770

NEBRASKA
OMAHA
Rabbi Mendel Katzman
402.330.1800

NEVADA
HENDERSON
Rabbi Mendy Harlig
Rabbi Tzvi Bronstein
702.617.0770

SUMMERLIN
Rabbi Yisroel Schanowitz
Rabbi Tzvi Bronstein
702.855.0770

NEW JERSEY
BASKING RIDGE
Rabbi Mendy Herson
908.604.8844

CHERRY HILL
Rabbi Mendy Mangel
856.874.1500

CLINTON
Rabbi Eli Kornfeld
908.623.7000

FORT LEE
Rabbi Meir Konikov
201.886.1238

FRANKLIN LAKES
Rabbi Chanoch Kaplan
201.848.0449

HILLSBOROUGH
Rabbi Shmaya Krinsky
908.874.0444

HOBOKEN
Rabbi Moshe Shapiro
201.386.5222

MADISON
Rabbi Shalom Lubin
973.377.0707

MANALAPAN
Rabbi Boruch Chazanow
732.972.3687

MEDFORD
Rabbi Yitzchok Kahan
609.953.3150

Mountain Lakes
Rabbi Levi Dubinsky
973.551.1898

NORTH BRUNSWICK
Rabbi Levi Azimov
732.398.9492

RANDOLPH
Rabbi Avraham Bechor
973.895.3070

ROCKAWAY
Rabbi Asher Herson
Rabbi Mordechai Baumgarten
973.625.1525

TEANECK
Rabbi Ephraim Simon
201.907.0686

TENAFLY
Rabbi Mordechai Shain
Rabbi Yitzchak Gershovitz
201.871.1152

TOMS RIVER
Rabbi Moshe Gourarie
732.349.4199

WAYNE
Rabbi Michel Gurkov
973.694.6274

WEST ORANGE
Rabbi Efraim Mintz
Rabbi Mendy Kasowitz
973.731.0770

WOODCLIFF LAKE
Rabbi Dov Drizin
201.476.0157

NEW MEXICO
S. FE
Rabbi Berel Levertov
505.983.2000

NEW YORK
ALBANY
Rabbi Yossi Rubin
518.482.5781

BEDFORD
Rabbi Arik Wolf
914.666.6065

BINGHAMTON
Mrs. Rivkah Slonim
607.797.0015

BRIGHTON BEACH
Rabbi Zushe Winner
Rabbi Avrohom Winner
718.946.9833

CEDARHURST
Rabbi Shneur Zalman Wolowik
516.295.2478

DIX HILLS
Rabbi Yaakov Saacks
631.351.8672

DOBBS FERRY
Rabbi Benjy Silverman
914.693.6100

EAST HAMPTON
Rabbi Leibel Baumgarten
631.329.5800

FOREST HILLS
Rabbi Eli Blokh
Rabbi Yossi Mendelson
718.459.8432 ext.17

ITHACA
Rabbi Eli Silberstein
607.257.7379

KINGSTON
Rabbi Yitzchok Hecht
845.334.9044

LARCHMONT
Rabbi Mendel Silberstein
914.834.4321

NYC GRAMERCY PARK
Rabbi Naftali Rotenstreich
212.924.3200

NYC KEHILATH JESHURUN
Rabbi Elie Weinstock
212.774.5636

OSSINING
Rabbi Dovid Labkowski
914.923.2522

PORT WASHINGTON
Rabbi Shalom Paltiel
516.767.8672

RIVERDALE
Rabbi Levi Shemtov
718.549.1100

ROCHESTER
Rabbi Nechemia Vogel
585.271.0330

ROSLYN
Rabbi Yaakov Reiter
516.484.8185

SEA GATE
Rabbi Chaim Brikman
Mrs. Rivka Brikman
718.266.1736

STATEN ISLAND
Rabbi Moshe Katzman
Rabbi Shmuel Bendet
718.370.8953

STONY BROOK
Rabbi Shalom Ber Cohen
631.585.0521

SUFFERN
Rabbi Isaac Lefkowitz
Rabbi Shmuel Gancz
845.368.1889

WOODBURY
Rabbi Shmuel Lipszyc
516.682.0404

NORTH CAROLINA
ASHEVILLE
Rabbi Shaya Susskind
828.505.0746

CHARLOTTE
Rabbi Yossi Groner
Rabbi Shlomo Cohen
704.366.3984

RALEIGH
Rabbi Aaron Herman
919.637.6950

RALEIGH
Rabbi Pinchas Herman
Rabbi Sholom Ber Estrin
919.847.8986

OHIO
BEACHWOOD
Rabbi Yossi Marosov
216.381.4736

BLUE ASH
Rabbi Yisroel Mangel
513.793.5200

COLUMBUS
Rabbi Areyah Kaltmann
Rabbi Levi Andrusier
614.294.3296

DAYTON
Rabbi Nochum Mangel
Rabbi Dr. Shmuel Klatzkin
937.643.0770

TOLEDO
Rabbi Yossi Shemtov
419.843.9393

OKLAHOMA
OKLAHOMA CITY
Rabbi Ovadia Goldman
405.524.4800

TULSA
Rabbi Yehuda Weg
918.492.4499

OREGON
PORTLAND
Rabbi Moshe Wilhelm
Rabbi Mordechai Wilhelm
503.977.9947

PENNSYLVANIA
AMBLER
Rabbi Shaya Deitsch
215.591.9310

BALA CYNWYD
Rabbi Shraga Sherman
610.660.9192

CLARKS SUMMIT
Rabbi Benny Rapoport
570.587.3300

DEVON
Rabbi Yossi Kaplan
610.971.9977

DOYLESTOWN
Rabbi Mendel Prus
215.340.1303

NEWTOWN
Rabbi Aryeh Weinstein
215.497.9925

PHILADELPHIA: CENTER CITY
Rabbi Yochonon Goldman
215.238.2100

PITTSBURGH
Rabbi Yisroel Altein
412.422.7300 ext. 269

PITTSBURGH: SOUTH HILLS
Rabbi Mendy Rosenblum
412.278.3693

READING
Rabbi Yosef Lipsker
610.921.2805

RYDAL
Rabbi Zushe Gurevitz
215.572.1511

SOUTH CAROLINA
COLUMBIA
Rabbi Hesh Epstein
803.782.1831

TENNESSEE
BELLEVUE
Rabbi Yitzchok Tiechtel
615.646.5750

MEMPHIS
Rabbi Levi Klein
901.766.1800

KNOXVILLE
Rabbi Yossi Wilhelm
865.588.8584

TEXAS
HOUSTON
Rabbi Moishe Traxler
Rabbi Dovid Goldstein
713.774.0300

HOUSTON: RICE UNIVERSITY AREA
Rabbi Eliezer Lazaroff
Rabbi Yitzchok Schmukler
713.522.2004

PLANO
Rabbi Mendel Block
Rabbi Yehudah Horowitz
972.596.8270

S. ANTONIO
Rabbi Chaim Block
Rabbi Yossi Marrus
210.492.1085

UTAH
SALT LAKE CITY
Rabbi Benny Zippel
801.467.7777

VERMONT
BURLINGTON
Rabbi Yitzchok Raskin
802.658.5770

VIRGINIA
ALEXANDRIA/ARLINGTON
Rabbi Mordechai Newman
703.370.2774

FAIRFAX
Rabbi Leibel Fajnland
703.426.1980

NORFOLK
Rabbi Aaron Margolin
Rabbi Levi Brashevitzky
757.616.0770

RICHMOND
Rabbi Dr. Shlomo Pereira
804.740.2000

TYSONS CORNER
Rabbi Levi Deitsch
703.356.3451

WASHINGTON
BELLEVUE
Rabbi Mordechai Farkash
Rabbi Sholom Elishevitz
425.957.7860

OLYMPIA
Rabbi Cheski Edelman
360.584-4306

SEATTLE
Rabbi Elazar Bogomilsky
206.527.1411

SPOKANE COUNTY
Rabbi Yisroel Hahn
509.443.0770

WISCONSIN
MEQUON
Rabbi Menachem Rapoport
262.242.2235

MILWAUKEE
Rabbi Mendel Shmotkin
Rabbi Shais Taub
414.961.6100

PUERTO RICO
CAROLINA
Rabbi Mendel Zarchi
787.253.0894

ARGENTINA
BUENOS AIRES
Rabbi Hirshel Hendel
5411 4807 7073

AUSTRALIA
BRISBANE
Rabbi Chanoch Sufrin
617.3843.6770

MELBOURNE
Rabbi Schneier Lange
613.9522.8222
Rabbi Shimshon Yurkowicz
613.9822.3600

SYDNEY
BONDI
Rabbi Pinchas Feldman
612.9387.3822

DOUBLE BAY
Rabbi Yanky Berger
612.9327.1644

DOVER HEIGHTS
Rabbi Benzion Milecki
612.9337.6775

NORTH SHORE
Rabbi Nochum Schapiro
Mrs. Fruma Schapiro
Rabbi Shmuly Kopel
612.9488.9548

AUSTRIA
VIENNA
Rabbi Shaya Boas
431.369.1818 ext. 123

BELGIUM
ANTWERP
Rabbi Mendy Gurary
32.3.239.6212

BRAZIL
RIO DE JANEIRO
Rabbi Yehoshua Goldman
Rabbi Avraham Steinmetz
21.3543.3770

S. PAULO
Rabbi Avraham Steinmetz
55.11.3081.3081

CANADA
ALBERTA
CALGARY
Rabbi Mordechai Groner
403.238.4880

BRITISH COLUMBIA
RICHMOND
Rabbi Yechiel Baitelman
604.277.6427

VICTORIA
Rabbi Meir Kaplan
250.595.7656

MANITOBA
WINNIPEG
Rabbi Avrohom Altein
Rabbi Shmuel Altein
204.339.8737

ONTARIO
LONDON
Rabbi Eliezer Gurkow
519.434.3962

NIAGARA FALLS
Rabbi Zalman Zaltzman

OTTAWA
Rabbi Menachem M. Blum
613.823.0866

GREATER TORONTO
REGIONAL OFFICE & THORNHILL
Rabbi Yossi Gansburg
905.731.7000

LAWRENCE/EGLINTON
Rabbi Menachem Gansburg
416.546.8770

MIDTOWN
Rabbi Shlomo Wolvovsky
416.516.2005

MISSISSAUGA
Rabbi Yitzchok Slavin
905.820.4432

RICHMOND HILL
Rabbi Mendel Bernstein
905.770.7700

BJL
Rabbi Leib Chaiken
416.916.7202

UPTOWN
Rabbi Moshe Steiner
647.267.8533

YORK UNIVERSITY
Rabbi Vidal Bekerman
416.856.4575

QUEBEC
MONTREAL
Rabbi Berel Bell
Rabbi Ronnie Fine
Rabbi Leibel Fine
514.342.3.JLI

TOWN OF MOUNT ROYAL
Rabbi Moshe Krasnanski
514.739.0770

COLOMBIA
BOGOTA
Rabbi Yehoshua B. Rosenfeld
Rabbi Chanoch Piekarski
571.635.8251

DENMARK
COPENHAGEN
Rabbi Yitzchok Lowenthal
45.3316.1850

GREECE
ATHENS
Rabbi Mendel Hendel
30.210.520.2880

GUATEMALA
GUATEMALA CITY
Rabbi Shalom Pelman
502.2485.0770

NETHERLANDS
DEN HAAG
Rabbi Shmuel Katzman
31.70.347.0222

ROTTERDAM
Rabbi Yehuda Vorst
31.10.466.9481

RUSSIA
MOSCOW
Rabbi Shneor Leider
Rabbi Yanky Klein
749.5783.8479

SINGAPORE
SINGAPORE
Rabbi Mordechai Abergel
656.337.2189

SOUTH AFRICA
CAPE TOWN
Rabbi Mendel Popack
Rabbi Pinchas Hecht
27.21.434.3740

JOHANNESBURG
Rabbi Dovid Masinter
Rabbi Yossi Hecht
Rabbi Dovi Rabin
27.11.440.6600

SWEDEN
STOCKHOLM
Rabbi Chaim Greisman
468.679.7067

SWITZERLAND
LUGANO
Rabbi Yaakov Tzvi Kantor
091.921.3720

UNITED KINGDOM
EDGEWARE
Rabbi Leivi Sudak
44.208.905.4141

LONDON
Rabbi Gershon Overlander
Rabbi Dovid Katz
502.2485.0770

Rabbi Bentzi Sudak
020.8800.0022 ext. 103

LEEDS
Rabbi Eli Pink
44.113.266.3311

URUGUAY
MONTEVIDEO
Rabbi Eliezer Shemtov
5982.709.3444 ext. 109/110

VENEZUELA
CARACAS
Rabbi Yehoshua Rosenblum
58.212.264.7011

NOTES

NOTES

JEWISH LEARNING INSTITUTE

THE JEWISH LEARNING MULTIPLEX

Brought to you by the Rohr Jewish Learning Institute

In fulfillment of the mandate of the Lubavitcher Rebbe, of blessed memory,
whose leadership guides every step of our work,
the mission of the Rohr Jewish Learning Institute is to transform
Jewish life and the greater community through the study of Torah,
connecting each Jew to our shared heritage of Jewish learning.

While our flagship program remains the cornerstone of our organization,
JLI is proud to feature additional divisions catering to specific populations,
in order to meet a wide array of educational needs.

THE ROHR JEWISH LEARNING INSTITUTE
is an affiliate of *Merkos L'Inyonei Chinuch*,
the educational arm of the Chabad-Lubavitch Movement.

TORAH STUDIES

Torah Studies provides a rich and nuanced encounter with the weekly Torah reading.

MYSHIUR
TALMUD LEARNING INITIATIVE

MyShiur courses are designed to assist students in developing the skills needed to study Talmud independently.

SINAI SCHOLARS SOCIETY
IN PARTNERSHIP WITH CHABAD ON CAMPUS

This rigorous fellowship program invites select college students to explore the fundamentals of Judaism.

JLI TEENS
YOUNG SMART JEWISH
IN PARTNERSHIP WITH CTEEN: CHABAD TEEN NETWORK

Jewish teens forge their identity as they engage in Torah study, social interaction, and serious fun.

TORAH I
IN PARTNERSHIP WITH CHABAD ON CAMPUS

The rigor and excellence of JLI courses, adapted to the campus environment.

TORAHCafé™

TorahCafe.com provides an exclusive selection of top-rated Jewish educational videos.

BRILLIANT LEARNING, NATURALLY
National JEWISH RETREAT

This yearly event rejuvenates mind, body, and spirit with a powerful synthesis of Jewish learning and community.

ROSHCHODESH society

The Rosh Chodesh Society gathers Jewish women together once a month for intensive textual study.

PEDAGOGY · CURRICULUM · MARKETING
JLI ACADEMY

Select affiliates are invited to partner with peers and noted professionals, as leaders of innovation and excellence.

the LAND & the SPIRIT
Mission to Israel

Mission participants delve into our nation's rich past while exploring the Holy Land's relevance and meaning today.